Praise for Strategy from the Outside In

"Getting your company to organize around what customers value most sounds easy in theory, but it's very hard to do consistently well. Day and Moorman provide a thoughtful, realistic, and actionable blueprint for delivering the most value to your most valuable customers."

—**Beth Comstock,** Chief Marketing Officer, GE

"Only a few books can really help marketing professionals make a difference in their organization. Strategy from the Outside In *falls into this category. Creating superior customer value is or should be a priority of all marketers. Day and Moorman provide a clear path for delivering on such value. Most important, their work is based on the real-world successes (and failures) of organizations which they have studied.*"

—**Dennis Dunlap,** CEO, American Marketing Association

"Strategy from the Outside In *offers a refreshing reminder that answers to managers' most pressing questions always start by looking outside the organization and meeting consumer needs better than the other guys! It provides a combination of solid evidence and user-friendly frameworks that can be put to use immediately. A must-read not only for today's challenged CMO but for the rest of the C-suite as a guiding framework for the entire enterprise.*"

—**Rob Malcolm,** President, Global Marketing,
Sales and Innovation, Diageo PLC

"Strategy from the Outside In *provides a handbook to re-imagine a business through the eyes of customers. It is full of current case studies, research, and practical frameworks that senior marketers can use to refine their own thinking and influence their colleagues.*"

—**Greg Gordon,** SVP Consumer Marketing,
Liberty Mutual

"Day and Moorman advise companies to leave their comfortable positions of controlling their businesses to the uncomfortable position of allowing their customers control. This is a book only for companies courageous enough to listen to their customers instead of themselves."

—**Ron Nicol,** Senior Partner and Managing Director,
Boston Consulting Group

STRATEGY
FROM THE
OUTSIDE IN

PROFITING FROM
CUSTOMER VALUE

GEORGE S. DAY
CHRISTINE MOORMAN

New York   Chicago   San Francisco   Lisbon   London
Madrid   Mexico City   Milan   New Delhi   San Juan
Seoul   Singapore   Sydney   Toronto

To my family—my proudest legacy
—*George*

To Ed, my touchstone, my rock, my greatest love
—*Chris*

The **McGraw·Hill** Companies

15 16 17 18 19 20 QVS/QVS 21 20 19 18 17

ISBN   978-0-07-174229-0
MHID   0-07-174229-8

McGraw-Hill books are available at special quantity discounts to use as premiums and sales promotions or for use in corporate training programs. To contact a representative, please e-mail us at bulksales@mcgraw-hill.com.

This book is printed on acid-free paper.

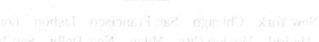

Contents

Part One

Seeing Outside In:
Shifting Your Perspective

1

Strategy from the Outside In

With the wreckage of the Great Recession still smoldering and slow economic growth expected for the foreseeable future, it's not surprising to see that many companies are turning inward and hunkering down. Profits, growth, and value creation seem to have become stretch goals rather than baseline expectations. Companies that were praised over the last decade for delivering shareholder value have largely fallen on hard times; buried under debt, they have no clear plan for capitalizing once customers are willing to spend again. The Fortune 500's top 25 at the beginning of the century included companies such as General Motors, Ford, Citigroup, Bank of America, AIG, Enron, and Compaq. Measured by market value, only 8 of the 25 largest companies in the world in 2000 can claim that distinction today.

Yet a number of companies operating in the same challenging environment have gained market share, grown revenues and profits, and created more value for customers, in contrast to their competitors' intense focus on budget cutting. Indeed, there are companies that have managed market share, profit, and customer value growth throughout the vertiginous boom-and-bust business cycles of the last 20 years. These companies may not have been favorite stock picks, nor have all of them topped the lists of the decade's most profitable corporations. But what they have done is found a way to build value over the long term. These are not flash-in-the-pan companies, world-beaters one year and stragglers the next. They are companies like

Johnson & Johnson, Procter & Gamble, Fidelity, Cisco, Walmart, Amazon, Apple, IKEA, Texas Instruments, Becton Dickinson, and Tesco, among others.

These companies have been successful because they have remained true to the purpose of a business (as stated by Peter Drucker): to create and keep customers. They've kept that purpose not by focusing on shareholders and meeting quarterly numbers, by playing games with their financial statements, or by focusing just on competitive advantages. Instead, they've done it by consistently creating superior customer value—and profiting handsomely from that customer value.

We've spent years looking at these companies—and many not-so-successful ones—looking for patterns and commonalities that explain their stellar results, and we've concluded that they offer three very important lessons for any executive who wants to consistently create superior customer value and generate economic profits over the long term. There is no step-by-step formula, but there are consistencies in how these companies think, how they make strategic decisions, and, most important, how they operate to ensure they are maximizing the value they create and the profits they capture.

- These companies approach strategy from the outside in rather than from the inside out. They start with the market when they design their strategy, not the other way around.
- They use deep market insights to inform and guide their outside-in view.
- Their outside-in strategy focuses every part of the organization on achieving, sustaining, and profiting from customer value.

Two Paths to Strategy

The first thing that distinguishes these value- and profit-creating companies is that they drive strategy from the perspective of the market—in other words, from the *outside in*. This may sound trivial, but it is shockingly uncommon. For all the talk about "putting the customer first" and "relentlessly delivering value to customers," most management teams fail to do this. Put most simply, outside in means standing in the customer's shoes and viewing everything the company does through the customer's eyes.

Far more common than outside-in thinking is inside-out thinking and inside-out strategy. Inside-out companies narrowly frame their strategic thinking by asking, "What can the market do for us?" rather than, "What can we do for the market?" The consequences of inside-out versus outside-in thinking can be seen in the way many business-to-business firms approach customer solutions. The inside-out view is that "solutions are bundles of products and services that help us sell more." The outside-in view is that "the purpose of a solution is to help our customers find value and make money—to our mutual benefit." Some differences in the two ways of framing strategic issues are shown in Figure 1-1.

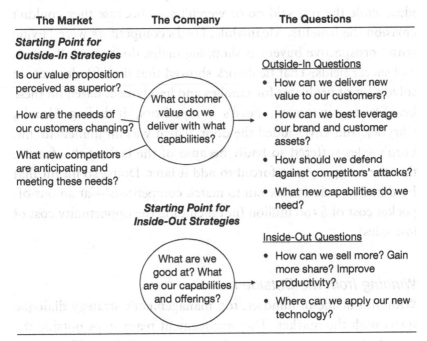

The Market	The Company	The Questions
Starting Point for Outside-In Strategies		**Outside-In Questions**
Is our value proposition perceived as superior?		• How can we deliver new value to our customers?
How are the needs of our customers changing?	What customer value do we deliver with what capabilities?	• How can we best leverage our brand and customer assets?
What new competitors are anticipating and meeting these needs?		• How should we defend against competitors' attacks?
	Starting Point for Inside-Out Strategies	• What new capabilities do we need?
		Inside-Out Questions
	What are we good at? What are our capabilities and offerings?	• How can we sell more? Gain more share? Improve productivity?
		• Where can we apply our new technology?

FIGURE 1-1 Which Path to Strategy?

Inside-out thinking helps explain why a large database company that was looking to grow by leveraging its deep information about the companies' finances spent several million dollars to develop a product for small and medium-sized enterprises without first having in-depth conversations with potential buyers. Management, seduced by the seemingly vast potential of this market, relied on the assurances of the sales force that customers would buy. During the process, no one asked what value the company would be offering customers, or how the company's new product would offer customers more value than the status quo. Instead, managers focused on what customers could do for the company. As a result, the new product flopped and was abandoned in less than a year.

An even more costly example is Ford's unfortunate decision not to add a sliding door on the driver's side of its Windstar minivan.[1] The extra cost of the fifth door was the major factor in this decision, but just to be sure, the designers asked a sample of buyers their opinion. Only one-third of the sample thought it was a good idea, while the rest said no or weren't sure because they couldn't envision the benefits. Meanwhile, Ford's competitors were "living with" prospective buyers at shopping malls, do-it-yourself stores, and soccer fields. That fieldwork showed that the fifth door could solve a lot of problems for families and handymen. Based on these benefits to customers, Ford's competitors, including Honda, Chrysler, and GM, added the door, which was an immediate hit. Ford's sales suffered so badly because of the lack of this feature that the company was forced to add it later. Doing so meant that Ford had to redesign its van to match competitors'—at an out-of-pocket cost of $560 million (not including the opportunity cost of lost sales).

Winning from the Outside In

With an outside-in mindset, top management's strategy dialogue starts with the market. The management team steps outside the boundaries and constraints of the company as it is, and looks first at its market: How and why are customers changing? What new needs do they have? What can we do to solve their problems and help them make more money? What new competitors are lurking around the corner, and how can we derail their efforts? This perspective expands the strategy dialogue and opens up a richer set of opportunities for competitive advantage and growth.

Jeff Bezos, the founder and chairman of Amazon.com, is a champion of the outside-in approach. He explained how Amazon was able to meet the needs of its customers for Web services by offering access to its cloud computing network and for a more convenient reading experience with the Kindle. He describes it as a "working backward" mentality:[2]

> *Rather than ask what we are good at and what else can we do with that skill, you ask, who are our customers? What do they need? And then you say we're going to give that to them regardless of whether we have the skills to do so, and we will learn these skills no matter how long it takes.... There is a tendency I think for executives to think that the right course of action is to stick to the knitting—stick with what you are good at. That may be a generally good rule, but the problem is the world changes out from under you if you are not constantly adding to your skill set.*

The difficulties faced by Dell Computer over the last four years illustrate the need for outside-in thinking. For several decades, Dell's celebrated mastery of logistics allowed it to deliver leading-edge computer hardware at prices and speeds that no rival could match. The whole organization could concentrate on assembling and shipping PCs, laptops, and servers as cheaply and quickly as possible. This single-minded emphasis on efficiency made Dell the worldwide market share leader in 2005. Growth came by expanding globally and broadening the range of hardware sold through its direct-to-customer model. Everything was viewed through the prism of this business model and how to leverage it further.

But this inside-out emphasis also kept Dell from seeing and responding to a sea change in its market. More and more customers wanted to buy at retail and own products that conveyed a sense of personal style. Both Apple and Hewlett-Packard (HP) had seen the trend building and were ready to oblige. HP redesigned its machines with a focus on customer experience and distinctive value, beyond price or the latest technology. It advertised, "The Computer Is Personal Again."[3] The market responded, and HP assumed market share leadership in 2006. Dell, on the other hand, faltered and lost sales. Nevertheless, the efficiency focus was so embedded in Dell that manufacturing executives resisted offering distinct designs, even at a premium price.

As one commentator put it, "Dell began to treat consumers and even some business customers like they were passengers on a Greyhound bus."[4] Between 2Q 2008 and 2Q 2009, Dell's share of the U.S. personal computer market dropped from 31.4 percent to 26.3 percent. On top of that, many of Dell's advantages were neutralized as HP and other competitors improved their supply-chain management and lowered costs.

Anecdotes aside, there is abundant evidence for the superiority of outside-in thinking. Much of it comes from studying the relative profit performance of market-driven companies.[5] These firms have an inherent advantage over their more self-absorbed rivals because of their superior ability to understand markets, provide superior value over time, and attract and retain customers.

Inside-Out Myopia

Given both the intuitive and the data-driven appeal of outside-in strategy, why is the inside-out approach to strategy so pervasive? There are many subtle forces that converge to encourage inside-out thinking and slowly disconnect the business from its market.

Positive Reinforcement

Inside-out strategic thinking ultimately relies on gaining maximum returns from existing assets—in other words, increasing efficiency. Increasing efficiency usually produces positive results. However, the quest for steady improvement in operations crowds out the question of whether the operations are worth doing in the first place! While the efficiency of the existing assets may be rising, the market is shifting, and customer value is slipping away. By the time companies that are caught in this cozy positive-feedback loop notice they are no longer delivering customer value, it's too late—competitors have seized the initiative.

Competing Priorities

For most executives, there are often many stakeholders who are closer at hand than customers. Employees, boards, partners, suppliers, and regulators all stand closer to executives than customers do. This proximity means that their concerns can easily become more urgent than those of customers. Meanwhile, within the organization, internal concern about resource allocation, budgeting, and turf wars with other functions become the most pressing priorities.

Contemporary Strategy Theories

The capabilities- or resource-based view of the firm is one culprit. These ideas have inadvertently tilted the dialogue within firms toward an inside-out view. Their supporters argue that the source of a firm's defensible competitive position lies in its distinctive, hard-to-duplicate resources and capabilities. Excellent service operations, strong supply chains, and superior human resource practices are advantages that are cultivated slowly over time. They are hard for competitors to copy, but they also limit the ability of the firm to adapt. In this theory, these resources exist to be used, and the task of management is to improve and fully exploit them. This is certainly a worthwhile goal to be eventually achieved. But as a starting point for strategic thinking, it myopically narrows and anchors the dialogue prematurely.

Darwin in the Enterprise

A contributing factor to the lure of inside-out thinking that can't be ignored is employees' inherent drive for self-preservation. Because firms (and business units, departments, and teams) are made up of human beings, they are inevitably tempted to put their own survival first. This instinct naturally accords with an inside-out view, since the outside-in view often requires a firm to reinvent itself—to employ creative destruction internally to meet ever-changing customer value expectations.

Going with the Flow

Another human trait that also drives inside-out strategy is the tendency to go with the flow and behave like the others around us. Social scientists call this social norming or "groupthink" when they study social dynamics, but companies and organizations are susceptible to social norming, too. Over time, the companies in any industry or sector tend to behave in the same way and to focus on the same issues and strategies—usually inside-out ones. When these industries or sectors are truly shaken up, it is usually because a new entrant makes a breakthrough in delivering customer value that the incumbents have overlooked.

These factors and others continually push executives toward inside-out strategy. Without constant effort and vigilance, inside-out thinking comes to dominate in the firm, and outside-in strategy disappears.

Detecting Inside-Out Thinking

The myopia of inside-out thinking is hard to detect when it becomes embedded in our mental models and shapes the way we do business. Mental models are simplifying frameworks that include prevailing assumptions, norms, and even the vocabulary used to talk about customers. They help impose order and provide handy rules of thumb. The problem is that these inherent simplifications and untested ideas don't announce themselves. Table 1-1 illustrates some that we have encountered in our study of inside-out and outside-in thinking.

TABLE 1-1 Mental Models and Strategy Approaches

Outside-In	Inside-Out
• All decisions start with the market and opportunities for advantage	• We'll sell to whoever will buy
• Profits are gained through a superior value proposition and leveraging the brand and customer assets	• Profits are gained through cost cutting and efficiency improvements. Six sigma, TQM and replicability of processes take priority
• Customer knowledge is a valuable asset and channels are value-adding partners	• Customer data are a control mechanism and channels are conduits
• We know more than our competitors	• If competitors do it, it must be good
• No sacred cows—cannibalize yourself	• Protect the cash flow stream
• Customers buy the expectation of benefits	• Customers buy performance features
• Superior quality is defined by customers as "fitness for use"	• Quality is conformance to internal standards
• The best ideas come from living with customers	• Customers don't know what they want and they can't tell you if they're asked
• Customer loyalty is the key to profitability	• Expanding the customer base is what matters

Market Insight

An outside-in approach to strategy is a clear necessity. However, it will not necessarily lead to a superior customer value proposition or outstanding economic profits unless it is guided by deep market insights. This brings us to the second lesson we've gleaned from the companies we have studied: that it is not sufficient to simply view the firm from the vantage point of the market. It takes smart investments in market intelligence and an organization-wide commitment to sensing and acting on the resulting market insights.

Within inside-out companies, market data usually reside in reports of competitors' moves, unrelated compilations of market research reports, and the occasional analysis of activity in the customer database. But data are not knowledge or insight! Valuable market insights are based on much deeper and more integrated knowledge that reveals patterns and identifies opportunities. Market insights are the difference between simply observing market trends and probing further to explain and exploit those trends.

Casella Wines saw the same trends in the wine market as its rivals did. Its deep dive underneath these trends uncovered a large nonconsumption market that was turned off by the myriad of confusing choices, the haughty nature of the category, and the dense vocabulary. Its answer was the Yellow Tail brand, with a simple and fruity taste, few choices, no vintages, and an endearing kangaroo symbol, which it parlayed into the most popular imported wine in the United States.[6]

The most valuable market insights are (1) accurate reflections of reality, not just what managers want or expect to see, (2) actionable, with the potential to mobilize and inspire the entire organization to develop new strategies or improve the current strategies, (3) not seen or understood by competitors, and (4) used in novel ways to influence strategy.

When distiller Diageo applied the insight that "Men want to progress in life," the power came not from its inherent novelty, but from its application to Johnnie Walker's label (turning the man so that he is walking forward, not backward) and a mass advertising campaign that used paintings on buildings to show the walking man's progress. The campaign increased sales 50 percent (to $5 billion) over a nine-year period.[7]

The Strategic Case for Market Insights

The case for timely and widely shared market insights has been made persuasively by Anne Mulcahy, chairman and former CEO of Xerox Corporation and *Chief Executive* magazine's 2008 CEO of the Year. Mulcahy believes that marketing and innovation are even more important in an era of demanding customers, information overload, and economic recession.[8] To create personalized solutions for data-intensive customers in law firms and health care, Xerox needs new learning capabilities, Mulcahy says.

In Mulcahy's view, learning about the market in which you compete starts at the top, and every senior manager has to be attuned to the voice of the customer, with marketing having overall accountability for what is learned and how it is used. To keep Xerox's management team focused on the market, its top 500 accounts are assigned to senior officers, who take responsibility for fixing customer problems. Mulcahy speaks enthusiastically about "dreaming with customers" by bringing customers into Xerox labs to identify their pain points and guide Xerox's innovation efforts.

Market-leading firms stand out in their ability to continuously sense and act on trends and events in their markets. They are better equipped to anticipate how their markets will respond to actions designed to attract and retain customers and to perceive emerging segment opportunities. In these well-educated firms, everyone from first-line sales and service people to the CEO is sensitized to listen to latent problems and opportunities. They achieve this with market-focused leadership that shapes an open-minded and inquisitive culture and a well-honed market learning capability that infuses the entire strategy development process.

Market insight is difficult for a company to master and for competitors to imitate, making it a basis for a durable competitive advantage. However, like all capabilities, it is vulnerable to creeping complacency and turning inward to focus on cost cutting, and/or an emphasis on short-term results that leads the firm to stop listening to the voice of the customer.

Intuit fell into this trap despite a history of providing superior relational value to customers that earned it the dominant share of the tax preparation market. By May 2000, its products dominated the retail market—Quicken had an 84 percent share, QuickBooks an 87 percent share, and TurboTax a high 60 percent share—and had 83 percent of the online market! Then Intuit began doing things that irritated loyal customers, such as raising the cost of customer service calls and limiting software licenses to one per computer. This caused growth to flatten and made the company vulnerable to attacks from venerable competitors such as H&R

Block's TaxCut and easier Web-based financial planning services, such as Mint.com, that also provided storage and better support for customers.

How Market Insights Enable Outside-In Strategies

Strategically useful insights address such questions as: What are our customers' real needs? Where are competitors likely to attack? Why are valuable customers defecting, and how can we keep them? How far can we stretch our brand? What happens if we selectively cut prices? What social media should we use? Market insights that answer such questions contribute to strategy decisions in four ways.

Making Fact-Based Decisions

Outside-in companies have a superior ability to make decisions based on accurate and up-to-date information rather than relying on gut instincts and familiar heuristics. This means the extensive use of databases that capture what is known about market structures (how are segments evolving and competitive positions changing?), market responses (what are the drivers of customer value?), and market economics (where is the firm making or losing money, and what moves will improve profitability?). The knowledge value in the data is unlocked with statistical analyses and predictive models.[9]

Anticipating Competitors' Moves and Countermoves

We are living in an interdependent world, where the success of strategy depends on the actions of present and potential competitors. The long-run success of the new Boeing 787 Dreamliner commercial jet depends on the way Airbus positions, prices, and markets its new A350 and A380 planes. Any intelligence about potential Airbus moves has high value to Boeing, and vice versa.

Deep insights into competitors' strategies can also reveal market opportunities.[10] Nintendo took advantage of the constraints that

Sony and Microsoft imposed on themselves with their mutual emphasis on superpowerful video-game consoles that appealed to hard-core gamers. Nintendo, with the Wii console, focused on an enjoyable game experience that appealed to all demographics. Because the console didn't have the expensive digital hub features of its rivals, it was launched at half the price. Best of all, Nintendo learned that because Sony PlayStation and Microsoft's Xbox were so closely associated with hard-core gamers, neither had the consumer's permission to enter the Wii space. This meant that Wii was not likely to suffer attacks from these electronic giants.

Connecting with Online and Networked Customers

The Internet has reshaped markets in many profound ways. Foremost is the shift in power to customers. Many information asymmetries have been wiped away, enabling consumers to ignore traditional push marketing and instead to go online to decide what to buy. This shift began with books and electronics and has steadily expanded to include most products and services. For example, currently almost 60 percent of baby boomers, not exactly the most tech-savvy demographic, go online to supplement their doctors' advice, and many more do so to search for information about products that they want to buy. The era of the passive consumer has ended.[11]

Proliferating media types and new distribution channels feed and are fed by increased consumer choice. The traditional three television channels and daily print newspapers have been displaced by targeted social media, online magazines, blogs, and newsgroups. New media and channels are promising more points of access to customers, but at a cost of fragmented strategies that dilute the efficiency of marketing spending. Traditional communications approaches that rely on one-way broadcast of a brand message over mass media are losing their efficacy. Instead, market insight will come from engaging in two-way dialogues with customers to understand what they want, and when and where they want it.

The possibilities can be imagined from Hewlett-Packard's experience with an online contest to design the skin of a new special-edition entertainment laptop.[12] The competition was launched with a low-key announcement via the Web and MTV. But word spread virally, and eventually 8,500 entries were submitted from 112 countries. The contest site got more than 5 million hits, prompting HP to quintuple its forecast of potential sales. These and other stories of new ways to collaborate and interact with customers magnify the need for clear outside-in thinking.

Guiding Growth and Innovation

Firms that are armed with deep insights into their markets become adept at sensing and acting on growth opportunities ahead of their rivals. Walmart found that its pharmacy customers routinely broke pills in half because they couldn't afford their full prescription. Their solution was $4 prescriptions for a limited list of popular generic medications. This offered a real benefit, especially to the uninsured, and attracted new traffic to Walmart stores.

Deep market insights are essential to the pursuit of new opportunities. By 2001, Toyota (in America) understood that its worthy, reliable brand had little appeal to Gen Y (the generation born between 1980 and 1994)—a group that it knew little about. Ethnographic and clinical research with Gen-Yers of a car-buying age uncovered key differences: these consumers were much more social, time-pressed, and able to multitask with technology, and they had a preference for personalizing their possessions with accessories. Toyota designed and then tested different car concepts and mock-ups to ensure that they were in tune with the market. One small, boxy, 108-hp model tested particularly well and became the basis of the new Scion line of cars. Toyota also learned that Gen-Yers would use only the Internet for initial research and did not want to negotiate price. This meant that dealers offering the Scion brand had to be transparent and accept a fixed price. The ROI on these market insights was impressive. By 2006, sales had reached 175,000 units, and the median age of buyers was 31, compared to 54 for Toyota and Lexus buyers.[13]

Designing Strategy from the Outside In

The third and final lesson from the companies we've examined is how they operationalize an outside-in strategy and deploy market insight to create customer value and maximize profits. Just as an outside-in perspective doesn't guarantee success without market insight, market insight and an outside-in strategy do not guarantee success without a series of intentional actions to build and reinforce customer value creation and profitability.

These actions are the major focus of this book because we find they are what really distinguish market leaders from other companies that are just muddling through. We call them the four *customer value imperatives*, because they are crucial to success. Moreover, they are imperatives for the top management of the firm. Without constant attention to these imperatives from the very top of the organization, any firm will quickly succumb to the centripetal forces pulling it toward an inside-out approach, and its position in the market will soon erode.

The Four Customer Value Imperatives

The first imperative is to *be a customer value leader* with a distinct and compelling customer value proposition. This requires the disciplined choice of where the firm will stake a claim in the market, what value it will offer its target customers, and how the organization will deliver that value.

All firms have to balance the short and the long term. A business strikes the right balance by earning superior economic profits in the short run, by maintaining its customer value leadership, and then by investing in a portfolio of innovations that will deliver results in the medium and long term. This is the second customer value imperative: *innovate new value for customers.*

Customer value and innovation benefit the firm when they are transformed into valuable customer and brand assets. The third imperative is to *capitalize on the customer as an asset.* This requires selecting and developing loyal customers, protecting them from competitive attacks, and then leveraging that customer asset by deepening and broadening relationships with customers.

Strong brands attract and retain customers and hence need to be explicitly managed. Thus, the fourth imperative is to *capitalize on the brand as an asset.* This means strengthening the brand with coherent investments, protecting it against dilution and erosion, and then leveraging it fully to capture new opportunities in both adjacent and international markets.

These imperatives build on each other, just as they build on the outside-in perspective and market insights. Different companies tend to be better at different imperatives—and companies' strengths in these imperatives also tend to vary over time. But the most profitable companies do all four better than their rivals over the long term.

Top-Management Focus on the Four Imperatives

The four customer value imperatives are the responsibility of the entire top-management team, or C-suite, and require the engagement and understanding of every part of the organization. The imperatives belong to the C-suite for four reasons.

First, as we've discussed, the pull of inside-out thinking is powerful and can knock even the best companies off course. If the senior management team is not committed to the four imperatives, then inside-out thinking will inevitably take hold, customer value will wane, and profits will erode. There is simply no way that a company can maintain an outside-in perspective if all of the C-suite has not fully bought in and committed to the four imperatives.

Second, executing on the customer value imperatives requires clear strategic choices about the allocation of resources and the capabilities to nurture. If the chief financial officer is attempting to cut working capital to the bone while the chief operations officer is attempting to deliver customer value via best-in-class inventory management, the value proposition is going to collapse. Executing on the imperatives requires every part of the firm's governance and operations to be properly aligned in the pursuit of delivering customer value—rewards and incentives, hiring strategy, risk tolerance, finance and budgeting, and sales. If any of these areas is marching to the beat of a different drummer, the firm's profits will be significantly impaired. Therefore, the C-suite doesn't just need to be familiar with the four imperatives, it needs to deeply understand them and embrace them. Ultimately, strategy is all about choices; the four imperatives crystallize these choices and provide a path toward making better decisions.

Third, these four imperatives have wide-ranging ripple effects throughout the organization. In the best companies, the imperatives resonate with all functions and at every level of the organization. Employees can readily see how their activities contribute to superior customer value. For example, the accounting group creates value when it develops flexible options based on the needs of different customer segments. The logistics/IT group enhances customer value when it works with a major account to coordinate supply chains. Service operations improve customer value by learning to anticipate and solve service problems—even before they happen!

Fourth, the imperatives are fundamental drivers of economic profit. Throughout this book, we'll show how each imperative contributes in direct and measurable ways to each of the components of economic profit: revenue, margins, and asset utilization.

Who Should Be Accountable for the Four Imperatives?

If everyone in the C-suite is responsible, then no one may be accountable in the sense of being answerable for these actions. The potential cost is lack of strategic consistency, which leads to ambiguous market positions and reactive, not proactive, decisions. Increasingly, firms are recognizing this reality and holding a specific member of the executive team accountable. Someone must be the focal point for orchestrating all the company's activities on behalf of the customer. Many entities within the company come in contact with the customer; but if no one individual is accountable, the total experience will be uneven, the brand will suffer, and customers will defect to rivals.

In many firms, this executive carries the title of chief marketing officer (CMO), and that's the term we'll use throughout the book for simplicity's sake. But make no mistake—the key issue is the role and *not* the title. A number of the best companies we've studied do not have a CMO; another executive in the C-suite leads the firm's response to one or more of the customer value imperatives. In fact, in many companies that we've studied, the person holding the title of CMO either does not have the authority, does not have the trust of other C-suite executives, or does not have the ability to succeed in this role.

The role of CMO is crucial to the success of an outside-in company, and therefore it must be earned. Executives within a marketing organization should not take it for granted that they will assume this role, nor should C-suite executives simply hand off the imperatives to the marketing function. The key skills, organizational investments, and choices needed to execute on the four imperatives are the topic of the last section of the book. There we'll also look at how several CMOs at outside-in companies have earned their position and used it to help keep their companies on track to superior profits.

A New Perspective

The next chapter describes each of the imperatives in more detail and explains how they fit together and how they create customer value and company profitability. Each imperative is then developed in detail in two chapters. The book closes with a deep dive into the supporting insight, organizational, and leadership conditions necessary to consistently apply strategies that respond to the four imperatives.

2

Profiting from Customer Value

Anyone who passes even a single day in the UK today is virtually certain to have an encounter with Tesco. But back in 1992, surprising as it may seem now, Tesco was in a state of crisis. The firm was an undifferentiated also-ran among grocery stores, steadily losing market share. Today it dominates its markets with three types of stores: big-box stores that would fit seamlessly into Korean or American suburbia, small-footprint urban stores that turn their inventory between lunch and dinnertime, and convenience stores near gas stations. Between 1995 and 2010, Tesco's market share doubled despite intense competition from archrival Sainsbury's, Marks & Spencer, and aggressive deep discounters such as Asda (a unit of Walmart).[1]

How did Tesco move from also-ran to titan? It began viewing everything it did from the perspective of customers. Tesco began its journey to an outside-in strategy in 1995, when it adopted a statement of core purpose: "To create value for customers to earn their lifetime loyalty." All questions about operations, human resources, finance, and retailing were answered by assessing whether the firm's target customers would see value. This customer-centric lens, known as "The Tesco Way," means that employees and managers obsess over delivering value to customers—whether in the form of a clean restroom, short lines at checkout, or lower prices on staple goods—and ignore any ideas that don't do so. With this quiet pragmatism, Tesco has become the third largest retailer in the world, entered 15 international markets, expanded into non-food businesses such as banking, and battled and often bested the world's most powerful competitors.[2]

Market leaders like Tesco bring together all the elements we introduced in Chapter 1—the four customer value imperatives, deep market insights, and an outside-in approach. By 2010, industry experts considered Tesco's market insight capability, in conjunction with a customer-first culture, to be the essence of its ongoing advantage. The foundation for this advantage was laid in 1995 by Terry Leahy, the CMO at the time, who later became the CEO. He began the turnaround from shrinking market share to global leadership by asking, "Why exactly are customers leaving?" Over many months, Leahy and his team dug deeply for the answers. From these insights, he crafted a proposal to the board of directors with three messages. First, if Tesco was to win, it had to first stop copying Sainsbury's and find a different path. In other words, Tesco needed to stop chasing Sainsbury's value proposition and find one of its own. Second, listening to customers had to happen at every level and across the entire firm. Third, the retail strategy and merchandising offers would be based on what Tesco's customers valued—not on what the company could do.

What Is Customer Value?

It is not too much to say that everything in this book is built on the pursuit of customer value. Customer value is a foundational idea in outside-in strategy. Perceptions of value drive customer choice, satisfaction, loyalty, and word of mouth. So what is customer value?

Unfortunately *value* may be one of the most overused and misused terms. Thus, the term *value price* is often wrongly used to mean a low price or a bundled price. Low-priced products can offer customers excellent value. However, equating customer value with low price obscures the more fundamental role that customer value plays in how markets operate and how firms must compete.

Ultimately, customer value is about the trade-off between the benefits that customers perceive they are getting from an offering and the perceived cost of obtaining these benefits—adjusted for the riskiness of the offer. We have found it useful to think about customer value using the following approach: Customer value = (1 − perceived risk) × (perceived benefits − perceived life-cycle costs).[3] The greater the perceived benefits and/or the lower the perceived total costs of a product, the greater the customer value and the higher the likelihood that the customer will choose that product. Let's look at each component in detail.

Ted Levitt, the author of the classic *Harvard Business Review* article "Marketing Myopia," famously observed, "People don't want to buy a quarter-inch drill. They want a quarter-inch hole!" *Perceived benefits* are the outcomes that customers associate with a product, service, or relationship with a company. What people want from a high-speed copier is high machine uptime, speed of throughput, and print quality, but customers also make copier choices based on the quality and speed of customer service. What people want from a video game is fun, excitement, and escape.

Customers' *perceived costs* also have many dimensions. For simple products, such as fasteners, the only relevant cost may be the initial price paid. With complex industrial products, though, many other costs are incurred over the life cycle of the product. In the personal computer market, most large buyers estimate that the total life-cycle costs incurred by the firm are six to eight times[4] the initial price paid for the hardware because of acquisition costs (including searching, ordering, processing, receiving, and installing), operating costs (notably energy consumption), psychological costs of learning a new system, and maintenance and disposal costs (including the cost of software upgrades, technical assistance, and repairs).

Buyer choices are also swayed by differences in *perceived risks* among vendors. The degree of risk depends on the buyer's uncertainty about the answers to the questions, "Can I trust the supplier's promises? Will the offering perform as expected? Will the vendor stay in business long enough to support the product in the future?" Small vendors with unknown brand names, no recommendations, and limited track records are at a real disadvantage because the perceived risks sharply offset the gains from superior perceived benefits. Therefore, the customer value framework requires outside-in thinking deeply informed by market insights for the following reasons:

- First, attributes do not replace benefits. Every manager we know endorses Levitt's powerful insight, but most of them proceed to ignore the message. Instead, they segment their markets by product attributes (type of drill, power, price point, and so on) or customer demographics, rather than by customer needs. This is inside-out thinking. It rarely yields deep insights into what customers want or how they are making choices. The result is imitative strategies and missed market opportunities.

- Second, within markets, customers vary in their emphasis on certain costs and benefits. Some segments of video-game customers want high-tech performance features that make a game it more realistic or futuristic, such as *Grand Theft Auto*; other segments want to personalize characters and the experience, such as in *The Sims*. The nature of the costs depends on the customer segment and the particular offering. Not all buyers will recognize these costs and incorporate them into their buying decisions. Furthermore, costs that will be incurred far in the future may be discounted back to their present value (consciously or not) at such a high discount rate that they virtually vanish.

- Third, customer value is dynamic. At any point in time, customers have a preference and know what they value.

However, as customers become more experienced and competitors shift priorities, value changes. This happens within specific customers and across markets as they morph and fragment over time.

Customer Value as a Goal

The centrality of customer value to outside-in strategy begs the question of not just *how* to define customer value, but *why* it should be the goal at all! For the last 20 years at least, the conventional wisdom has been that the goal of a firm is to maximize shareholder value. The durability of this goal is a tribute to the elegance of the argument and the speed of the feedback from the stock market on the achievement of the goal. If the stock price goes up, the right moves are being made.

The Great Recession has finally put a dent in the presumption that shareholder value is the best measure of a firm's success. Shareholder value as measured by equity prices is first and foremost a reflection of the expectations of future earnings. On average, less than 4 percent of a company's current stock price is a reflection of current earnings, while the other 96 percent is investors' expectations of future earnings. And so the only way to continually increase shareholder value is to continually increase shareholder expectations! But it is impossible to raise expectations indefinitely. Therefore, the pursuit of shareholder value inevitably leads to the manipulation of expectations and ultimately fails to deliver shareholder value except in the shortest of time frames.[5] This is not to say that shareholder value is not a critical outcome—only that shareholder value is not an outcome that can be or should be pursued *directly*.

If maximizing shareholder value is not a sustainable overriding goal, what should replace it? The answer was given long ago by Peter Drucker, who said, "It is the prospect of providing a customer with value that gives the corporation purpose, and it is the satisfaction of the customer's requirements that gives it results."[6]

Long-term shareholder value is the outcome of consistently generating economic profits. Economic profits are the outcome of creating and capitalizing on customer value. Simply put, the business has to get cash from customers before shareholders can receive it. This is why we put the four customer value imperatives at the center of an outside-in strategy—when effectively implemented, they drive long-run shareholder value.

Leading companies are following the path to shareholder value via customer value with more relevant objectives. When A. G. Lafley became the president and CEO of Procter & Gamble (P&G), bonus compensation for executives and senior managers was based on total shareholder return (TSR), which was defined as the increase in share price plus reinvested dividends over a three-year period. The flaw in the TSR metric is that great TSR performance in one year is generally followed by poor TSR in the next because earnings expectations have been reset to an unrealistic level that has no connection with strategy. Now P&G uses operating TSR,[7] based on three measures of how well the company delivers superior customer value (sales growth, profit margin improvement, and asset efficiency). The premise is that operating TSR drives the stock price over the long run. Moreover, the decisions of operating managers can directly influence operating TSR, unlike the market equity–based TSR.

The Customer Value Imperatives

So how does a firm that wants to pursue customer value via an outside-in strategy actually reach its goals, not just in the short term, but over the long term, as Tesco and others have done? Our work with and study of these leading companies led us to the four imperatives of customer value that we introduced in Chapter 1. These operational approaches ensure that a firm remains focused on creating and profiting from customer value. This chapter will feature Tesco as an example of how to apply the imperatives.

Imperative 1: Be a Customer Value Leader

Customer value leaders are companies that outperform their rivals by delivering superior value to a distinct segment of the market. They know that their target customers want as much value as they can get: the best product, at the best price, with the best service. They also know that these demanding customers have to make trade-offs and will give up one kind of value in return for another that is more important to them.

These trade-offs lead to the formation of three distinct customer segments in almost every market: (1) performance value buyers, who seek a product that meets their demanding requirements for quality, fashion, and/or functionality, (2) price value buyers, who simply want the best price for an adequate level of performance or service, and (3) relational value buyers, who put a premium on total solutions that meet their needs beyond product attributes, including service, financing, technical assistance, and so on.

Customer value leaders understand that they cannot be all things to all these segments. They make the hard choice of which segment to target, offer a value proposition that is distinct from those offered by their competitors, and deliver this value with a business model that is optimized for their market, while realizing that what they offer may underperform in other segments.

Nike is a *performance value leader*. When it burst onto the scene in the 1980s, Nike married its performance advantages with a fashion sense that swept the world. From this beginning, it has introduced technological innovations such as cross-trainers and Air Jordans. Its newest products have upheld that reputation—Flywire footwear that is super lightweight and uses threads stronger than steel, Proplayers sportswear that wicks and breaths with a second-skin fit, and the SUMO2 590 driver that takes a golfer's moment of inertia to exceptional levels.[8]

Zappos is a *relational value leader* in shoes, apparel, handbags, and related products. It creates strong brand affinity by going to extremes in customer service—free shipping on all purchases (and both ways, so that customers feel comfortable ordering multiple sizes and returning what doesn't fit), a 365-day return policy, staffing its call center 24/7, and surprise upgrades such as overnight service. Like all relational value leaders, Zappos has intensely loyal customers and gets approximately 75 percent of its sales from repeat customers. Behind the scenes is a strong customer-focused culture and the best customer relationship management system in the retail trade. The system not only tracks products and inventories, but also reminds employees to call customers back if there are problems and calculates the margin impact of putting an item on sale.

Family Dollar Stores is a *price value leader*. This "small-box" discounter leads its industry by staying tightly focused on its target customer, who, in 2010, earned just $35,000 per year. The business model looks like that of the other price-focused stores, with an emphasis on cheaper second- and third-tier brands and small stores in low-cost locations. This keeps prices comparable to Walmart's. Family Dollar gained its advantage because it acted on an insight that customers spent about the same amount—$10 per shopping trip in 2004—whether they shopped once a week or once a month. Clearly, the way to boost sales was to increase the frequency of shopping trips. To accomplish this, Family Dollar focused on becoming the place that people would go when they ran out of grocery staples like milk or frozen pizza. This was not easy to do; it meant adding refrigerators and redesigning the supply chain, while keeping costs low. Direct competitors were slow to see the same opportunities for creating customer value. Because the Family Dollar Stores were more convenient, it was able to avoid direct competition with much larger Walmart stores.

The Value Tesco Creates
Through convenient store locations, tailored assortments, targeted promotions, and outstanding customer service, Tesco has emerged as a relational value leader. Tesco's position is captured in its slogan "Every little helps." As an example of its commitment to

service quality, when managers learned that customers were upset by but resigned to long checkout lines, Tesco introduced its "One in Front" policy and publicly committed to keeping lines short. Cashiers were to signal for help if more than one person was waiting at checkout. While this sounds straightforward, the entire organization had to get behind this move and accept the added costs and responsibilities. Tesco's business model gives it an edge by simplifying every aspect of the business in order to pass its savings on to the customer.

Customers believe that Tesco's prices are on a par with those of all but the so-called hard discounters that offer a no-frills experience. Tesco may not have the lowest prices on every item, but it knows the market so well that it can pick out the products that customers use to decide which store is cheapest and selectively match rivals' prices. The quality and presentation of Tesco products are competent but not outstanding. Sainsbury's and Waitrose are recognized for higher-quality products, but at a significant price premium. Meanwhile, Asda offers rock-bottom prices that appeal to the 15 to 20 percent of the UK market that is very price-sensitive.

Imperative 2: Innovate New Value for Customers

It is not enough to win the battle for current customers' needs. This will not grow a firm beyond the inherent constraints of its served market. Thus, the second customer value imperative is to drive growth by innovating new value for current customers and attracting new customers.

Superior market and financial results are a reward for past efforts, but they cannot be used as an excuse for complacency, and they are certainly not a guarantee of future profits. If you want to maximize profits over the long term, you have to be not only a customer value leader today but a *customer value innovator* for tomorrow. A constant push for innovation is fueled by superior market insights into how customers are changing and what competitors are doing. As a result, customer value innovators are able to anticipate where markets are going and preempt challengers who are trying to match or leapfrog them.

Customer value innovation is not restricted to technology advances. Too many firms narrowly define innovation this way and miss opportunities to innovate new customer value. Being a customer value innovator requires a full-spectrum view of innovation, including new markets, product features, pricing models, business models, supply chains, and so on. Customer value innovators see opportunities for growth along every dimension of a competitive strategy—they pursue new geographies and new customer segments, create new and enriched customer experiences, rethink the profile of features in ways that competitors can't match, and reconfigure the way they create and capture value.

Customer value innovators also see that profits are maximized through a good mix of incremental innovations that yield low returns at lower risk, augmented by more ambitious undertakings that produce higher returns but push the firm outside its comfort zone into adjacent markets, technologies, and business models. Risks associated with these more aggressive innovations are mitigated through careful strategic moves.

The New Value Tesco Innovates

Tesco has also mastered the second customer value imperative. Its global revenue increased by 80 percent between 2003 and 2008, and before-tax profits grew by 105 percent. Tesco has grown its business by reaching current and new customers with alternative retailing approaches. For example, its city Metro stores switch from providing sandwiches at lunchtime to providing prepared dinners for the same customers to pick up on the way home. Express stores are smaller convenience stores, often located near gas stations. The Tesco Extra "big-box" stores are 10 times bigger than Metro stores and carry an expanding array of nongrocery items. Tesco has reached new customers abroad by expanding into 12 new geographic markets over the last 15 years. The success of Tesco's geographic growth is attributed to its ability to balance localization (to meet diverse needs) and standardization (to contain costs) through one of the best purchasing and distribution networks in the world.

Tesco has also recognized the huge opportunity in the adjacent market for retail financial services in the UK. Tesco's move capitalizes on the trustworthiness of its brand, the ubiquity of its locations, and the deep-seated customer distrust of big banks after the bailouts in the wake of recent financial crises. Indeed, Terry Leahy pledged to transform the supermarket chain into a "people's bank." Yet the risks were sizable. The record of retailers selling financial services was mixed, and some observers doubted whether Tesco had the depth of financial resources needed to compete effectively. To contain these risks, it started small with limited services, such as credit cards, and followed up with more complex products, such as bank accounts and mortgages.[9] Tesco's not-so-secret weapon in this battle is its vast transactional database, which has allowed it to learn about the market. As one analyst warned, "Tesco's skill at customer analytics is better than anyone in financial services. That ought to keep a number of retail banks awake at night."

Imperative 3: Capitalize on the Customer as an Asset

Customer value and innovation benefit the firm only if they can be transformed into valuable assets. Companies that master this imperative have found a way to consistently turn customer value into valuable customers. For these *customer asset managers*, customers produce profits by purchasing more in a category, purchasing across categories, purchasing new products, responding faster to company marketing activities, defecting less to the competition, investing in the relationship, and promoting the company more by word of mouth and by word of mouse. These behaviors influence the level, speed, and volatility of company cash flows. These profit effects are why managing customers should be viewed as managing an important asset of the company, despite the fact that customers are not owned and are not on the balance sheet.

Insurance company USAA has a customer retention rate of 96 percent in an industry that averages 80 percent. This relational value leader has built its strategy on excellent service with a deep connection to its customers' (members of the military and their families) lives. By synthesizing demographic information, purchasing behavior, and key life events, such as deployment, the birth of child, or a marriage, USAA customizes both the products it offers and when and how the offer is made. This strategy has produced strong relationships with customers, who have given the company permission to enter all aspects of their financial lives—from banking to insurance products to financial services.

When a firm has moved a customer from a focus on the single transaction or purchase to a sense of loyalty to the company, profits accelerate. This means both a strong commitment to the company and what it offers and a regular habit of purchasing from the company when the need arises. For performance value leaders such as Nike, customers trust that the company will improve the technologies and designs used in sneakers, clothing, and music systems. Customers are loyal to the resulting new products. For the price value leader Family Dollar Stores, customers give their loyalty in return for low prices and convenience. For the relational value leader Zappos, customers are loyal to a customized product or service experience that offers them outstanding and specific service.

How Tesco Manages the Customer as an Asset

Tesco has also mastered this imperative. It extended its relationship with customers by creating three convenient store formats that can be found near homes and places of work. Stores are stocked with products that reflect the tastes and preferences of customers in the area. For example, a Polish immigrant who moves into a neighborhood where he will be close to old friends will discover that the Tesco store carries the sausages he was used to buying at home. Tesco is also open and responsive to customer inputs. When planning to drop a poor-selling brand of bread, Tesco learned that the so-called milk loaf was a destination product for a loyal customer cohort that would shop elsewhere if the bread disappeared. While the bread itself sold poorly, it was a gateway product for a profitable customer segment. Tesco kept the bread.

Managing customers as assets requires the regular collection, integration, and utilization of customer information. Tesco's Clubcard offers customers a penny rebate per pound (sterling) spent, but to Tesco, the card is primarily an opportunity to gather detailed customer data and only secondarily an opportunity to offer discounts. Through this loyalty card, which is carried by 14 million customers, Tesco learns who buys what, when, and where.

Armed with this massive database and a superb analytical capability (the company continually wins awards in technology circles), Tesco adjusts its marketing appeals, its range of products, and the way the products are displayed within each store. By tailoring its product offerings to customers' needs using insights gained through the Clubcard, Tesco has earned customers' view of it as a trusted friend that understands what they need. The Clubcard also provides Tesco with information on customer margins and retention that can be used to invest in profitable customers and to grow others into a stronger relationship.

At Tesco, insights arise not only from the Clubcard but from employees' and managers' interactions with customers. Employees are encouraged to share their views on customer interactions and are often put in focus groups to gather customer experiences. Through the "Tesco Week in Store Together," or TWIST, program, corporate managers run the cash registers and stock shelves. This experience offers a deeper understanding of what customers experience in Tesco stores and an opportunity to learn directly what they want and need.

Imperative 4: Capitalize on the Brand as an Asset
Brands can also be valuable assets for companies. However, many companies fail to *capitalize on the brand as an asset*. A strong

brand makes a credible promise to reliably deliver a meaningful benefit. For example, GE "brings good things to life," "Think different" at Apple, and "Volvo is safety" lay claim to value propositions that attract customers, reduce perceived risk, and simplify the choice process. Strong brands don't automatically follow from strong value propositions, however. *Brand asset managers* devote sustained attention to three issues: building the brand by adopting a long-run investment perspective, protecting the brand against competitive attacks and loss of relevance in the market, and then optimizing the value of the brand asset by leveraging it prudently.

Brands can be destroyed by timid execution and confused strategies. An especially unfortunate example of what *not* to do is GM's offshoot Saturn brand, which emerged in 1991 as a "Different Kind of Car Company" and was finally shut down at the end of 2009 as part of the restructuring of General Motors. It was an early success with its strategy of no-haggle prices, a customer-friendly dealer network, and affordable cars. But sales peaked in 1994 as Saturn lost focus. The slide in the value of the brand asset started when the original car model wasn't replaced for a decade. Positioning became confused as Saturn lurched from one brand message to another. In 2001, it became the "Forward-Thinking Company," and when that didn't resonate, the new slogan was a meaningless "Like Always, Like Never Before." Then the once-affordable brand name was abruptly attached to a large sedan with Lexus-level features. This might have worked had Saturn spent several years reaching out to affluent buyers, but it hadn't. Saturn was so compromised by erratic decisions over its short life that its brand promises weren't believable.[10]

Why should marketers worry about strong brand reputations if the firm is already managing the customer as an asset? Most obviously, because positive thoughts and feelings can exist independent of customer purchase behavior. Brand reputation can serve as the "warranty" that customers rely on when making purchases.

Brand reputation not only enlarges the customer's relationship with the company, but also protects it. Customers are easier for rivals to pick off when a purchase of the brand is not coupled with positive associations and a sense of loyalty. Brand reputation is also helpful when the company fails the customer. Customers with strong beliefs about a company or its products rarely toss them aside after a single service or product failure. Instead, a strong brand can help a customer rationalize the event as an outlier and give the company another chance. Finally, brand reputation can be held and shared by those purchasing and not purchasing from the company. This buzz, propelled by e-commerce and social media, is more valuable to the firm than advertising or a sales force.

This imperative is critically important to a firm's economic profit because a strong brand is a vehicle for future growth activities among both new and current customers. Brand can help the firm penetrate existing markets, enter new geographic markets, and grow into new categories.

How Tesco Manages the Brand as an Asset

During the early period of Leahy's reinvention of Tesco, he was clear that Tesco would compete between the hard discounters and the more upscale stores, such as Sainsbury's. Everything Tesco did communicated a focus on "customer value" and a great love for the customer. Leahy's strategy was calculated, focused, and easy to communicate. This helped convert employees, who were often the first brand impression experienced by customers. And customers learned fast that Tesco was there for them.

Everything that Tesco does beams that love of customer. A visit to Tesco.com reveals a breadth of online offerings, personal development, and community activities. In discussing the move into personal banking, Andre Higginson, chief executive of retailing services, notes, "We believe in creating value for all our customers because that is how we earn their loyalty. Over time customers have come to trust Tesco to deliver value whether they are buying their weekly shop or opening a savings account."[11] This kind of trust pays off when Tesco is leveraging the brand into new categories.

How the Imperatives Work Together

At Tesco and the other companies we discuss, there are impressive profit payoffs from managing each imperative well. However, to unlock their full potential, it is necessary to understand how the imperatives work together in a system that the company can coordinate as it designs and executes its strategy.

Figure 2-1 shows the paths along which the imperatives reinforce one another over time. The process begins when a company creates value that customers are willing to pay for. As a relational value leader, Tesco stands out relative to competitors in the customers' eyes, and that is why customers are willing to pay for the value it offers.

We think it is useful to view customer value leaders as having created a real option by meeting the first imperative. Over time, these firms have the choice of building on their success in three ways—by innovating new value and by creating and leveraging valuable customers and brands.

Tesco acted on this option by driving innovation, by making decisive moves to capture a greater share of its customers' wallets across longer relationships, and by leveraging the brand into everything from online shopping to financial services. As shown in Figure 2-1,

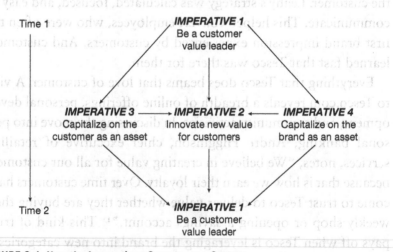

FIGURE 2-1 How the Imperatives Operate as a System

both the customer asset and the brand asset are sources of important growth opportunities for innovation. Tesco leveraged both of these assets as it entered new markets and new categories and invented new business models for online shopping and in-store banking.

Finally, if they are done well, innovation, customer management, and leveraging the brand strengthen the value associated with the original and evolved offering. Loyal customers bring renewed trust and commitment to the company, strong brands ensure that the company's offerings are in the customer's consideration set and top of mind in the marketplace, and innovation improves value over the original offering and gives the customers confidence that they can return to the company to meet a broader set of needs. So it has been with Tesco. These profit-making activities have not distracted the company or customers from Tesco's mission: "To create value for customers to earn their lifetime loyalty."

How the Imperatives Pay Off: Making Profits from Customer Value

We've repeatedly made the argument that pursuing customer value via these four imperatives leads to superior profits. You may very well be asking at this point how exactly profits arise in this system of outside-in management. Any reader who has been a senior manager for an enterprise knows that a company's profit model is complex, and therefore the answer to that question must take such complexity into account. In the next eight chapters, we will be answering the profitability question as it must be answered—in detail, with plenty of examples across various industries. In the meantime, though, let us offer a snapshot of some of the many paths to superior profitability that the successful pursuit of customer value yields.

We begin by defining what we mean by profits. We believe that economic profit is the ultimate measure of profitability. The simplest definition of economic profit is net operating profit (after taxes) less a charge for the opportunity cost of capital used.[12] Thus, there are two ways of increasing economic profit: increasing net operating profit or lowering the total cost of capital (which includes reducing the amount of capital needed).

The first imperative, *be a customer value leader*, can affect both elements of economic profit depending on the path to customer value a company chooses. Performance and relationship value leaders, for instance, can often charge a price premium and increase their margins. Price value leaders relentlessly reduce their costs but pass most of those cost savings on to customers. However, each time they lower their prices, price value leaders have the potential to capture market share and grow total operating profits.

The second imperative, *innovate new value for customers*, can increase economic profit in almost innumerable ways. New value can increase profits by opening up new markets, improving customer acquisition efforts, increasing customer loyalty, and increasing the firm's profits through business model innovations. When innovation is done properly from an outside-in perspective, risk is reduced, which in turn reduces expenses and capital charges.

The third imperative, *capitalize on the customer as an asset*, affects economic profits by proactively managing customers for maximum loyalty. The payoff comes when the firm captures more of a customer's wallet, experiences fewer defections, gains powerful endorsements, and spends less money on customer acquisition and retention. The customer asset is valued as the sum of the discounted long-term profits associated with these customer purchasing and influence behaviors.

The fourth imperative, *capitalize on the brand as an asset*, can play a critical role in growing profits over the long term. For example, as a company learns to leverage its brand to pave the way into new markets, operating profits can grow faster as market penetration time decreases. Similarly, another way in which the fourth imperative can enhance economic profit is that strong brands can help insulate customers from negative experiences and prompt endorsements even among people who don't purchase.

These are just a few simple examples, and the applicability of each example will vary from firm to firm, industry to industry, and context to context. The point is not to provide an exhaustive survey of the connections between the four imperatives and economic profit, but to show that the four imperatives are inextricably linked to growing economic profits. The better a firm executes any one of them, the greater the impact on economic profit. When a firm executes all of them well, the effect on economic profit is multiplicative.

Applying a New Perspective

Customer value is at the heart of an outside-in strategy. It is the right goal for firms that seek to maximize long-term profits. The leading firms we've studied take that conviction and turn it into effective action via the four customer value imperatives. As always, this is easier said than done. We'll spend the next eight chapters digging deeply into the four imperatives. For each, we'll first examine the "why"—the ways in which the imperative drives superior performance—and then, in the subsequent chapter, explain the "how," illustrating how leaders apply the imperative to capture profits.

Part Two

Operating Outside In:
The Four Customer Value Imperatives

3

The First Imperative:
Be a Customer Value Leader

Astride every competitive market stand one or more leaders that reliably deliver superior customer value and firm profits. What do these market leaders have in common? They figure out a way to maximize benefits for the customer and for the firm, while minimizing costs and risks. This sounds abstract in principle, but in practice it's quite concrete—it begins by first understanding the customer's priorities and then progresses by translating those priorities into a clear value proposition that drives company strategy and business model choice. In this way, companies as diverse as IKEA, Texas Instruments, and Apple achieve *customer value leadership*.

Being a customer value leader is the first and most important customer value imperative because it defines the strategic direction of the business. It shapes the investments that the firm must make and the capabilities that it needs to develop.[1] Customer value leadership is also the prerequisite and foundation for the other three imperatives. A company cannot capitalize on the economic value of customers and brands without first establishing itself as a customer value leader.

Of course, there is more than one way to be a customer value leader, since customers perceive value in different ways. An outside-in approach always begins, then, with a deep understanding of the value priorities for a target market in order to form a corresponding value position. The value position is what the customers and competitors see and explains why the offerings of the business are chosen or spurned. In this chapter, we'll examine the key concepts and frameworks for understanding these value positions.

Customer Value Priorities

Customers want as much value as they can get. They say, "Give me outstanding product performance, wide selection, and knowledgeable service, at the lowest price—all at once!" While customers demand the impossible, in reality they are constantly making trade-offs based on their needs. A frugal bank customer with many small withdrawals and little savings will opt for a no-fee account with unlimited ATM use and no personal service, whereas a customer with significant assets and a complex financial life willingly pays more for hands-on guidance. These trade-offs in product attributes and benefits fall into three categories of value: performance value, price value, and relational value. Customers tend to fall into one of three segments based on the type of value that is most important to them in a particular purchase situation.

Performance Value Priorities

For customers in the *performance value segment*, the main concern is whether the product is best at meeting their demanding requirements. This may mean having the highest perceived quality, the best functionality, or the most innovative features. This is why so many buyers of earthmoving equipment are attracted to Caterpillar, auto enthusiasts to BMW cars, and casual athletes to Nike footwear. As these three examples attest, performance value is also gained through fashion, style, and design superiority. The main driver of performance value is the perceived quality of the core offering (the shoe itself, the car, the device, or the meal in a restaurant). Does it meet or exceed customer expectations on each of the performance attributes?

Apple, for instance, delivers performance value. It achieved iconic status with the iPod digital audio player through its intuitive operation, its easy connectivity to a vast library of music, and a trusted brand. Apple is also known for superior design: The distinctive look and feel and trendy user base almost immediately established the iPod as a status symbol. Yet Apple's excellence most fully resides in the fact that its products are reliably easy to use. Apple protects that ease zealously and works just as hard to limit complexity as it does to add innovative functionality.[2]

Price Value Priorities

The top priority for the *price value segment* is to get the best price for an acceptable level of quality and performance. The emphasis is on the perceived total cost part of the customer value equation. These customers relentlessly seek bargains on the Internet, consult with like-minded friends who comparison-shop for bargains, and are acutely aware of prices. As a result of their being highly "deal-conscious," they are less loyal to their suppliers and may appear fickle in their choices. Their finely honed price sensitivity, however, does not mean that they will accept "cheap" offerings that are low-priced because of subpar performance or inadequate service.

IKEA meets these requirements by staking out a "low price with meaning" position in the fragmented furniture market. Most furniture retailers offer a wide selection of brand-name items with lots of sales help. IKEA's self-serve value proposition eliminates these familiar elements. IKEA does not provide in-store sales assistance and requires customers to do everything from taking their own measurements to pulling their own furniture off warehouse pallets. Customers have to transport their purchases home and assemble them. Costs are further reduced by limiting furniture to modern Scandinavian designs and moving manufacturing to low-cost countries. Product design is utilitarian, and IKEA makes no pretense that its products will last forever.[3] Yet IKEA is not a low-end big-box store selling cheap furniture in dingy warehouses in out-of-the-way locations. Its showrooms have a cheerful, airy, modern ambiance, with unexpected amenities such as playgrounds for children and cafés.[4] This means that, overall, IKEA measures up on basic service features of the retail experience while offering rock-bottom prices.

Relational Value Priorities

The decision process for customers in the *relational value segment* is to first screen the available offerings for acceptable price and performance and then make a choice based on the best service. These customers look at the total offering for augmentations such as technical assistance, integrated bundles of complementary products, repair service, knowledgeable sales staff, or help with financing. They put a premium on "solutions" that simplify their lives or operations and reduce the total life-cycle cost. In the home entertainment products market, these are the customers who are overwhelmed with the convergence of products and need credible help choosing among and installing the myriad of televisions or computer-based devices. They are more risk averse and therefore give greater weight to warranties, endorsements, and service.

Texas Instruments has prevailed over Intel in the market for semiconductor chips for portable electronic devices by cultivating a relational approach to managing its customers.[5] It does this by acting as the design lab for realizing its customers' ambitions. A relationship with Nokia provided the template for this strategy. Texas Instruments customized its chip for Nokia's cell phone software, which enabled the processing of large amounts of digital information quickly, with the result that this chip became the core of a generation of Nokia cell phones.

Texas Instruments further refined its strategy of working closely with aspiring companies when it provided the tailored light-processing chips that helped Samsung Electronics enter the large-screen, high-definition TV market. Texas Instruments' ability to direct its development efforts toward meeting customer design needs also helped advance its technology and enabled it to enter other device markets.[6]

How Do Customers Choose?

Customer value leaders need to have a good understanding of how customers choose in order to manage their value positions, both initially and over time. If customers see no meaningful differences among alternatives, they may simply take the best deal, take the first they see or remember, or stick with what they chose the last time. This is why brand familiarity and reputation are especially important in mature markets. Customers may be aware of four or five courier services and regard them as equally capable of meeting their needs. If they had a good experience with UPS, they are likely to use it again the next time. This apparent loyalty doesn't mean that the customer is emotionally attached to the company or even believes that it has a better offering—only that it worked last time.[7] There are several key points that customer value leaders should emphasize.

Customers Focus on a Subset of Offerings

The company should begin by getting a sense of the target customer's consideration set. This is not all firms! Saks and Neiman Marcus are usually competing in a different market from Walmart, Kmart, or Dollar General. Customers judge the relative positions of the offerings that are in their consideration set.[8]

In some cases, the target customer's consideration set will be the other brands in the same category. For example, Coca-Cola, Pepsi-Cola, and RC Cola compete head-on in the soft drink category. In other instances, the frame of reference might be brands in disparate categories. Even though Coke, Gatorade, and Snapple compete in the soft drink, sport drink, and iced tea categories, they all have a claim on a customer's "share of thirst." Roberto Goizueta, the legendary CEO of Coca-Cola, understood this when he observed that Coca-Cola accounts for only 8 ounces in an average customer's consumption of 64 ounces. He told his staff, "We must be resolutely focused on the other 56 ounces."

Customers Weight the Value Vectors

Once the consideration set has been assessed (or reassessed, as it should be vigilantly monitored), the firm needs to understand how target customers weight the different sources of value we have described. Given the three customer priorities and associated segments, it follows that customers will not evenly weight all sources of value that they see in the market. Instead, at any point in time, they will give greater weight to the source of value that they prioritize. The "value vectors" in Figure 3-1 reflect the three types of value that customers use when making a choice among competing alternatives.

This does not mean that customers will ignore the other sources of value. Instead, they will simply give these issues less weight as

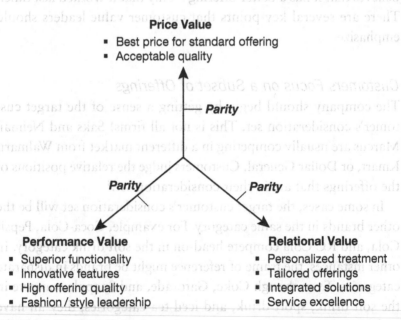

Price Value
- Best price for standard offering
- Acceptable quality

Parity

Parity   Parity

Performance Value
- Superior functionality
- Innovative features
- High offering quality
- Fashion / style leadership

Relational Value
- Personalized treatment
- Tailored offerings
- Integrated solutions
- Service excellence

FIGURE 3-1 The Value Vectors

they make their choice. If, for example, a product is very strong on performance but terrible on customer service or outrageously expensive, the customer may select an alternative that provides an acceptable level of service and price but is slightly lower on performance relative to the strongest product. Once an acceptable level is met (something that we will define as parity), the customer will pick the product that gives him the best weighted combination of the three types of value.

Customers Assess Offering Performance: Below, At, or Above Parity

Customer value leaders must also realize that actual differences between products are irrelevant. When customers choose, they do so on the basis of their perceptions of the product. Therefore, the value vectors are a handy aid to outside-in thinking because the customer's views can be easily located relative to competitors.

Each vector has a parity position. This is the level of performance that must be achieved if the customers are to judge that a firm's offer is credible. Will their next car be a Hyundai, an Audi, or a Ford? In the minds of prospective customers, each of these three auto brands, and many more, has a position that is above, below, or at parity on each vector.

This parity level is more than just the minimum requirements for playing the game. Instead, it usually means at least a moderate, and often a high, level of perceived competence. This level of competence is reached by most competitors. As a consequence, customers do not see a meaningful difference among the offerings. Parity is an outside-in concept. The question is not whether there is an *actual* difference between competitors on a specific axis. It is whether customers *perceive* a meaningful difference. Inside-out companies often deceive themselves by believing that their carefully managed differentiation efforts matter to, or are even noticed by, customers.

How does a firm judge whether its offerings are at parity? The arbiter is always the customer, including those who buy from the firm now, those who have never bought from the firm, and those who have stopped buying from it. One way to assess parity is to ask a sample of customers to rate the firms or brands on key features and benefits. The rating scale could ask, for example, whether Xerox desktop copiers are ahead of, equal to, or behind competitors on print quality, technical support, price, and so forth. The comparisons could be against the market leader and/or against top competitors for the target segment of customers. A consistent rating of equality across offerings in a category is compelling evidence of parity.

In the worst case, competitive alternatives are all seen as being close to parity on all three vectors. The markets are essentially stalemated, since no leader is established on any value vector. Without meaningful differentiation, the conversation between buyers and sellers usually deteriorates to a negotiation about price. The resulting downward pressure on margins means that few firms have economic profits that exceed their cost of capital.

The Dynamics of Customer Value Positions

There is a law in economics that every situation bears the seeds of its own reversal. This is the law of nemesis—nothing good lasts indefinitely, because others will want to share it.[9] The corollary for customer value leaders is that no competitive advantage is ever secure in the long run, and, unfortunately, the definition of the long run is getting shorter in every market. This means that the top management team must have a clear outside-in understanding of the possible scenarios for the evolution of the market it serves if it is to stay ahead of rivals.

How Markets Evolve
The product life cycle is the reigning framework for describing how markets are presumed to evolve through the well-known stages of introduction, growth, maturity, and decline.[10] There is a misleading

inevitability to this stylized treatment of market evolution that seriously undermines its contribution to strategic thinking. Instead, savvy strategists understand that each market has its own rhythm, which is shaped by the interactions of customers and competitors. These managers have deep insights into the following forces that shape the rate of market growth and its long-run size, which they turn to their advantage.

Diminishing Consumer and Competitor Uncertainty over Time[11]
During the introduction of a new product or category, consumer uncertainty about quality, benefits, and value is at its highest. Some uncertainty is due to the fact that the first offering of a break-through product may not be as good as established products and is usually more costly to produce. For example, early versions of digital watches and cellular phones were bulky and power-hungry, with limited capabilities. Additional uncertainty arises during the introduction stage because customers can't envision the product's benefits, and therefore adoption is slow. Facing these customer dynamics, powerful competitors may adopt a "wait and see" attitude. This makes it difficult for firms competing in young markets to fully appreciate how the industry will develop. Over time, customers will gain confidence, and the rules of the competitive game—the accepted assumptions about how value is created and captured—will be clearer. Hence, companies need to "think forward and reason back" about where customers will be moving and how competitors will be acting in the future.

Coevolution of Products and Markets
As markets unfold, their growth potential may still be limited by what prospective customers can envision from their experience. This usually underestimates the latent potential demand, which emerges only after the market gains experience with the product or service. The latent market potential of an emerging technology can be difficult to anticipate, as illustrated by the introduction of

the Apple LaserWriter printer in the 1980s. This printer was positioned by Apple as being much quieter than the existing daisy-wheel and dot-matrix printers. But Apple's incorporation of Adobe's PostScript page description language did something else that became much more important. Unlike existing printers, which were essentially computerized typewriters, the PostScript devices could print both text and graphics. When this capability was unleashed with new computer software, the field of desktop publishing emerged, and laser printer sales greatly exceeded the forecasts.[12]

Morphing Market Boundaries
The traditional strategy playbook is anchored on fixed and well-defined markets—the competitors are familiar and stable, and product functions are well defined and distinct from adjacent categories. As markets evolve, firms find themselves in increasingly dynamic and competitive environments. In the new game, competition to satisfy customers' requirements comes from unexpected places—especially in the fast-converging computing, telecommunications, and entertainment industries. Market boundaries have evolved from fixed to fuzzy, with overlapping substitutes and complex role reversals in which customers become competitors and vice versa.

Globalization is further intensifying and complicating the competition for customers. Plummeting communication costs and diffused manufacturing capabilities permit the entry of hordes of low-cost competitors into many industries. As emerging-market firms build their capabilities, they expand their reach. Some people foresee a world in which companies from every part of the world compete with one another in every market. Products and services flow from many locations to many destinations,[13] and firms that do not solidify their value leadership soon find their customers being enticed away by firms that were not even on their competitive radars.

Misleading Market Measures

Industry conventions and entrenched practices can lull market-share leaders into a false sense of security. Artifacts as innocent as the way market data are classified in research studies, sales reports, and government classifications/categories can contribute to these inside-out blinders. At one time, for example, markets for breakfast cereal, energy bars, and candy bars were considered separate because the products were sold in different aisles of the grocery store. Then came "breakfast cereal bars" (cereal in the shape of a candy bar), which served as a catalyst for consumers to eat portable cereal throughout the day, and thus mixed the categories. Taking a 5.4 percent share of the U.S. snack market over the 35 years since their introduction, these offerings dramatically changed the competitive landscape of the cereal market.[14] However, many firms missed the threat and failed to see the opportunity to create new customer value because they were focused only on familiar market metrics about cereal.

Changing Value Priorities in Evolving Markets

In most markets, a relatively large price value segment eventually emerges. The timing depends on two reciprocal processes: customers gaining confidence in their ability to make choices, and credible price value leaders entering.

Customers Gain Confidence

With experience and repeat purchasing, customers become ever more knowledgeable about the characteristics, appropriate usage patterns, and applications of a product or service. It is no longer a novelty or the purview of enthusiasts and early adopters. For many customers, the performance value that first attracted their patronage becomes a given, and they feel less need for technical support, education, or even prestigious brands as a signal of quality. These buyers are increasingly confident in their choices and may not believe that there is much difference among the available alternatives.

When this happens, the dominant companies in the market are likely to overshoot the requirements of segments of their target market. In their zeal to keep ahead of their rivals on the performance vector, these companies deliver more functionality and quality than customers in the lower tier of the market can utilize or are willing to pay for. Customers will not keep paying ever-higher prices for benefits that they do not need.[15]

Price Value Players Enter

Customers with confidence become even more price sensitive when there are credible suppliers available to meet their core needs. This sets the stage for a rush of price-focused entrants or the expansion of niche players that previously operated on the fringes of the market. These firms leverage forces such as globalization, deregulation, and supply-chain innovation to offer dramatically lower prices for standard, plain-vanilla offerings of acceptable quality. This was the path taken by companies that now command significant market share, such as Ryanair, IKEA, Huawei, and Vanguard Investments.

When buyers with significant purchasing power emerge in a given market, it creates even more incentive for price value aspirants to enter the fray and create more profound price pressure. This kind of power shift is seen when shrinking perceived product differentiation justifies delegating the choice of vendor to the purchasing function of a firm, or when the purchasing function itself becomes more powerful and takes aggressive action to make price the primary choice factor. This kind of power shift is seen, for example, with the ascendance of hospital buying groups that pool the purchases of affiliated hospitals and in the concentration of purchasing power among powerful retailers such as Walmart.

Evolving Customer Value Positions

As growth slows, the struggle for competitive position intensifies, and the strategies of incumbents start to converge. This results in difficult strategy problems: escalating parity and the value vectors changing in importance.

Parity Is an Escalating Target

There is a well-known "herd mentality" among incumbents that leads to continuous jockeying to establish "points of parity" along the value vectors. It is not enough for a mid-tier hotel to offer cable TV and room service; to meet the competition, it must offer high-speed Internet access and down duvets. From toothpaste to credit cards to orthopedic devices, the degree of perceived differentiation steadily diminishes because of the relentless process of imitation.

Keeping pace with rivals in the served market is a requirement for staying in the game. Falling noticeably behind on any one of the three value vectors erodes the overall customer value position. One effect of everyone keeping pace is that the parity level on each vector steadily moves outward: performance improves, real prices drop, and service is better.

As parity advances on all three vectors, companies have to spend more just to stay in the game. Customers, especially business customers with dedicated purchasing resources, are more informed and more willing to play one competitor against another. As customers' expectations about acceptable performance on each attribute rise, they are less willing to accept below-parity performance on any vector.

These pressures require firms to pay increasing attention to all three value vectors, not just the value vector on which they seek value leadership. Performance value leaders can't allow their prices and costs to be badly out of line or their service to be viewed as unacceptably poor. If they do, such leaders will be forced to offset the deficiencies in the total value of their offering by lowering their prices.[16]

One culprit in this escalation is the tendency to try to improve operational performance by imitating the best practices of other companies. Such improvements seldom produce sustainable leadership, however, because best practices diffuse so rapidly. Consultants share their experience with other clients in the same industry, employees regularly move between firms, and managers attend the same industry meetings or read the same blogs, journals, and newsletters. Hence, the irony of best practices competition is that it leads to an absolute improvement in productivity and performance across all competitors, but a relative improvement for no one. Parity reigns. The absolute gains are more likely to be captured by customers.

The Value Vectors Change in Relative Importance

Figure 3-2 shows a common pattern of change in the importance of the value vectors as the market evolves. The length of each value vector is a linear representation of its relative importance compared to the other two. Both the price value and the relational value vectors become larger relative to the performance value vector as the market evolves toward maturity. At the same time, the parity level continues to move out along each vector (from t_1 to t_n).

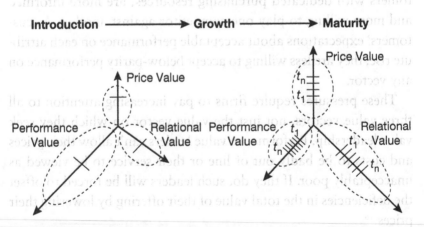

FIGURE 3-2 Evolving Strategic Positions

If a firm can read this transition effectively and jump on the opportunity, it can be a great success. The story of Commerce Bank (see the sidebar that follows) illustrates both the tendency of price players to enter and the tendency to prioritize relational value to emerge. While this does not always happen in such a textbook manner as it did for Commerce Bank, we observe this type of evolution and impressive disruption in other industries as well.

Commerce Bank realized that customers had become accustomed to—but were not especially happy with—high prices and poor service. There was a segment that increasingly valued a relational strategy—perhaps in part as a backlash to the price focus, and also in part as a more enduring need.[17] Commerce Bank attracted a large segment of customers with a superior retail experience as the relational value vector became more salient.

Learning from Retail Banking

Retail banking in developed countries is mature and highly competitive. The core loan and deposit offerings are undifferentiated. Rate differentials and service improvements are matched quickly. Another sign of maturity is the long-run trend toward consolidation and a polarized industry structure. Within the U.S. banking market, many mid-tier banks were acquired or squeezed out during the 1980s and 1990s, leaving large banks (e.g., Bank of America and Wells Fargo) competing on the basis of scale and coverage, while local niche players specialized in meeting the idiosyncratic needs of their community.

As the forces of consolidation played out, the big banks converged on similar strategies to gain scale and reduce operating costs so that they could afford their acquisitions. They expanded their branch networks to attract the deposits they needed and targeted their most valuable customers with bundled offerings, while reducing service levels and actively pushing most customers to use low-cost ATMs and Internet banking. This exacerbated a tendency toward a transactional rather than a relational mindset, as reflected in their selection of front-line employees for their ability to perform repetitive tasks, comply with processes, and accept relatively low pay.

Retail banking customers were not pleased. By 2001, only 53 percent were very satisfied with their bank. Because these customers were also better informed, they shopped around and became less loyal. The result was that a retail bank could lose up to a third of its customer base each year to moves and defections.

In these conditions of deteriorating service and more demanding customers, Commerce Bank prospered with a value proposition that emphasized relational value. From 1999 to 2008, the bank expanded from 120 to 400 branches in the northeastern United States, with average revenue and asset growth of 28 percent and 36 percent per year, respectively, and a customer defection rate half that of its larger rivals. Between 1999 and 2004, deposits grew from $5.6 billion to $27.7 billion, and loans tripled from $3 billion to $9.4 billion. In 2001, deposits grew by almost 40 percent, compared to the nation-wide average growth rate of 5 percent.

There were many facets to Commerce Bank's outside-in strategy:

- Think like a retailer, not a banker. Focus on delivering a superior customer experience, with branches designed to look more like retail stores, with roaming tellers, no desks, and children's play areas.
- Compete on convenience as defined by the target customers. This meant weekend and evening hours, responsive service, leading online banking services, and reimbursement of fees for use of out-of-network ATMs.

- Build a customer-centric culture, with "customer first" values woven into everything from training and selection of front-line employees to the operation of the call center.
- Stay close to parity on the price value vector, but don't match rivals with the lowest costs. This trade-off was necessary to cover the costs to provide greater relational value.[18]

The presumption behind the declining relative importance of the performance vector is not that performance becomes less highly valued. As time passes and technology diffuses, features are matched and customers become more knowledgeable about how to use the product, so that performance value becomes "table stakes," or a requirement for participating. Performance is still crucial, but to most buyers it is no longer a differentiator and thus is given a lower priority in their choice process. Most rivals will deliver a very competent core product. This "normal" evolutionary process may be disrupted by an innovation that initiates a new life cycle because it delivers a 2 to 10 times improvement in performance. This is the aim of pharmaceutical firms seeking a blockbuster drug for a crowded category.

This trajectory of relative vector importance is neither foreordained nor irreversible. Incumbents can either facilitate or inhibit the seemingly inexorable growth of the price value vector by their actions. Also, the relative importance of each value vector depends on the choices that are available in the market. As the Commerce Bank story illustrates, if no firm offers superior relational value, this vector will remain stunted because customers usually can't visualize what they are missing.

Anticipating Changes in Value Positions

Vigilant management teams have a deeply informed outside-in view of how their competitive position will evolve, and they use this knowledge to shape the forces of change to their benefit. Each member of the team will have a functional viewpoint that will provide important input to the strategy process. The COO will have insight into how the supply chain may shift, and the CTO may have her finger on the pulse of new research that will influence new product development.

The transition to maturity creates a number of dilemmas for customer value leaders. As revenue growth slows, pricing pressures may cause earnings growth to slow. To sustain growth, it is tempting to match each move that competitors make and, in turn, challenge them in their target segments. While this may be expedient in the short run, the long-run consequence is usually a loss of focus, a blurred position in the market, and rising costs of complexity in strategy and offerings.

That doesn't mean that customer value leaders can ignore the competition. The evidence[19] is that while most experienced executives (70 to 75 percent) do consider the current competition when making product or pricing decisions, only 8 percent report thinking through *future* competitive responses to product introductions, while 15 percent consider reactions to price changes. One way for value leaders to stay ahead is to anticipate competitive moves and reactions, and concurrent shifts in customer value priorities, then reposition the firm to shape the shift to its advantage.

A case in point is Redpath Sugar. Few markets are as undifferentiated as refined sugar. Brand names are weak; the soft-drink, baked goods, and retail customers are powerful and insist on dual sourcing; and the market is barely growing. Two big competitors—Redpath Sugar and Crystal—were locked in a stalemate, which was reinforced by a collective inside-out mindset that emphasized scale and production efficiency to drive down costs. Both rivals competed on price value with the same products and sales approaches. Customers got the message and based their purchasing decisions solely on price and delivery terms.

To escape the profit-draining stalemate, Redpath Sugar first sent most of the C-suite to "live with" its 17 largest customers. The results were discouraging, because they discovered that the two suppliers were considered equally competent, but no different. The results were also encouraging because they discovered that the needs of these customers were changing. Customers wanted shorter production runs, faster deliveries, more varieties of product and packaging, and smaller inventories on hand. None of these emerging requirements could be met with the current business model of large refineries and regionally centralized warehouses.

Redpath's selection of a relational value strategy, based on partnering to manage the customer's total requirements, was obvious in retrospect but daunting in prospect. The necessary changes in the supply chain (more decentralized warehousing and just-in-time dispatching and delivery) and in the costing and tracking systems required a different mindset and a significant investment (a $40 million modernization and capacity expansion project completed in 1997).[20] Many of the traditional salespeople could not adapt to the sophisticated solutions approach to selling. There were intense demands that the leadership delay the organizational changes. However, with town hall meetings and extensive conversation at all levels, this resistance was eventually overcome. The new strategy was validated within two years, as customers slowly integrated their production process with the company's logistics system and gave Redpath a growing share of their business because of the associated cost savings.

Customer Value Leaders

Customer value leaders create value that their customers will pay for by formulating their strategy from the outside in. The strategy development process begins by asking: "Which needs of which target customer segments are we going to serve better than anyone else, while being seen as competent and competitive in meeting the rest of this market's needs?" This choice provides a positioning theme around which an organization can mobilize its resources.

Managers must also develop a point of view concerning how their company's target markets might evolve and the strategies that should be adopted to shape the market to their advantage.

In summary, top management's task is to decide how to create and sustain the firm's customer value position. In the next chapter, we look at these choices more deeply to understand how value leaders gain and sustain their positional advantage.

4

Becoming a Customer Value Leader

oth IBM and McDonald's have faced near-death experiences by
failing to keep customer value their highest priority. At the turn
of the millennium, McDonald's had become a fast-food "fuel
depot," beset with serious problems, including a decline in food
quality, shoddy service, a hazy brand promise, and a poor bottom
line. The company was resuscitated by speaking directly to its core
customer's desire for an effortless service experience, with the
promise of "simple, easy, enjoyment."[1] In 1993, IBM was on the
verge of breaking itself up into independent product and service
companies before it realized that it had everything it needed to solve
its customers' information technology problems. Under Louis
Gerstner, IBM's new strategy was to marry strong technology with
powerful customer solutions that were in sync with emerging
network and Internet trends.[2]

Both these turnarounds and the sustained success of customer
value leaders like UPS and Caterpillar have their genesis in crystal-
clear customer value strategies. These leaders don't try to straddle
the entire spectrum of value positions. They accept the familiar
adage, "You can't be all things to all people." Many executive
teams initially reject this premise because they don't want to make
choices that will limit the market that they can serve. This inside-
out delusion is dangerous on two grounds. To begin with, both customers and employees are likely to be confused about the firm's

positioning. The brand message is murky, the selling appeals lack consistency and clarity, and the product or service bundle is a series of compromises. Such a strategy is also vulnerable to attacks by more focused competitors.

These leaders are more profitable because of their disciplined outside-in strategic choices. There are several paths to their profitability. Customers of performance and relational value leaders are willing to pay a premium price for the superior value that these leaders deliver. Price value leaders win with lower costs because of superior scale utilization and cost discipline. Leaders also work hard to stay at parity on the other two vectors.

Profitability will be penalized if the firm is noticeably below parity on one vector—even if it clearly leads on another vector. This is especially true with inadequate service. Customers may tolerate missed deadlines or partial order fulfillment from firms with a material performance advantage that can't be matched by competitors, but they will demand a sizable price discount as compensation for the aggravation.

Winning strategies are distinctive, hard-to-imitate, and closely aligned combinations of the customer value proposition and the business model. The CEO and CFO take the lead role in setting the objectives to balance financial capacity (what can we afford?), equity market expectations (what do we need to achieve?), and the aspirations of the organization (what will realistically motivate and challenge the organization?). The CMO or her counterpart takes the lead role in specifying the value proposition (target customer segment, offering, and competitive profile). The entire C-suite works together to craft a business model that can reliably deliver superior value to customers.

In this chapter, we explain how customer value leaders gain their advantage and convert it into superior profits. But gaining an advantage is only the beginning of the journey. Outside-in strategists are always prepared to defend their leadership position from competitive attacks.

Elements of a Customer Value Strategy

Every business needs a customer value strategy to allocate resources and to give direction to the organization. Yet there is little agreement about what belongs in a strategy statement.[3] Sometimes strategy is confused with aspirations, such as becoming a technology leader, or actions, such as outsourcing. If the aim of a customer value strategy is to help firms make tough choices about where and how to compete, it must start by asking three questions from the outside in:

- What is our primary business objective?
- What is our customer value proposition?
- What is our business model for delivering and monetizing customer value?

Business Objectives

Objectives specify the ends that the strategy intends to achieve. For an objective to be actionable, it must be specific, measurable, and time-bound. Objectives should be aspirational, but they should also be clear. Aspirational objectives such as "we seek to grow profitably" are confusing because they don't say what takes priority—growth or profits.

The choice of a dominant objective has profound consequences for the rest of the strategy. It will guide the selection of the customer value proposition and the business model used to achieve it. Hence, all three elements must share an outside-in focus.[4]

The Customer Value Proposition

The phrase *customer value proposition* is often heard but rarely defined consistently. Three different uses of the phrase are common.[5] For many people, the phrase means all the tangible and intangible benefits that managers imagine target customers receive from their offering. The more benefits listed, the better! Another usage considers only points where a product is superior to the next best alternative, whether or not customers value these differences.

We prefer a third variant that we see in use among customer value leaders. A customer value leader bases its value proposition on a resonating theme—a few elements where the firm is distinctly better than the competition that really matter to a target market. An effective customer value proposition offers superior performance, price, or relational value and communicates that value in a way that shows that it has a deep appreciation of the customer's value priorities.

The choice of value proposition is also the choice of *target customer segment*—and vice versa. The integrity and consistency of these two interlocking choices explains why Edward Jones, the fourth largest brokerage firm in the United States, has outperformed its rivals in all kinds of markets.[6] Its relational value proposition is to offer "trusted and convenient face-to-face financial advice to conservative individual investors who delegate their financial decisions." Unlike rivals that define their target segment by net worth or income, Edward Jones works closely with investors defined by their needs. In particular, its customers are long-term investors who are uncomfortable making investment decisions without the guidance of a trusted advisor.

When we take apart a distinctive value proposition, we find that three interlocking choices have been made:

- **Target customer segment.** The business has a shared view of the segment(s) to be served based on the type of value that is most important to those customers. Well-positioned firms also know which segments they don't want to serve. Thus, Edward Jones chose not to pursue day traders.
- **Offering.** What will the firm offer the target segment(s) to meet its needs? Will it be just the core product, or will it be a

complete solution that augments the core product with personalization and support services? What products or services will *not* be offered because they are inconsistent with the value proposition? For example, Edward Jones does not offer any proprietary mutual funds to avoid compromising the independence of its financial advisors and undermining the trust of its clients. It is important to remember that the offering includes all aspects of the customer experience—everything that the customer sees, hears, and feels when interacting with the firm.

- **Competitive profile.** How well does the firm's offering compare to competitors' offerings on the key value attributes? The key is to have a distinctive profile on these attributes that meets the needs of the target segment.

These elements intersect to create a winning value proposition for the Ginger budget hotel chain, launched in India in 2004 by the Tata Group (which also runs the Taj Hotel chain). The chain was designed to meet the needs of frequent business travelers who wanted a place to stay that was not as earthy and unpredictable as a low-price hotel, but who could not pay the sky-high prices of a five-star hotel. Patrons have compared the experience to Holiday Inn Express, UK Travelodge, and Hampton Inn.[7]

The Ginger brand promises a customer experience that is "consistent, simple, light-hearted" at the best price. The small rooms are strictly no frills, with dorm-style furniture, but with state-of-the-art new mattresses. Costs are tightly controlled by locating the hotels in business districts, away from high real estate cost areas, and using self-check-in and minimal staff. The resulting competitive profile shown in Figure 4-1 clearly sets Ginger apart from the competing hotels and aligns the hotel with the needs of its target segment.

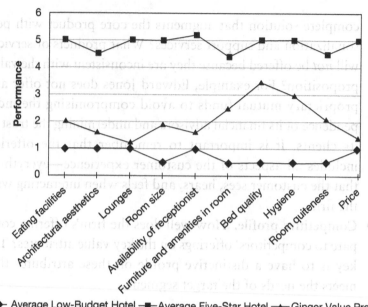

—◆— Average Low-Budget Hotel —■—Average Five-Star Hotel —▲—Ginger Value Profile

Source: Published materials, site visits, and hotel reviews.

FIGURE 4-1 The Budget Hotel Market in India

The Business Model

If the value proposition is *what* the company offers to the target segment, then the business model is *how* the business profitably fulfills this promise.[8] Effective business models of outside-in companies are tightly synchronized to fit the value proposition—not the other way around. What distinguishes Edward Jones from Bank of America (Merrill Lynch) and Wells Fargo is that it has only one financial advisor per office. Because there is no branch office infrastructure to give direction and support, each financial advisor has to be entrepreneurial and self-directed. These offices are located in strip malls and retail districts of suburbs so they are convenient to clients. This helps the firm deliver personalized attention and builds trust. However, this reduces profits because operating 10,000 separate offices imposes high real estate and advertising costs.

The word *model* suggests a complex and abstract representation. Good business models are anything but abstract. They answer two enduring questions: (1) "What business activities are necessary to create the value that we promise our customers?" (What is the value-creating system?) and (2) "How do we make money while creating value for our customers?" (What is the value-capture system?).[9]

The Value-Creating System

The value-creating system comprises all the activities that the firm links together to create and deliver customer value, from basic inputs to create products and services through to the channels used to sell, service, and distribute an offering. It represents firms' choices of (1) which activities to perform, (2) how these activities are sequenced, and (3) who performs them.

Every business needs many capabilities to move its products or services through the value chain. Each capability, such as order fulfillment or service delivery, is a complex bundle of skills, knowledge, and systems, exercised through a distinct process for coordinating the sequence of activities.

There are, however, only a few distinctive capabilities or core competencies within each business that really contribute to the creation of superior customer value. These should be lavished with management attention because they are so essential to the strategy. What sets Marriott Hotels apart from its peer competitors is a service operations capability performed with a fanatical attention to detail. This capability begins with recruiting and hiring and continues through standardized hotel operations. The payoff is a consistent service experience—Marriott customers seldom have unpleasant surprises. Marriott's other capabilities are done well enough to keep the company in the game, but they are not the basis of its advantage.

The question of who performs the value-creating activities is increasingly pressing as firms evolve toward a role as a controlling node in a network of intermediaries and partners. Consider

Li & Fung, the Asian trading company that supplies more than $14 billion in clothing, toys, and other products for top U.S. brands, but does not own a single factory. Instead, a single order can be sourced from a network of about 10,000 suppliers around the globe. This gives Li & Fung incredible flexibility and speed that customers value.

The Value-Capture System

The business model must also account for how the firm will capture profits. This value-capture system is the "monetizing" part of any business model. It includes the ways in which the firm gets paid and the firm's choice of fixed and variable costs to create the value. These together determine the pattern of cash flows. There is a high degree of complementarity between value creation and value capture, as when Gillette subsidizes the price of razors to sell more profitable replacement blades.

Zara, the international clothing retailer, is a fashion imitator. Its value-creating system is built on a well-tuned system of designers who observe and quickly copy popular fashions, and a manufacturing system that can create and move clothing into centrally located stores all over the world at record speed. Store managers provide feedback on customer purchases, which in turn provides designers with ideas. The firm captures value because the clothing, often supplied in small batches to create a sense of scarcity, sells fast and no inventories are held. Prices are low, but discounts are rare. Zara also captures value because its stores don't advertise, but use central locations to attract customers and remind them to visit often for the latest in "fast fashion."[10]

Achieving a Customer Value Advantage

The first step in achieving a customer value advantage is to select the thrust of the value proposition—whether it will be performance value, price value, or relational value leadership.

Performance Value Leadership

For performance value leaders, the value proposition is all about having the best product or service offering, usually at a price premium. A leadership position on this vector is achieved through relentless innovation aimed at superior or unique functionality, features, and/or design, coupled with superior quality. It takes real focus and skill to make products and services that customers recognize as the best available and that deliver demonstrable benefits and performance.

One of the defining features of a performance value strategy is peerless quality. This is quality not in the narrow sense of compliance with standards, but in the broad sense of fitness for customer use. For Medtronic, which dominates the market for implanted cardiac devices such as pacemakers and defibrillators, this means reliability (variance in mean time before failure or malfunction) and longevity (since it is extremely costly and risky to replace a device that has been implanted in the chest cavity). Many respected companies have failed in this market because they could not master the rigorous discipline and inculcate a quality-first culture.

In other markets, performance value is achieved through an experiential or emotional impact. Thus, Nike basketball shoes, Omega watches, Bang & Olufsen stereos, and Louis Vuitton handbags indulge their customers' desires for high-fashion design, association with sports heroes, or peer recognition. Electronic Arts (EA) became the leading interactive games publisher by launching a continuous stream of new games, such as *The Sims*, that fed gamers' desire for new experiences, including the ability to create simulated characters, assign them roles and personalities, and then control their lives. Within two years of its launch in 2000, *The Sims* and its various elaborations sold more than 16 million units worldwide to become the most successful PC game up to that time.[11]

Price Value Leadership

Price value leaders are not performance innovators, nor do they cultivate close relationships with their customers. Instead, they provide reliable products or services positioned in the middle of the market space at the *best price*. The best price is seldom the cheapest, but offers the lowest total life-cycle cost to the customer.

Exemplars such as Vanguard Group, IKEA, Aldi, and Walmart work on all the factors that customers consider when comparing total cost, such as (1) product reliability, which lowers the future costs of ownership by avoiding repairs and downtime, (2) reliable service, which cuts the tangible costs of annoyance and uncertainty about delivery or customer service, and (3) convenience and availability, which make shopping easier. But at the top of the list is always the price paid. Thus, the mutual fund giant Vanguard uses index funds that mirror the overall stock market and a bare-bones corporate structure to charge only 0.3 percent of assets for annual expenses. This is far below the average domestic stock fund, which charges approximately 1.5 percent for expenses.

There are many routes to price value leadership. The two most prevalent are applying highly disciplined cost management and using superior pricing acumen.

Disciplined Cost Management

These firms sell high volumes of standard products to gain the cost savings from economies of scale. But scale is not enough; further discipline is needed to limit variety and avoid product line proliferation. It also means minimizing overhead and installing a frugal culture. Facilities are usually austere, which sends a clear signal to customers. Procedures are highly standardized, and tight cost controls are in place. All firms need cost controls to be at least at competitive parity on the price value vector, but price value leaders are more thorough and rigorous and less accepting of cost variances. These leaders are also public about comparing their customers' total costs with those of target competitors.

Superior Pricing Acumen

To be able to offer the best price, a price value leader must have a well-defined pricing capability and deep insights into the price sensitivity and behavior of its target segment. This is how Progressive Corporation became one of the most profitable auto insurance companies in the United States. Auto insurance is a necessary, but it is *not* a desirable purchase for most customers. Most states require that all car owners carry some form of liability insurance. The net effect is that most customers are highly price-sensitive and put the most weight on the annual premium cost rather than on service benefits, such as the timeliness of processing claims or the location of agents.

Progressive uses a superior data mining and analysis capability to accurately assess the risk—and thus the expected cost—of each customer. For example, it has learned that getting a ticket for "failure to yield" makes a customer a higher risk (and hence warrants a higher premium) than getting a ticket for "speeding." It then uses targeted pricing schemes to attract profitable customers and to discourage the unprofitable ones. This has taken a long-term investment in creating massive data archives on consumer characteristics and behavior and sophisticated algorithms that can determine the best price. However, the investment is paying off, as competitors have not been unable to match this capability.

Relational Value Leadership

These companies are unlikely to offer either the lowest price or the latest performance features. Instead, they deliver service and offerings that are possible only with a deeper customer relationship. Two examples demonstrate the possibilities:

- Rolls-Royce, the global market leader in commercial jet engines, powered half of the wide-bodied passenger jets built in 2008. It overcame formidable competitors like GE and Pratt & Whitney with an engine design that was more costly to make, but that can be customized for a wider range of aircraft designs than its rivals. But in addition to supplying an excellent product, Rolls-Royce introduced an after-sale support option that addressed customers' concerns about engine maintenance costs. Rolls-Royce's airline customers don't buy the engines. Instead, as part of the "Power by the Hour" program, customers pay a fee based on the number of hours flown, which saves money. Relationships are tightened because Rolls-Royce maintains the engine and replaces it when it breaks down. It monitors every engine function while the aircraft is in the air to get an early warning of service needs. This means fewer emergency repairs and time saved for both the customer and Rolls-Royce. As the COO noted, "You could only get closer to the customer by being in the plane."[12]

• Fidelity Investments repositioned itself with a strategy of providing affluent investors with credible advice and investment solutions tailored to the individual investor's situation and delivered with exceptional service on the customer's own terms. This required careful identification of customer segments to nurture, the formation of dedicated service models and offerings for each segment, and personalized education and guidance appropriate to the profit potential of each segment. High-net-worth customers with more than $2 million in investments with Fidelity get their own account representatives, while investors with less than $100,000 are served through the Internet and a pool of account reps.[13]

Relational value leaders have several things in common. First, their relationships with their best customers are unusually tight, so there is mutual trust based on shared understanding and mutual commitments. These leaders are experts at their customers' businesses or lives. Second, they have broadened their offering far beyond their core product to include customer information and training, complementary products, support services, and financing as required. They compete on scope rather than scale. Third, their customers think they are getting an offering that has been tailored to their needs. It may be fully customized or simply personalized. This is not the "one size fits all" approach of price value leaders.

These common features conceal huge differences in how relational value is delivered in different markets.[14] Customer relationship management (CRM) approaches are used by firms like Fidelity Investments that serve mass markets with millions of customers. Comprehensive solution management approaches are applied by firms like Rolls-Royce when complex systems are sold to a small number of very valuable customers. Of course, there are many companies that use some of each approach.

Customer Relationship Management (CRM)
The essence of CRM is customizing products and services for each particular customer. More precisely, it is a cross-functional process that involves a continuing dialogue with customers, managing this dialogue across all customer touch points, and offering personalized treatment of the most valuable customers.

Only since the 1990s have information technologies harnessed to the Internet made it possible to have dialogues with customers cost-effectively and gain a coherent and comprehensive view of each customer, including his profitability. CRM uses these systems to customize products, services, and information for each customer.

But CRM is more than database management, data mining, call centers, and sales-force automation. In order to work, it should be managed as an ongoing learning relationship with the customer that the company must capture and use to personalize interactions. CRM infiltrates all aspects of the firm's operations and crosses traditional functions to achieve this personalization. All of the customer's touch points are aligned and synchronized around actual and expected customer behavior.

Comprehensive Solution Management

Solutions are bundles of products and related services that create value greater than the sum of their parts.[15] To offer a real solution, not just a repackaging of existing products and services, four criteria must be met:

- Each solution is *co-created* with customers.
- It is therefore *tailored* to each customer.
- The relationship between customer and supplier is unusually *intimate* and involves multiple relationships and connection points across the companies.
- Suppliers accept some of the *risk* through performance-based or risk-based contracts.

As with CRM best practices, the aim is to form a one-to-one learning relationship. But being able to co-create a real solution requires relationships that are much deeper and wider than those enabled by CRM, with social and information connections across many levels and functions of each partner organization. This is feasible only with high-value, long-term customers who warrant sizable investments of time and energy and are also willing to make a reciprocal commitment.

Customers who are partners can gain from such relationships in several ways. Overall costs may be lower and quality higher when customers are interacting with a single supplier for multiple activities. They may see benefits from superior performance through preferred access to the latest technology. Their risks may be reduced by sharing them with the supplier.

As an example, Asea Brown Boveri, a leading power and automation technology group, better known as ABB, has charged customers a daily rental fee for drilling pipe used on ocean-based oil and gas rigs. The daily rate was high (~$150,000 per day), but it was often inflated because drilling company customers ran into snags getting the equipment through customs in the country where the drilling was taking place. ABB saw an opportunity to shift the emphasis away from price to a focus on service. It did so by charging customers for the services required to get the pipes to the wells (including navigating customs). Because ABB was doing this for many of its customers across more than 100 countries, it was able to gain efficiencies in the importation process and share the cost savings with its customers.

A comprehensive solution is also much more than a bundle that enables one-stop shopping or even an option such as tailoring a PC to suit a customer's desired configuration. Thinking in terms of bundles of products and services offered is an inside-out approach that focuses on "how can we sell more?" True solutions come from the outside in to solve a customer's problem. These require deep insights into customer needs that come from "living together," and the ability to use these insights to help the customer make money and provide a better overall result. Not every customer will commit to such a deep relationship or even pay for a solution. Relational value leaders move these customers to other offerings or even "fire" them.

Aligning the Strategy with a Dashboard of Metrics

Customer value leadership requires tough choices of where and how to compete and the commitment to a distinct strategic thrust. This thrust is enabled by a business model that deploys value-creation and value-capture capabilities that competitors can't match. All other capabilities are in the service of these strategic capabilities.

Table 4-1 lists the strategic thrusts, the value-creating system in the business model, and a representative dashboard of metrics that customer value leaders are likely use to compete on each vector. Such a dashboard is essential for signaling strategic priorities, tracking performance, and diagnosing the reasons for poor performance. However, these metrics must be driven from the C-suite to achieve the top-to-bottom consistency that customer value leaders need.

TABLE 4-1 Customer Value Leadership Strategy, Organization, and Metrics

	Performance Value Leadership	Price Value Leadership	Relational Value Leadership
Strategic Thrust	• Continuous innovation • Technology leadership • Exceptional quality • Speed to market	• Lowest delivered cost with competent quality and reliability • Economies of scale	• Customized experiences • Comprehensive solutions • Economies of scope
Distinctive Value-Creating Capabilities	• Probe-and-learn market sensing • R&D: Open networks and/or strong internal processes • Product development/design teams	• Supply-chain management • Manufacturing • Inventory control • Pricing and yield management	• CRM to give integrated view of customers • Modular operations • Service operations • Information systems
How the Firm Operates	• Networked and decentralized organization • Loose-knit and fluid teams • Autonomous employees • Experimental mindset	• Vertically integrated and self-contained organization • Hierarchical structure • Directed employees • Frugal mindset	• Networked and team-based organization • Front-line autonomy • Empowered employees • "Have it your way" mindset
Metrics in the Dashboard	• Relative rate of growth in earnings and revenue • Time to market • % of sales from new products in the past N years • Customer satisfaction with new products • Customer willingness to pay a price premium	• Relative cost of value-creating processes • Trajectory of prices relative to competitors • Market share • Variance in output of customer-facing processes	• Segment profitability • Customer loyalty rates • Share of wallet • Share of requirements by segment • Customer lifetime value

How many metrics are needed to give a realistic picture of customer value leader performance? In our experience, most organizations are hard-pressed to manage more than six to eight metrics without losing focus on the areas of highest leverage. The key is to find the few metrics that truly reflect the strategic priorities of the firm's customer value leadership choices.

The metrics in the firm's customer value dashboard are the *drivers* of financial performance. Thus, each customer value strategy and the associated business model is evaluated on economic profit, accounting for both operating profits and the cost of the assets (fixed and working capital) being used. Firms should also collect diagnostic financial measures such as gross margins, days' receivables, and inventory turns to support the entire strategy.

Performance Value Leadership Alignment

Performance value leaders' path to profitability is through speed in bringing continuous innovation to market ahead of the competition. High margins are realized by appealing to a performance-sensitive segment that is willing to pay for the increased benefits of science, fashion, or outstanding functionality.

Performance value leaders often achieve superior financial results with fluid and open value-creating systems. In other words, they are willing to adopt useful technologies and ideas from whatever sources can do the job, and to partner with specialists along the value chain to get their concepts to market faster. They have mastered the deployment of flexible, cross-functional teams that stay close to their potential markets. There is a spirit of fast experimentation as a way to learn. These companies are also willing to cannibalize their previous generation of products and seek modular designs across products to cut costs and make innovations easier to produce.

Metrics

Dashboards designed for performance value leaders reveal the productivity and effectiveness of the innovation process. Useful effectiveness measures are time to market (the time from the beginning of development to the launch date) and time to breakeven (after entering the market). These can be used either for individual projects or for the full innovation portfolio. The aim of the whole portfolio is to achieve revenue and earnings growth that is better than that of the competition. Whether this is accomplished depends on the amount of innovation, as measured by the percent of sales from new products launched in the past N years, and how well these innovations were received by the market, as measured by the average customer satisfaction with and willingness to pay for the new offerings.

Price Value Leadership Alignment

Price value leaders play a different game that is worlds apart from the other value vectors. Their starting point is the same outside-in view based on deep market insights. But price value leaders move from the outside to the inside faster than those competing on other value vectors. Guided by market insights, these firms focus their attention on the rigorous pursuit of efficiency in operations, often using Six Sigma or total quality management methods. They know how to squeeze cost from their supply chains. What sets the leaders on this vector apart is an ability to keep their inside efforts inextricably linked to their outside perspective. They know which cost factors really affect the customer experience—it's not a question of doing everything cheaply, but of identifying which costs can be minimized without detracting from the customer's experience. Price value leaders apply their process and efficiency discipline to all customer-facing processes. To guide these decisions, these leaders invest in understanding how their target customer perceives all the life-cycle costs beyond the initial price paid.

These leaders often have a hierarchical structure in which the employees are more directed than enabled, and in which consistency in executing processes is emphasized. The path to profitability for a price value leader is all about achieving economies of scale, so that the firm can have the lowest delivered cost. These leaders have strong margins and are willing to cut prices to gain share and improve capacity utilization, if necessary. The trade-off between current profits and long-run market share depends on the leaders' objectives. A price-cutting entrant can exploit this trade-off if the incumbent price value leader is under shareholder pressure to increase profits. When this happens, the incumbent may concede the market rather than take a margin hit.

Metrics

The strategic priorities of price value leaders are economies of scale and consistency of operation. Whether they are winning the battle is signaled by a dashboard that highlights market share (as a proxy for scale), capacity utilization, and changes in their costs relative to those of the competition. To maintain tight control, they watch for changes in the costs of their inputs and of each process, and time spent traversing the supply chain. To maintain an outside-in perspective, they watch closely for variability in the customer-facing processes, such as delivery time compared to delivery promises, and monitor their price levels relative to competitors'.

Relational Value Leadership Alignment

Relational value leaders use economies of scope to give their best customers exactly what they want. Their business models are aligned with this end in many ways. The sharp end is a front-line team with autonomy. Although we advocate that all value leaders have direct and continuous exposure to customers, relational leaders have a long tradition of "living with" their customers to learn their needs and even get to know their customers' customer. When the front end of the organization devises a solution, it is up to the back end to leverage modular operations and provide service operations to deliver the solution. Network partners can play a crucial role in filling in any gaps in the solution.

This is a costly business model to implement, so it is essential that customers remain loyal. High customer acquisition costs have to be covered by locking the customer into the solution with contracts and other devices, or simply by keeping them so delighted that they don't defect. Superior margins are sustained by bundling services, products, and support in order to reduce costs and to gain a price premium.

Metrics

For relational value leaders, costs do matter, but the real drivers of economic profit are (1) low customer churn and/or defection rates, (2) deep penetration into the customer's spending in a category, which could be share of wallet for financial institutions or share of total requirements for B2B firms, and (3) the ability to move the customer to a broadening array of complementary products and services. The latter is revealed by metrics such as the lifetime value of customers, which we'll cover fully in Chapter 8.

Defending Customer Value Leadership

We chose the phrase *customer value leader* quite deliberately, as it illustrates the fleeting nature of this position. Leaders are not necessarily winners. There is a big difference between being the leader of a marathon at mile 10 and winning it at mile 26.2. The leadership position of any company is constantly under threat. Whether the company can maintain its leadership depends on its ability to defend its position against all comers. The most frequent focus of attack on a customer value leader is on the price vector.

To many performance leaders, the three scariest words in the English language are "the China price," which may be 30 percent or more below what a firm can possibly make something for in the United States or Europe. This is not just shoes and apparel: in 2009, Huawei, based in Shenzen, China, could produce sophisticated networking equipment for 25 percent below Cisco's comparable price.

But disruptive low-cost competitors can come from any direction. European retailers once dismissed Germany's hard-discount grocers, Aldi and Lidl, as local anomalies until the discounters attacked with their bare-bones price value strategy. Similarly, in B2B markets, incumbents usually ignore low-cost entrants. The technology and consumer packaged goods industries are littered with the remains of large incumbents who made this error.

Sustaining Performance Value Leadership

How should performance value leaders respond to the inevitable price value challenge?[16] A key question is whether the new rival is targeting their customers, as opposed to looking at a segment that they don't want to serve. If the low-cost rival seems to be avoiding the incumbent's customers initially, then a watch-and-wait posture is appropriate so long as it is laced with paranoia.

One thing these firms should *not* do is match or beat the low-cost attacker's prices in an effort to drive it out of the market. There are three possible options for *performance leaders* to consider, as shown in Figure 4-2:

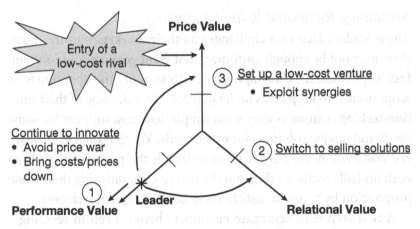

FIGURE 4-2 How Should a Performance Leader Respond?

1. **Continue to innovate.** This option best fits the genetic code of performance leaders. Depending on the market, this could mean superior design (Bang & Olufsen), 2 to 5 times improvements in technical performance (the next generation of Intel chips), a unique product assortment (Whole Foods), or a superior experience (Singapore Airlines). This will succeed in the long run only if consumers will continue to pay for the superior benefits. Because the market is steadily becoming more price-sensitive, it is essential that costs and prices are kept in line.

2. **Switch to selling solutions.** This is a feasible option for firms in markets where the firm's performance edge no longer means as much to the target segment.

3. **Attack with a low-cost offshoot.** This approach is feasible when the new and established operations can share high-fixed-cost assets, such as capital-intensive networks or a core production facility, to mutual advantage through greater utilization. In financial services, HSBC has a successful low-cost operation in the form of First Direct branchless banking. The low-cost offshoot should be at a different location, use a different go-to-market model, and have a different brand name that communicates that fewer services go along with lower prices.

Sustaining Relational Value Leadership

These leaders face two challenges as their markets mature. First, there may not be enough customers that want genuine solutions and fast, sophisticated, thorough service to support the economies of scope needed to keep costs under control. Second, some of their solution-seeking customers may want simple, low-cost support for some needs and unique solutions for other needs. Yet relational value leaders' costs will never permit them to match the prices of their low-cost, no-frills rivals, so they run the real risk of confusing their value proposition by trying to satisfy these conflicting requirements.

A first step is to segregate customers better. Even in seemingly undifferentiated markets, such as bulk chemicals, paper, and sheet steel, relatively few customers buy solely on price and ignore relational value attributes such as delivery speed, after-sales service, and the quality of their supplier relationships. One maker of industrial resins found that fewer than half of its buyers cared most about price and on-time delivery, but that even those buyers wanted technical assistance and sales access on occasion and were willing to pay for it.

The second step is to rethink the processes for delivering relational value in order to cut costs while enhancing valued customer services. To cut costs, many relational value leaders build a "lean backbone"—a high-reliability, cost-effective standard platform of sales support and service processes for interactions that cut across all customers.[17] To improve value-added services for individual customers, the key is to develop "high-touch" overlays for situations where customers value additional sales and service and competitors do not have the same deep knowledge and hard-to-match skills.

Customer Value Leadership Realism

Achieving and sustaining customer leadership is a never-ending task. It begins with a value proposition that is best at meeting the needs of a well-defined target customer segment. Leaders have the right offer and the right experience for the right customer. They invest heavily in a business model that is synchronized with their value proposition, to ensure that every function, activity, and process delivers what the customer expects.

Customer value leaders are also realists. They realize they can't afford to underestimate the competition or to fall behind shifts in technology and customer requirements. This takes the kind of continuous innovation that is discussed in the next two chapters.

5

The Second Imperative:
Innovate New Value for Customers

Companies such as Cisco, Nike, GE, 3M, Tesco, and Amazon have demonstrated a superior ability to increase their top line faster than their rivals through organic growth. Why are these *customer value innovators* able to outperform the competition in good times and bad?

The first contributor to a superior growth record is deep market insights and foresight. As John Chambers, CEO of Cisco Systems, says, "Customers always have more frontline knowledge about the technology in action. So, while most companies set their strategy based on competition or their own so-called technology religion, ours is set solely on two things: listening to our customers, who tell us what the market transitions are, and then capturing these marketing transitions."[1]

Second, customer value innovators have a more expansive approach to innovation.[2] They consider the full spectrum of possibilities for growth instead of limiting themselves to the narrower possibilities of product innovation. They surmount the constraints of inside-out thinking (which emphasizes developing products with better features and functions) by putting their emphasis on deciphering and satisfying the changing needs of their market. In this postindustrial world, where much of business is about service and the customer experience, these firms understand that a product focus is too confining. Business model innovations can be every bit as profitable as technical marvels on slivers of silicon.

Third, customer value innovators create a supportive climate that nurtures continuous innovation. This climate is shaped by an externally oriented culture, unwavering leadership commitment, and the right reward structure. Innovative cultures are based on trust; people understand that their ideas are valued and that it is safe to pursue them. Such cultures flourish when the top management team is fully immersed in the growth strategy. This doesn't mean micromanaging projects, but it does require an active and supportive role in following projects, giving people permission to take risks, and establishing the right incentives and metrics.[3] We examine these larger cultural issues in detail in Chapter 12.

How Should You Grow: Make, Buy, or Both?

There are two ways to reach ambitious growth objectives. The *make* option is to grow organically from within, using the firm's own resources, which include the resources of the firm's extended network of technology and development partners, suppliers, and channel partners. The other way is to *buy* your way into new markets through acquisitions. Both have their place in a growth strategy—and both can be managed with an outside-in guiding logic.

Buying another company can jump-start an entry into a new market or provide an immediate market share gain. A small acquisition can provide a toehold in a new industry from which to learn the realities of an unfamiliar market. This is a risky option, however, as the anticipated financial returns often don't materialize.[4] Eager buyers are prone to pay too much for acquisitions, and are often overly optimistic about their ability to integrate the new firm and extract the hoped-for synergies. Many failures result from an inside-out emphasis on the financial statements without taking the time to comprehend the market served by the firm to be acquired.

The benefits of the organic "make" option were well stated by Jeff Bezos in Chapter 1 as he explained the benefits of starting from the outside in to identify new opportunities and then building the capabilities to exploit them. While organic growth takes longer, it usually yields better risk-adjusted economic profits.

In this and the next chapter, we'll thoroughly explore how customer value innovators manage their innovation activities from the outside in. Their overriding question is the essence of the second imperative: How can we create new value for customers? The answer in this chapter focuses on the delivering that new value through a full spectrum of small and large innovations for both current customers and new customers. The second theme is that innovation is inherently risky, and that winning growth strategies find the best balance of risk and reward. In the next chapter, we draw from best practices to show how finding, selecting, and implementing a high-yield portfolio of organic growth initiatives can be driven by an outside-in innovation process.

The Organic Growth Challenge

Most top management teams are not confident that they will reach their ambitious organic growth goals.[5] Why do they find superior organic growth so hard to achieve? One school of thought emphasizes *external constraints*—companies are mired in saturated, "red ocean" markets, pressured by customers who themselves are being squeezed and forced to compete for incremental share gains against rivals who follow similar strategies.[6] Others point to *internal impediments*—short-term incentives that subvert long-term objectives, urgent demands from customers and salespeople that absorb scarce development resources, risk-averse cultures, and inferior innovation capabilities.[7]

The combined effect of these external and internal impediments is that "small i" (incremental) innovations displace "Big I" (discontinuous) innovations on the continuum of degrees of innovation in Table 5-1.

As evidence, research has shown that from 1990 to 2004, the average percentage of "major" innovations in firms' portfolios dropped from 20.4 percent to 11.5 percent even as the total number of initiatives increased.[8] Small i minor innovations make up 85 to 90 percent of most companies' innovation portfolios, but they rarely generate much additional growth.

The aversion to Big I initiatives stems from a belief that they are too risky and that their rewards (if any) will accrue too far in the future. The probability of failure certainly goes up sharply when the company ventures beyond incremental moves within familiar markets. This is no excuse for passivity, however. The solution is to assess the risks of new ventures properly and then use a disciplined process to manage these risks. The innovation risk matrix in Figure 5-1 can help companies do just that.

TABLE 5-1 The Innovation Continuum

"small i" Innovation	"Big I" Innovation
• Exploitation of existing capabilities	• Exploration of new market spaces
• Incremental	• Discontinuous
• Continuous improvement	• Disruptive
• "Red ocean" (from the blood of competitors)	• "Blue ocean" (uncontested open water)
• *Low risk—small rewards*	• *High risk—large rewards*

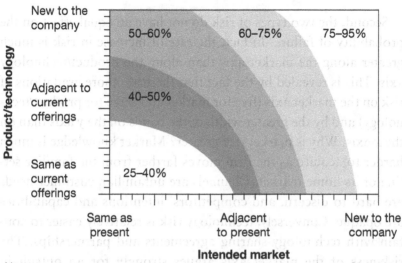

Notes:
- Probability of failure is reflected in percentages within the shaded bands.
- "Market" means customers, not geographic markets.

FIGURE 5-1 The Innovation Risk Matrix

The Innovation Risk Matrix

This matrix displays the probability of failure for an innovation project. Each project is plotted using two criteria: how familiar the firm is with the intended market (on the horizontal axis) and the similarity of the product or technology to existing offerings (on the vertical axis).[9] Project failure is defined as missing the original financial and market objectives used to justify the project by more than 35 percent. These failure estimate ranges have been thoroughly validated in dozens of interviews with consultants and senior managers and are consistent with recent surveys that place the overall failure rate of new products at close to 40 percent![10]

Several important conclusions can be reached by looking at this matrix of plotted projects. First, the likelihood of failure increases as the firm moves further from its current markets and current offerings.

Second, the two types of risk do not have an equal effect on the probability of failure. In fact, the rate of increase in risk is much greater along the market axis than along the product/technology axis. This is revealed by the fact that there are more gradations of risk on the market axis (five for market and three for product/technology) and by the greater width of the bands on the y axis than on the x axis. Why is market risk greater? Market knowledge is much harder to acquire as the firm moves farther from the familiar setting of its home market. Channels are unfamiliar, customer needs are hard to discern, and competitors' intentions and capabilities are opaque. Conversely, technology risk is relatively easier to contain with technology-sharing agreements and partnerships. The riskiness of the market axis argues strongly for an outside-in approach to innovation grounded in deep market insights.

When they plot their innovations on the matrix, most firms find that the majority of their innovation projects are clustered in the low risk–low return lower left corner. Relatively few projects can be classified as Big I initiatives, which can yield substantial organic growth, but with higher risk.

While this imbalance is unhealthy, it is not surprising for several reasons. Discounted cash flow analysis and other financial yardsticks for evaluating development projects are usually biased against the delayed payoffs and uncertainty inherent in Big I innovations. What's more, small i projects tend to drain R&D budgets as companies struggle to keep up with customers' and salespeople's demands for a continuous flow of incrementally improved products.

To be sure, small i innovations are often needed for continuous improvement and to blunt competitive moves. But the painful experience of all industries, and especially fast-moving consumer goods, is that these innovations are poor at improving either revenue or earnings growth. In fact, Big I innovations produce the majority of profits accruing from innovations. According to one study, only 14 percent of new products were Big I innovations, but they accounted for 61 percent of all profits from innovations.[11] Likewise, a study of 135 product launches by 10 consumer goods companies found that 131 were line extensions or incremental/small improvements to an existing product, and only 4 were truly novel developments in consumer value.[12]

Take the yogurt market, for example. The sales of small i extensions, such as new flavors, averaged between 1 and 4 percent of sales. The Big(ger) I innovations, such as Activia, a line of yogurt with special live culture bacteria with health benefits, had sales of 26 percent of its categories. This is a sales success almost 13 times greater than the average small i launch.

Adjacencies: The Sweet Spot for Profitable Growth

Figure 5-1 also points to a middle ground—adjacencies. Adjacencies achieve a better balance of risk and reward by striking into new territory while drawing on the business' resources and market knowledge. A market adjacency is a market that is new to the business, but that has some relationship with the firm's current market. For USAA, the families of military members are adjacent to the original "military" market. Innovations that rely on market adjacencies often leverage the firm's current offerings, brand, distribution, and sales activities. Some changes may be necessary to reach the adjacent market, such as using mobile and Internet technologies to reach the grown children of military members. There will also be some similarities in the competitive set, so competitive moves can often be anticipated.

Product or service adjacencies are new offerings that have some overlap with the company's technology and manufacturing competency, quality standards, and intellectual property. These linkages reduce the risk of innovation and also give the firm important efficiencies as it leverages its knowledge. Firms can also reduce their risk by introducing adjacent offerings to current customers. This type of compensatory strategy further mitigates risks.

Most firms steer clear of very risky Big I initiatives that take the business beyond adjacencies to the point where there is no connection to the current business. Customer value innovators fuel sustained growth[13] by carefully sequencing their adjacency moves, first understanding and containing the risk by proximal moves, then building on the expanded business to reach more distant adjacencies. Seldom do these companies make these moves in one jump. For example, Otis, the elevator maker, started with elevators and spare parts. With customer insight and market credibility, it moved into "building, maintaining, and operating" contracts by offering services such as financing, maintenance, and intelligent monitoring of elevators.

Contrast Walmart's history of methodical movement into product adjacencies such as groceries and electronics, related business models such as Sam's Club, and geographic adjacencies such as Mexico, Canada, and Germany with Kmart's abortive moves into the unfamiliar territory of book chains, drugstores, home improvement stores, and office supplies. While Walmart was becoming the largest retailer in the world, Kmart went bankrupt by 2003 and merged with Sears, Roebuck, & Co. Each of Kmart's moves distracted management and diverted resources from the core business. Indeed, Kmart violated an important rule of organic growth, which is to protect the core business and extract the full potential from current products and markets before stepping into new opportunities.

Sun Tzu, ancient Chinese military general and strategist, once said, "The more opportunities I seize, the more opportunities multiply before me."[14] In the same way, successful adjacencies create new platforms for growth. Amazon has become much more than an online book retailer by adding downloadable videos, streaming movies, and selling the Web services it uses to run its business to other companies. Its most audacious adjacency move was to enter the hardware business of e-book readers with the Kindle, an e-reader that can download tens of thousands of books, magazines, and newspapers with an always-on high-speed wireless connection.

Amazon entered the e-book market to leverage its distribution power and brand strength. According to Jeff Bezos, CEO of Amazon, the company based its e-book strategy first and foremost on customer needs instead of trying to match or leapfrog Sony, which was already in the market. What customers wanted was, "a device that made it very, very frictionless to buy and read electronic books."[15] The resulting Kindle enables Amazon to make money from both device sales and book purchases. The publishing platform is open to any content provider who wants to offer something for sale. But e-books also point the way toward a separation of content from platform, threatening the publishing industry with the same disruptive effects of digital change that have transformed the music industry. Amazon is positioned to profit no matter when or at what pace this happens—it has protected its core business while aggressively moving into adjacencies.

Full-Spectrum Innovation

Consider what these two highly successful growth initiatives have in common:

- DuPont has been making sulfuric acid since 1865, when it supplied John D. Rockefeller's first oil refinery with barrels of acid on horse-drawn wagons. This is a slow-growth, price-competitive market with too much capacity—surely a profit wasteland. So why is DuPont still in the business? Because it found a large and profitable growth opportunity with a service for efficiently regenerating spent sulfuric acid. This is highly valued by petroleum refiners, as they have to use more acid to process high-sulfur crude while reducing their emissions. DuPont builds, owns, operates, and maintains sulfuric acid production facilities within gasoline refiners' plants that not only regenerate the refiners' spent acid, but also capture the acid's gas emissions.[16]

- Netflix is a dot-com survivor that transformed the movie rental market with an online, rent-by-mail service for DVDs that has no due dates or late fees. Its value proposition is access to a vast library of DVDs and fast, free delivery. By 2008, Netflix had a strong brand that dominated the online market, a highly satisfied customer base, and unmatched expertise in providing personalized movie recommendations with average growth. It had leveraged these resources to make a profitable defensive move into the video-on-demand market. Net income rose steadily from $21 million in 2004 to $83 million in 2008. Year-over-year subscriber churn decreased from 4.2 percent to 3.9 percent in the last quarter of 2009.[17]

Both DuPont's sulfuric acid recovery business and Netflix succeeded by innovating new customer value. The petroleum refiners got better quality, fewer emissions, and lower operating costs plus balance sheet benefits because they didn't have to invest in equipment. DuPont also absorbed the risk of equipment failures and obsolescence. Netflix offered real cost savings on each rental, but what its customers valued most was the wide selection and the convenience of not having to drive back and forth to the rental store. There was also less risk of picking the wrong movie because of Netflix's recommendation engine. These innovations have made it difficult for competitors to find ways to offer enough additional value to compel customers to switch.

When thinking creatively about ways to grow by creating new value for customers, we recommend starting with the current strategy that drives Imperative 1. We advocate stretching, pushing, and reimagining each dimension of this strategy—the customer value proposition (the target segment, the offering, and the competitive profile) and the business model (the value-creating and value-capture systems).

The full spectrum of innovation requires expansive outside-in thinking. This is contrary to the DNA of many businesses, which traditionally follow several familiar inside-out pathways. We see most growth paths as being driven by (1) inertia (this is how we've always grown), (2) path dependency (this is what we know and can do), and (3) the necessity to match rivals (they did it, so we should follow).

In industries in which the competitors move in lockstep, there is a steady convergence toward a conventional wisdom about what customers value and how to innovate. Software companies tend to focus on developing code. Bioscience companies concentrate on curing cancer or cardiovascular disease. Advanced materials companies devote most of their innovation efforts to customer applications. These are important avenues for innovation, but they should not preclude other pathways. All innovation pathways need to be considered.

Pursuing a different innovation pathway can be a game changer because it takes competitors a long time to understand the move, and it requires new capabilities that these rivals cannot develop quickly. These are also ingredients of a first-mover advantage.

As the first step in overcoming innovation myopia, managers should look at every dimension of the strategy to find possible growth paths. Using previous research[18] and interviews with executives in many leading firms, we have found nine pathways for innovating the customer value proposition, and a further six pathways for innovating the business model. These are summarized in Table 5-2. These fifteen growth pathways are interconnected. A change in the value proposition will often require supportive moves along other dimensions of the business model. DuPont's sulfuric acid recovery innovation succeeded with a complete solution and required a massive companywide undertaking. Carefully selected customers participated as partners, new design and production capabilities were developed, and financing and technical support were necessary to make customers comfortable with reliance on a single supplier.

In the remainder of this chapter, we'll drill down on these pathways and show how customer value innovators use them to create

TABLE 5-2 The Full Spectrum of Innovation Pathways

Innovation Pathways for the Customer Value Proposition	**Customers**	1. Expand the market potential by stretching the market boundaries to serve other needs of current customers.
		2. Meet the needs of those who are not currently buying anything in the category (nonconsumers).
		3. Find new customers by satisfying unmet or latent needs.
		4. Penetrate new geographies.
	Offerings	5. Develop new core products or services that serve new and existing customers.
		6. Create integrated solutions that save customers' time and/or money, reduce customer risk, or enable customers to make more money.
		7. Redesign the customer experience across all touch points.
		8. Extend the brand into new domains (see Imperative 4).
	Competitive Profile	9. Reconfigure the competitive profile by eliminating, reducing, increasing, or adding key aspects of the offering relative to the prevailing industry standards.*
Innovation Pathways for the Business Model	**Value-Creating System**	1. Create new channels or innovative points of connection where the customer can interact with the firm.
		2. Change the organization by compressing the core of the business and extending the periphery with partners.
		3. Create new value through new procedures, partnerships, human resources, and so on.
		4. Reconfigure the activities in the value chain to improve the firm's performance, speed, quality, or cost structure.
		5. Improve/enhance the firm's ability to perform distinctive capabilities better than rivals.
	Value-Capture System	6. Redefine how the company monetizes and captures the economic value that it creates.

*This is the familiar four questions framework recommended by W. Chan Kim and Renee Mauborgne, *Blue Ocean Strategy* (Boston: Harvard Business School Press, 2005).

new value and capture additional profits. Of course, along each of the fifteen pathways, there is a range of reach and ambition from small i to Big I. Companies choose where they want to innovate on this continuum.

Innovating with the Customer Value Proposition

Firms can innovate by focusing on the customer, the offering, and/or how the offering compares to competition.

Customers

Many new innovation pathways are created by expanding the market arena. Most market definitions are artificial constructs, so outside-in thinking begins by challenging the boundaries with two questions: (1) "What other needs of our current customers can we serve?" and (2) "What other customers could use our capabilities?" This is the antithesis of pursuing market share. Instead of a 30 percent share of a familiar but narrow market, the business might have only 5 percent of a larger arena. An exemplar of this expansive mindset is the game maker Nintendo, which has set its sights on expanding its appeal well beyond traditional video gamers.

Another innovation pathway looks at past, present, and prospective customers in the currently served market. Customer value innovators are constantly asking, "Are there new or emerging growth segments that are not being served? Are there latent needs that our business can satisfy?" Often the biggest opportunities come by overcoming the barriers that inhibit consumption of the product or service.[19] It takes insightful outside-in thinking to step into the shoes of nonusers to understand these barriers. Are they inhibited because they don't have the skills to use the product, because they can't afford the available versions, because they can't find the product easily, or because it takes too much time? Google has grown mightily by reaching small businesses who found its targeted ad services much more affordable and effective than the traditional media. Google has a 60 percent market share in the online ad business, and advertising revenues represented 97 percent of Google's 2008 revenue.[20]

Penetrating new geographies is a compelling innovation pathway in an era in which developing countries are major growth engines. Big opportunities are being found at the "base of the pyramid" in these countries, with their vast but individually poor populations.[21] This prospect is very tempting to Procter & Gamble (P&G). Its logic is simple: Americans spend about $110 a year per capita on P&G products. The worldwide per capita figure is $12. Sales in Mexico are $20 a year per capita, with sales in China and India being between $1 and $3 per year per capita.[22] P&G's aim is to get the per capita numbers in China and India closer to that in Mexico. Succeeding in these countries requires more than stripped-down versions from the developed world. Instead, these consumers respond when offerings are developed that meet their unique needs.

Offerings

Offerings that create superior customer value are often found at the intersection of technology advances and customer needs. For instance, there is an enormous need for a stent that can open arteries and not cause problems years after insertion.[23] Abbott Laboratories responded by developing a stent made of bioabsorbable plastic that simply dissolves back into the bloodstream within a year or two after its work of opening an artery is done, similar to the way sutures or bone screws are ultimately absorbed. This stent, launched in Europe in 2006 and in the United States in 2008,[24] is a huge benefit to customers, who no longer have to worry about stent thrombosis, the rare but fatal clotting caused by stents that stay in blood vessels years after being inserted. Abbott's worldwide sales of coronary stents grew 38 percent from 2008 to 2009.[25]

Innovations can also involve bundling products, services, and information in ways that create value beyond the sum of their parts. This is what DuPont has done with its sulfuric acid recovery services. Salesforce.com provides a solution by selling software as a service. For years, large corporations have been dependent on complex and temperamental "enterprise" software to manage everything from sales support to shipping, invoicing, and payroll. Salesforce.com offers on-demand software through the Internet for the single key application of customer relationship management and hosts all the data from geographically dispersed sales forces so that real-time analyses are available.

The offering extends to the entire customer experience. Innovation considers everything that customers see, hear, and feel in order to become a meaningful part of their lives. This means rethinking all points of contact with the customer. American Girl and Cabela's stores have become retail destinations for buyers of girls' dolls and outdoor sporting equipment, respectively. Whether you're having an ice cream sundae with your doll at the "parlor" or taking rifle practice near a waterfall, the stores reinforce the value of their products. Nestlé has transformed its Nespresso coffee system into a richer customer experience. Its system centers on high-quality espresso coffee packets that work only in a special machine to emulate a true café taste in the home. To extend the experience, Nespresso stores across Europe sell appliances and specialty coffees to coffee aficionados.

Competitive Profile

This profile reveals the different levels of product features offered by competitors.[26] Innovations come from challenging the established profiles by asking which features can be eliminated, added, or modified to be below or above the industry standard. The key is that the competitive profile should include all the factors beyond the product itself that customers use when making a choice.

This outside-in logic explains how Curves Fitness Centers became the largest fitness and health club franchise in the world in 2010, with 10,000 locations in 70 countries.[27] The fitness industry has traditionally been served by high-end full-service health clubs, catering to both women and men and offering a full range of equipment at a high monthly fee. Curves has a very different competitive profile. It is positioned as a women's gym that provides a total body workout in 30 minutes at one-third the fee. Its equipment is specially designed for women, the equipment is arranged in a circle to encourage conversation, and timed music moves users from machine to machine to make the overall experience pleasant. Curves eliminates all the aspects of the traditional clubs that don't appeal to its target segment. Gone is the profusion of special machines, spas, juice bars, pools, and showers, and locker rooms are replaced with a few curtained off changing areas (which dramatically reduces Curves' capital costs).

Innovating with the Business Model

Innovation can occur in both the value-creating system and the value-capture system.

The Value-Creating System

This is the firm's value chain—the sequential activities that take the product from supply to channels for reaching the market. With each activity, the product gains some value, but the way the chain is designed and managed should create more economic and customer value than the sum of the parts. Advances in coordination devices and information technology have opened up many avenues for innovation by combining activities or outsourcing to a network.

Sometimes the aim is to lower costs and increase efficiency. An example is Sam's Club's adoption of a new milk jug that looks like a rectangular block. The benefit of the new jug is that it is stackable, so that it doesn't require special crates. This means that 400 more jugs can be loaded in a trailer—50 percent more than the amount loaded using the old jugs! With the use of recyclable cardboard and shrink-wrap, bacteria growth and contamination caused by reusing crates is significantly reduced.[28] These are small gains, perhaps, but for Sam's Club, this innovation was a cost saver and hence a profit maker.

In the same way, Medco essentially reinvented the way people buy maintenance prescriptions by promoting mail-order delivery of drugs and getting doctors and pharmacies to accept electronic delivery of prescriptions. This creates value for companies by reducing drug costs for their health plans.

As another example, Bharti Airtel became the largest mobile phone company in India by limiting its in-house value chain to customer care, marketing, and the regulatory interface, and outsourcing all the rest of its value-chain activities. This increased the focus on customers, shortened time to market, and cut risks by reducing fixed assets.

The Value-Capture System

This involves innovations in the way the company gets paid for the value it creates. Innovation in value capture may mean finding untapped revenue sources, developing novel pricing schemes, and otherwise adopting a partnership approach with customers and suppliers. For example, Praxair created more value for its customers (and gets paid more) by delivering gases right to the manufacturing station, rather than by leaving them in a tank car.

Xerox went from selling copiers to leasing them to create new value for customers who did not want to carry the copier as an asset on their balance sheets. Leasing allowed the copier to be expensed. This benefited customers, as they no longer had to tie up scarce capital in a depreciating machine. This increased Xerox's customer acquisition and retention until IBM imitated the strategy.[29]

The best-known value-capture or "monetization" mechanism is Google's paid search, which yields Google revenues each time auctioned words are clicked through. Beginning as just another search engine, the firm provided value to users by providing improved results. It then captured the value of having many users via the cost-per-click pricing model of AdWords.[30]

Customer Value Innovators

Customer value innovation that powers superior organic growth takes the understanding and engagement of the entire management team. Without it, the ingrained inside-out growth process is likely to direct money, technology, and human resources toward efforts that bolster the current business and follow familiar growth pathways. For a business to break out of this growth-inhibiting trap, it needs to adopt an outside-in growth process that uses deep market insights to uncover and select the best possibilities along high-yield growth pathways. In addition, management needs to be sure that different growth initiatives are treated differently in the process. Holding a risky high-potential adjacency or a Big I initiative to the same short-run criteria as small i initiatives guarantees that Big I initiatives will have less funds. In the next chapter, we describe a robust growth process that overcomes these problems.

Sustaining organic growth is one of the primary responsibilities of both the CEO and the C-suite. As with all leadership tasks, there needs to be someone within the C-suite who has strategic oversight and ongoing accountability. In "pure-play" technology companies, where growth comes mainly from technology innovation, the point person is appropriately the CTO. A more expansive, full-spectrum view of innovation as anything that creates new value for customers usually requires a broader set of outside-in skills. Acceptance as the full-spectrum innovation leader within the C-suite requires a mindset and track record of bringing deep insights into both market opportunities and the potential of emerging technologies to solve customers' problems. A CMO aspiring to this role must deliver such insight consistently.

6

Innovating New Value for Customers

Innovation is inherently inefficient—that is the essence of its exploratory, trial-and-error, and risk-taking nature. The innovation process has to balance divergence, which widens the search for opportunities, with convergence to focus on the best bets. This balance is easy to lose. As top-down pressure for organic growth intensifies, the number of growth initiatives usually expands faster than the capacity of the organization to bring them to market. The inevitable result is an internal traffic jam of projects that causes delays, frustrations, and disappointment.

As an example, a leading firm in hydraulic activator systems (used to lift elevators and move airplane flaps) suffered from having too many projects to absorb. It was entering a number of new markets and expanding its product lines while shifting from hydraulic to linear induction technologies. Few projects were completed properly. Instead of fully prepared "product releases" with tested new products, it had "product escapes." The company felt pressured to push new products out the door without adequate sales training, documentation, or support, which spawned a host of problems that had to be fixed later.

Customer value innovators have evolved a disciplined outside-in process for overcoming these problems and maximizing the returns from their investments in innovation. Organic growth leaders such as Xerox, 3M, GE, Philips, and Procter & Gamble all employ similar processes for managing their growth portfolios that do the following:

- Set ambitious growth objectives and support them with resources, along with visible and vocal top management commitment.
- Systematically search for growth opportunities along the full spectrum of innovation pathways.
- Overcome the centripetal pull of innovation resources toward cautious, lower-yield small i initiatives, and deliberately shift the balance of the growth portfolio toward opportunities with higher risk-adjusted returns.
- Encourage managers to take calculated risks. Their mantra is: think big . . . start small . . . fail cheap . . . scale fast.
- And above all, ground every step in the process with deep customer insights. As Sophie Vandebroek, the CTO of Xerox, recently observed, "If you innovate and it doesn't end up as something that the customer benefits from, then it's not innovation."[1]

The process in Figure 6-1 incorporates the best practices just described. But living up to these best practices is a challenge. Here is what GE had to do to evolve from a productivity company, steeped in efficiency, Six Sigma, and core process improvement, to an outside-in growth company. In 2005, CEO Jeff Immelt started by boosting the organic growth goal from 5 percent to 8 percent per year, which meant finding an additional $3.4 billion in organic growth each year. This stretch goal (set before the economic meltdown in 2008) challenged the organization to think more expansively about new geographies and adjacencies. It also signaled top management's commitment to organic growth because it was backed up with adequate resources.

Many steps were taken to encourage fresh thinking at GE, including diversifying the top ranks with outsiders (in a break from

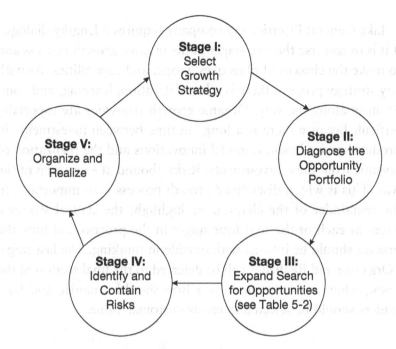

FIGURE 6-1 Managing Value Innovation as an Outside-In Process

the company's "promote-from-within" history), keeping executives in their positions longer so that they became deeply immersed in their industries, and tying executive compensation to new ideas, improved customer satisfaction, and top-line growth.

The leaders of each GE business were required to submit at least three "Imagination Breakthroughs" (i.e., stretch ideas that had the potential to become $1 billion businesses). However, the lead role in managing the Imagination Breakthroughs growth initiatives was given to the marketing team within each of the 11 business units. This was a startling departure for a company with a mindset that emphasized superior products and technology.[2] The GE Imagination Breakthroughs program was also aimed at shifting the balance of the portfolio toward adjacencies by giving the organization permission to break away from the tyranny of past success and to take calculated risks.

Like General Electric, any company requires a lengthy dialogue if it is to traverse the five stages in the organic growth process and to make the choices of objectives, scope, and capabilities. As with any strategy process, there is a lot of iteration, learning, and compromise along the way. Organic growth strategies are especially difficult because there is a long lag time between investments in product/service/business model innovations and the realization of revenue from these investments. Risks abound at every step of the way. This is why a disciplined growth process is so important. In the remainder of the chapter, we highlight the central strategic issues at each of the first four stages in the process and how the process should be infused with outside-in thinking. The last stage, "Organize and Realize," will be deferred to the final section of the book, where we examine how a firm should organize and how leaders should be selected to create customer value.

Stage I: Select the Growth Strategy

The purpose of the growth strategy is to establish resource requirements, guide the search for opportunities, and mobilize the organization. It is a statement of both ambition and direction—not in the sense of a road map, but more like a compass setting. A useful growth strategy addresses three issues.

- **Growth objectives.** What is the desired rate of revenue and profit growth? This strategic choice is shaped by the aspirations of management, equity market expectations for growth of the business relative to an industry benchmark, and the financial capacity of the business. Above all, these objectives must reflect a realistic assessment of what customers want and whether or not the company can deliver it.
- **Scope.** How broadly should the business search for opportunities? Are there limits on adjacencies that can be considered?
- **Emphasis on make versus buy.** A crucial choice is the relative emphasis on growth from acquisitions versus organic growth

that is achieved using the resources of the firm. Further, within organic growth, the firm must decide whether allying to gain access to key resources such as a partner's sales force, brand name, or channel will help it reach the market more quickly and/or more profitably. When McDonald's formed an alliance with Walmart to put restaurants in many stores, it was a calculated move to reach the market faster in key locations that were visited by many of its own customers without the expense of real estate and new bricks and mortar.

Praxair offers an example of the rewards from a clearly articulated growth strategy. In 2003, this global maker of industrial gases set out to find $2 billion in revenue growth in the next five years.[3] One half was to come from acquisitions. The other half required double-digit organic growth at the rate of $200 million per year. This was far beyond the annual growth that could be realized from repackaging helium, hydrogen, oxygen, and other gases. This goal was broken down into actionable categories. The first 15 percent would come from incremental growth in the base business and new channels for serving current markets. The rest would come from new services, such as injecting nitrogen into oil and gas wells, servicing the helium coolant used in MRI magnets, and developing new reactor cooling and nitrogen injection cooling methods for the bioscience industry.

These growth initiatives came from an intimate knowledge of changing customer needs that could be met with Praxair's existing capabilities in industrial gas production and delivery and its mastery of combustion, freezing, and metal fabrication technologies. While the leadership team—and especially the CEO—owned the growth process, the lead role in orchestrating the process was given to the CMO, who had a strong track record in managing innovation projects and was solidly grounded in the target markets. Revenues increased from $6.59 billion in 2004 (with net income of $697 million) to $9.40 billion in 2007 (with net income of $1.18 billion). About 40 percent of this growth came from the organic growth strategy.

Calibrate the Growth Gap

Since growth objectives are initially set by top management to meet stakeholder demands for revenue and profit growth, there is often a widening gap between increasingly aggressive targets and increasingly risk-averse portfolios. Given this, the pivotal question is whether these growth initiatives can close the growth gap shown in Figure 6-2 between growth objectives and the momentum of current strategies.

To understand what is achievable, management needs to dissect the sources of past growth and then set realistic goals for each source of future growth.[4] The barrier that has to be overcome is that most finance systems are designed from the inside out to keep score, control budget variances, and assess cost-cutting moves (just another reason that CFOs have to be on board with innovating new value for customers). These systems can tell you the details of the increase in revenue for each product or profit by sales territory, but nothing at all about the strategic questions concerning where the growth came from in the past and whether these sources can be sustained in the future. An outside-in finance system is centered on customers and markets. It should reveal what portions of the

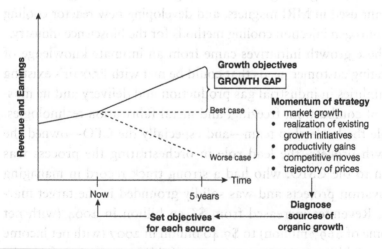

FIGURE 6-2 Calibrate the Growth Gap

revenue and earnings growth come from growth in the market, gains or losses in gross market share, gains from price changes, losses from churn or customer defections, and expansions into adjacent markets and new geographies.

Stage II: Diagnose the Opportunity Portfolio

Once you've settled on the growth strategy, the next stage is to assess the potential of the available growth initiatives in your portfolio to close the growth gap. There are many ways to display the portfolio of all growth initiatives that the business is actively pursuing.[5] We'll use the risk matrix from Chapter 5 because it provides a clear picture of how the projects fall on the spectrum of risk and the total profit and revenue growth potential of the portfolio.

The first step is to forecast revenues from each proposed growth initiative in the next three to five years. For many companies, compiling all the growth initiatives that are underway may be surprisingly difficult. R&D will know all about technology and new product initiatives, but other growth initiatives may be dispersed through the organization. Marketing may be exploring a new end-use market with a joint venture partner, while senior management may be investing in early-stage start-ups or considering a business model innovation.

The second step is to position each growth initiative in the risk matrix. This position is determined by the project's score on a range of factors, such as how closely the behavior of the targeted customers will match that of the company's current customers, how relevant the company's brand is to the intended market, and how applicable the company's technology capabilities are to the new product.[6]

Positioning a particular project in the matrix requires market insight. When McDonald's attempted to offer pizza, for example, it assumed that the new offering was closely adjacent to its existing fast-food items and thus targeted its usual customers. Under that assumption, pizza would be a product that was familiar to the present market and would appear in the bottom left of the risk matrix. But the project failed, and a postmortem showed that the launch had been fraught with risk. Because McDonald's could not figure out how to make and serve pizza in 30 seconds or less, orders for pizza caused long backups in the store and at the takeout window, thus breaking McDonald's service-delivery model and undermining customer value. The postmortem also revealed that the company's brand didn't give "permission" to offer pizza. Even though its core fast-food customers were demographically similar to pizza lovers, their expectations about the McDonald's experience didn't include pizza.

One common approach to positioning products in the innovation risk matrix is a portfolio review team. Typically consisting of members of the C-suite or other senior managers with strategic oversight and authority over development budgets and allocations, the team conducts the evaluation with the support of each project's development team. The overall health of the portfolio is revealed by the plot of all the initiatives (with each initiative being represented by a dot whose size is proportional to the project's estimated revenue). Sometimes a subjective assessment is all that is needed to reveal the health of the portfolio. Using this type of assessment, a European health-care product and beauty aid maker found that 95 percent of its development projects were package changes, line extensions, and other incremental improvements designed to match competitive moves and react to demands from important customers. New platform projects and breakthrough technology development were nearly absent from its portfolio!

The distribution of a typical portfolio, dominated by relatively low-risk, low-reward projects, is represented in Figure 6-3. There are more innovations in the lower left (as we saw in Figure 5-1), but the company reaps more rewards (hence bigger circles) as it moves out to the right and up.

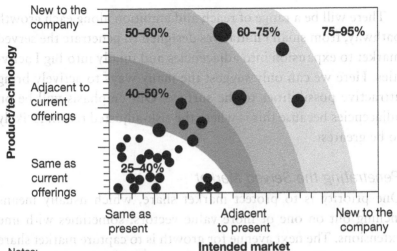

Notes:
- Probability of failure is reflected in percentages within the shaded bands.
- "Market" means customers, not geographic markets.
- The circles reflect the expected size of the company reward for an innovation project with the given market and product/technology features.

FIGURE 6-3 The Opportunity Portfolio

Once the available growth initiatives have been assessed, trade-offs in the objectives must be negotiated. It may be possible to achieve the revenue growth objective, but not the earnings objective—or vice versa. Regardless, there is almost always a widening growth gap to be filled with a directed search for better opportunities.

Stage III: Expand the Search for Growth Opportunities

The best growth opportunities will be found through a systematic search along each of the growth pathways of the full spectrum of possibilities described in the previous chapter (see Table 5-2 for a summary). This cannot be a *reactive* process that passively waits for ideas or suggestions from R&D, the sales force, customers, and employees. Their ideas may have merit, but they must be compared to a broader menu of possibilities in a system that proactively and systematically culls through the opportunities available to the company.

There will be a range of reach and ambition along each growth pathway, from small i initiatives designed to penetrate the served market to expansion into adjacencies and finally into Big I activities. Here we can only suggest the many ways to actively bring attractive possibilities to the surface. Our emphasis will be on adjacencies because this is where the risk-adjusted return is likely to be greatest.

Penetrating the Served Market

One priority is to protect market share, which usually means inching out on one or more value vectors, sometimes with line extensions. The next avenue for growth is to capture market share from rivals. This can be costly and counterproductive if it invites retaliation, which it is likely to do if the move is so clearly visible that it leads to price cutting, feature matching, or an escalation of marketing spending.

Though many market penetration strategies can be myopically imitative, yielding "me too" offerings and meager rewards, they can also be inspired "innovative imitations" that combine deep insights into changing market needs with an equivalent understanding of how their rivals succeeded. SoBe (South Beach Beverage Company) became a leader in "natural beverages" by learning from rivals such as AriZona Beverage Co., Snapple Beverage Corp., and Mistic Brands, Inc. SoBe also exploited three converging trends: the emphasis on healthier foods and beverages, the growing acceptance of natural or holistic treatments, and the aging of the baby boomer segment. Its irreverent brand attitude also helped it stand out from its rivals. Growth was further accelerated by line extensions such as herbal tonics that led toward the nutriceuticals market.

Expanding into Adjacencies

General Electric followed two growth pathways to enter the global wind turbine market. Its first step was a small acquisition in 2003 to learn about the market. It then leveraged its capabilities in making gas turbines and jet engines to develop a better wind turbine, while challenging the current competitive profile. At the time, the global market was heavily dependent on government subsidies, especially in Germany, which has a scarcity of open land. German competitors, such as Siemens, responded to market conditions by offering 20 different models that could fit on different-sized plots of land.

Deep immersion into the needs of current and prospective customers revealed two main drivers of customers' perceptions of economic value: gearbox reliability and efficiency in capturing wind energy. Existing wind turbines were unreliable, inefficient, and costly because of short production runs. These insights gave GE the confidence to challenge the prevailing business model, backed up with heavy investments in improving turbine efficiency and reliability. To get scale, it offered only one size of turbine that met the needs of markets where tight spaces were not a constraint. With design changes and high-volume production, GE improved reliability (uptime) from 85 percent to 97 percent. GE's engines also drew on aircraft technologies to design turbines that captured 20 percent more wind energy.

From this and other studies of successful adjacency moves,[7] we draw four lessons about how to expand the search for growth opportunities into adjacencies:

- **Anticipate emerging and latent customer needs.** Then immerse the organization in understanding customer value in different customer segments. Opportunities in adjacencies can be magnified by the convergence of supportive trends. Thus FedEx found opportunities in "global components handling" that emerged from trends in globalized freight flow, outsourcing demands, and Internet availability. Trends may emerge from fringe markets and extend outward. For example, snowboarding, microbreweries, and extreme sports have become popular with wider audiences.

- **Compete against nonconsumption.**[8] These are potential consumers who have a pressing need, but for a variety of reasons are not current consumers. For example, the biggest global markets for mobile phones remain in China and India, where the alternative is often no phone at all.
- **Leverage and extend the company's value-creating system.**[9] For example, price value leaders grow best by leveraging their low-cost value system within similar markets. The European low-cost airline easyJet has expanded into car rentals (easyCar), cruises (easyCruise), bus service (easyBus), hotels (easyHotel), and other ventures (see www.easy.com). The common denominator is a high-convenience, low-cost value-creating system that appeals to price-sensitive tourists, small business owners, and backpackers. All of these new businesses rely on a value-capture system built on "no frills" operations that vary prices according to demand, low-cost locations, Web-only sales, and high utilization rates that cover fixed costs.
- **Challenge the existing business model.** This exercise forces senior executives to consider how the value chain has to be modified to compete along a new dimension or serve existing customers in expanded ways. Note that successfully challenging existing models requires the absolute buy-in of the entire C-suite. Half-hearted attempts at business model change are almost certain to fail, as entrenched interests within the firm will revolt.

Exploration beyond Adjacencies

Some organic growth initiatives stretch the firm into unfamiliar territory on either the product or the market dimension. No expertise is available internally to help the firm navigate this terrain. At the extremes are discontinuities for which there is no discernible connection to the key success factors in the new market.[10] Such discontinuities may still be of interest if they fall into one of two broad categories of innovation.

The first type focuses on disruptive technology, such as nanotechnology in the chemicals and applied materials industry, or genomics and proteomics in the pharmaceutical industry. However, it is hard to predict disruptive or sustaining innovations or anticipate how they will be valued by customers.

The second type of discontinuity finds new ways to deliver customer value through creative outside-in thinking rather than a technological breakthrough.[11] Bloomberg rose to the top of business information providers by redefining the buyer as the trader and the analyst, rather than the IT manager.[12] While the former wanted feature-rich terminals and software with tailored analytical abilities, the latter wanted standardized systems at the best possible price. By understanding the actual customer for its products and services, Bloomberg was able to create and sell systems that increased traders' productivity and work satisfaction.

Stage IV: Identify and Contain Risks

A healthy portfolio of growth initiatives promises superior returns with a reasonable level of risk. While risk is unavoidable, it can be contained by delaying large and irreversible commitments as long as possible, sharing gains and losses with partners, and getting early warnings of problems so that corrective action can be taken. These aims can be achieved by screening for opportunity, investing in real options, and sharing risks with partners.

Screening for Opportunity

In the mid-1990s, 3M almost shut down a struggling project to develop a computer privacy screen that used its proprietary microlouver technology. Five years later, this product was the basis of one of 3M's fastest-growing businesses. A troubled development history with two unsuccessful launches, nagging concerns about the small size of the market for privacy screens, and sales force resistance had led the C-suite to put the product development team on probation. A rigorous screening of the project revealed flawed assumptions and numerous holes in 3M's understanding of the true opportunity in the adjacent markets for antiglare filters for computers. Armed with deeper insights into the market, and the potential risks, 3M launched a full line of computer "Privacy Filters" that leveraged its brand name and sales presence.[13]

To reduce the possibility of these types of screening errors, and to help identify areas where corrective action was needed, 3M has since adopted the Real-Win-Worth-It (R-W-W) screen (sometimes known as the Schrello screen)[14] to evaluate the 1,500 projects in its development portfolio. Many other firms, including GE and Honeywell, also use a version of the R-W-W screen. This is a robust and simple—but not simplistic—framework based on three sequential questions:

1. Is there a *real* market (Is there a need or desire for the product, can the customer afford it, will the customer buy it, and is the size of the market adequate?) and a *real* product (Is there a clear concept, can the product be made, and will the product satisfy the market?)?

2. Can we *win*? Are we a customer value leader? Does the innovation help us sustain and defend customer value leadership? Can our company be competitive?

3. Is it *worth* doing? Is the return adequate, at an acceptable risk? Are there other strategic considerations?

This is not an algorithm for making go/no-go decisions, but a disciplined learning process that can be employed at multiple stages of product development to expose faulty assumptions and gaps in knowledge, to identify potential sources of risk, and to ensure that every avenue for improvement has been explored. The R-W-W screen can be used to identify and fix problems that are slowing down a project, to contain risk, or expose problems that can't be fixed and should lead to terminating the project.

Figure 6-4 shows the structure of the screen. Perhaps the greatest benefit of the R-W-W screen is that it demands outside-in thinking.

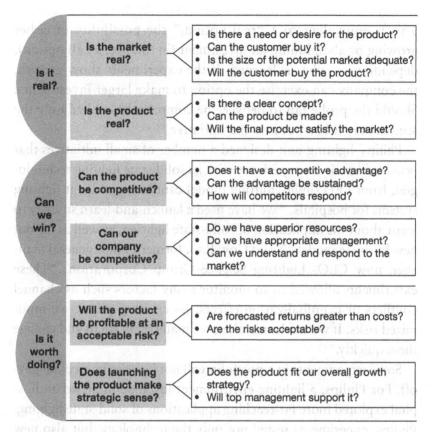

FIGURE 6-4 Real-Win-Worth-It Screen

When it is in the hands of a skilled facilitator, there is no way that even the most inwardly focused technical team can avoid challenging assumptions about the market opportunity and the firm's ability to gain an advantage. While testing these assumptions, the team learns more about the market and how to improve the growth project.

Investing in Real Options

Cautious investments can be made to reveal markets or to understand the potential of a new technology. The aim is to create an option that the firm can exercise if the early feedback is good.

This is equivalent to a "real option," the possibility of either growing or abandoning an investment (in finance, a call option), depending on what is learned. If the experiments show growth, the company can exercise the option to make larger investments. Should the probe fail to deliver, the company has risked only the seed money it has put into the initiative.[15]

Philips' lighting unit designed a number of small initiatives that provided hands-on experience with its solid-state lighting technologies, from LED (light-emitting diode) candles to ambient lighting systems for hospitals. "We have used a launch-and-learn strategy to learn about the application of solid-state lighting, as well as try out new business models," said Govi Rao, former Philips general manager, now CEO, Lighting Science Group Corporation. "These experiments allowed us to monitor many factors such as channel conflicts or cannibalization effects. By creating pilots, we minimized risks. If we made mistakes, we made them small and change them quickly."[16]

Some experiments in a portfolio will not have an immediate payoff. For Philips, a lighting environment installed in an urban hospital explored more far-reaching applications of solid-state lighting. Philips' experiments tested not only the technology, but also new business models, value chains, and market reactions. All of this helped to illuminate the potential of this new market space.

Collaborating and Sharing Risks

Partners, outside suppliers, and specialized contractors can absorb some of the risk or reduce it with their superior skills, experience, and market insights. This is a big departure from the "not invented here" mindset that still subverts many innovation processes. There are many ways to collaborate and share. Among them are the following:[17]

- **Use knowledge brokers.** With knowledge brokers, such as InnoCentive or Nine Sigma, a company can quickly tap into a much wider array of technology solutions than it could possibly reach on its own. These brokers facilitate a direct dialogue between a company with a need for a technology solution and a vast pool of potential problem solvers outside the company. Universities and research labs perform the same function by offering innovations for sale and inviting companies to sponsor research projects.

- **Open up the innovation process.** Most companies are genetically disposed to start with a product and then see if there is a market for it rather than aiming to create a better customer experience. However, a growing number are teaming up with design firms such as IDEO that have robust processes for designing better customer experiences. The design firm orchestrates the innovation process, but the client participates in all the consumer research, analyses, learning, and refinement of the innovation. By making outcomes concrete through rapid-prototyping processes, firms like IDEO help companies gain a better understanding of what might be possible, which inspires faith and investment in innovation activities.

- **Take equity stakes in innovators.** These investments offer early insights into emerging technologies or markets that are relevant but very risky. The stakes are not large, so the initial risk exposure is small, and further investments are made only when the opportunity becomes more promising. Used by companies such as IBM, Merck, Medtronic, and DuPont, this is also a way to bypass an entrenched business model and overcome corporate inertia.

Metrics for Managing the Value Innovation Process

A dashboard of innovation metrics has many uses. It is essential for identifying the weak links in the overall innovation process and costly disconnects between the growth strategy and the portfolio of growth initiatives. It is also needed to hold managers accountable by setting targets for improvement and linking incentives to reaching those targets. An adroitly chosen metric with a challenging target is a strong signal of a shift in strategic priorities. A. G. Lafley successfully transformed the innovation process at Procter & Gamble by setting a goal of acquiring 50 percent of the firm's innovations from outside the company.

A dashboard of metrics that brings an outside-in perspective to the innovation process should have a balanced coverage of three areas:

- **Innovation inputs,** such as R&D spending as a percentage of sales, number of R&D projects, human resources devoted to growth initiatives, and number of ideas or concepts in the pipeline. A valuable outside-in metric is the percentage of ideas sourced from outside the company.
- **Innovation process measures,** including the percentage of projects hitting gates on time, budget versus actual spending, average time to market, and innovation portfolio balance. Portfolio balance is required along several dimensions, including target domain, type of risk, and place on the small i/Big I continuum.
- **Innovation performance outcomes,** such as percentage of sales from new products in the past N years, success rates, revenue growth, customer satisfaction, net present value of the portfolio, and average time to breakeven. To sharpen the outside-in focus, we also recommend that companies track the percentage of profits from new customers, new usage occasions, and new categories.

An effective dashboard gives a holistic picture of the innovation process and the prospects for the portfolio to close the growth gap. The specific metrics are the basis for incentives that signal accountability for improving overall results. To achieve this end, the innovation dashboard should reflect the customer value strategy and be customized for the market. One size does not fit all, and there is no single "silver bullet" metric. A well-designed dashboard has to avoid these two pitfalls:

- **Emphasizing results over diagnostic insights.** The promise of results is used to justify investments in innovation. Therefore, results such as increases in revenue, profit, and customer satisfaction resulting from innovations and the return-on-investment in innovation matter, for the promise of these results is used to justify investments in innovation. Customer satisfaction reveals the ability of the firm to create compelling offerings and please customers. But suppose customer satisfaction is poor and the financial returns are disappointing? Without process effectiveness or input metrics, there is no gauge on the dashboard that will show the reason for these problems. Outcomes measures are also hard to interpret because they are the lagging result of a lengthy chain of decisions.
- **Encouraging incremental innovation.** Some of the most popular innovation metrics subtly or overtly encourage a focus on small i incremental innovations. Two metrics with possible toxic side effects are the percentage of sales from new products in the past N years and the new product success rate. The first metric measures the rate of change in the offerings and emphasizes the need to keep the products and services up to date. The second can be useful for measuring the effectiveness of the innovation process, but it may encourage too many minor projects that "succeed" because of their low thresholds for success.

The new product success rate metric is especially susceptible to gaming and manipulation. On the one hand, it is an essential indicator of the firm's ability to weed out unpromising projects as early as possible and bring the best ones to the market ahead of its rivals. But what is "success"? Was success achieved by setting an easy target? A big problem is underemphasis on riskier Big I innovations. It is tempting to defer spending on these projects when there is a bonus attached to reaching a target success rate.

Unbounded Innovation

Although internal and external forces may push firms toward investments in small i innovation, a disciplined process for managing organic growth initiatives can yield consistently higher rates of growth. A shift toward Big I organic growth requires a realistic assessment of the growth gap—in order to set achievable goals—followed by an outside-in search for new growth opportunities, properly screening those opportunities to reveal their potential, and managing them so that risks are contained.

Customer value innovators need a C-suite executive to formulate the organic growth strategy, to expand the search for new pathways of full-spectrum innovation, and to manage the overall growth process. CMOs earn this role by grounding the entire process in deep market insights to ensure the best fit between market opportunities and possibilities and by mobilizing the rest of the organization.[18]

7

The Third Imperative: Capitalize on the Customer as an Asset

In 2000, Fidelity Investments' leadership of the global mutual fund market looked shaky. The company was being squeezed between full-service financial advisors, which sold the same funds as Fidelity, and low-cost electronic brokers such as E*TRADE. But Fidelity climbed back to a leadership position. It did so by adopting three pivotal actions for its turnaround strategy.[1]

First, Fidelity embraced a relational value proposition that promised customers superior experience with a trusted provider of lifetime investment solutions.

Second, Fidelity segmented its customer base with an eye toward creating a differentiated service offering for its most profitable customers. After exploring different segmentation schemes, Fidelity settled on net worth of managed assets. Affluent investors scoring at the top of this metric, approximately 10 percent of the firm's customers, wanted to take control of their personal investing. This metric was also simple, readily understood by employees (who had to act on it), and correlated with client profitability, which would help Fidelity's bottom line.

Third, Fidelity began to treat different customers differently. Using the segmentation scheme, it devised customer tiers and designed service levels that corresponded to forecasted customer lifetime value. A customer profitability database (the result of an investment in market insight) allowed Fidelity to separate customer acquisition costs from retention costs, which increased the precision of lifetime value estimates. Individuals with a net worth greater than $2 million were given private access to highly trained personal investment reps; less affluent investors were steered toward pooled reps and a retirement consultant. Further service distinctions were made based on age and stage in the life cycle. The key was to have "high-touch" moments backed up with in-depth Internet-based investment guides for the most valuable customers.

Fidelity's shift from an undifferentiated service offering required a clear understanding of what value it wanted to offer to customers and which buyers and prospects should be nurtured into long-term customers. The turnaround required a complete restructuring of the service organization around segment teams, as well as redesigned incentives based on customer retention and segment profitability.

Was it worth the investment and effort? While Fidelity is a private company and does not need to report earnings, it is known that between 1998 and 2006, its share of wallet among its customers increased from 30 percent to 54 percent and its churn rate dropped from 11 percent to 6 percent.[2]

Fidelity Investments recaptured a leading position by acting on the third imperative: capitalize on the customer as an asset. The customer asset is the sum of the discounted long-term profits associated with the customer's purchases and referrals. Like that of other companies we have seen make the transformation to *customer asset managers*, Fidelity's strategy was based on three key principles:

- It made the distinction between customer transactions and deep customer commitment and loyalty. Customer asset managers know that loyalty is a gateway condition that portends important downstream benefits to the company.
- It looked beyond the current invoices to extract the full lifetime value that loyal customers can offer the company. Customer asset managers know that to maximize long-term profits, they

must not only create customer value, but also explicitly manage customers to elicit a full range of behaviors that make them even more profitable over the long run.

- It developed and deployed a capability for capitalizing on the customer as an asset. This capability involves valuing customers and using lifetime value information to differentially develop, defend, and leverage customers.

This chapter addresses the first two steps taken by customer asset managers. Chapter 8 describes the third step.

From Customer Transactions to Customer Loyalty

In the late 1990s, Schwab had passed Merrill Lynch to become the stock-brokerage industry leader in terms of market capitalization.[3] A darling of Wall Street, Schwab seemed unstoppable. A few years later, however, the firm was faltering. Its new products were not well regarded, and its market capitalization plummeted. What went wrong? Analysts argue that Schwab failed to hold on to its position as a price value leader—a low-cost, no-frills brokerage firm. Account fees rose, and client service declined. In our view, Schwab had dropped below parity on the basic relational behaviors that even price-conscious investors require. Customers felt abandoned, and Schwab ranked 27 among 38 financial services firms on the degree to which the firm was perceived to be a "customer advocate."

To turn the firm around, new leadership decided to focus the whole firm on customer loyalty. Beginning in 2006, using a campaign called "Through Clients' Eyes," Schwab took several steps to regain customer trust. It reallocated resources so that by 2008, 84 percent of the retail staff was client-serving, up from 60 percent in 2004. This resulted in a reduction in wait times for callers from 2 minutes to 19 seconds. Schwab also adopted the policy of giving the customer a "direct callback number" if a problem was not resolved with one call. Schwab began measuring client satisfaction, and clients with a low satisfaction score received a personal call from a manager to investigate the problems. It also made pricing for CDs, money market funds, margins, and home loans transparent to the customer. Finally, the company changed its internal reward system to focus on client satisfaction, not on whether the client bought products with certain types of fees.

The change in customers' ratings of Schwab was astonishing: "honoring promises and guarantees" increased from 40 percent to 91 percent, "willing and able to assist me" increased from 68 percent to 88 percent, "always on my side" increased from 57 percent to 86 percent, and facilitating the "ease of comparing prices" increased from 42 percent to 67 percent. The number of customers rating the firm high on the Net Promoter score—a willingness to recommend a firm to friends and family—rose from 35 percent to 50 percent. The number of customers willing to consider Schwab for two or more additional products increased from 49 percent to 71 percent. The company ended 2007 with record sales of $1.1 billion, up 26 percent from 2006. Market cap was at $25 billion, up from $8 billion in 2004.[4] Pretax profit margin was 37.1 percent, up from 34.3 percent in 2006.[5]

Customer Loyalty to the Relationship

Charles Schwab understood the importance of moving the customer from a focus on the single transaction to a sense of loyalty to the company. As a contrast, consider the paradoxical situation with British banks during the 1990s.[6] Only 50 percent of retail banking customers were "very satisfied" with their bank, a level of satisfaction lower than in any other retail sector. Yet only 1 in 30 British customers switched banks in a given year. As the joke of the time went, "They changed their spouses more frequently than their bank." Among the reasons for the apparent stability were inertia, high switching costs, and lack of perceived differences among the banks.

This circumstance demonstrates that duration and customer loyalty are not the same thing. British banks were vulnerable to attack by competitors offering more relational value or price value. The latter is just what happened with the successful launches of both telephone and Internet banking services.

So what distinguishes a long sequence of purchases from real loyalty? Here it is helpful to distinguish behavioral loyalty from attitudinal loyalty. *Behavioral loyalty* is how frequently the customer purchases from the company when the need arises. Behavioral loyalty alone produces revenues for the company. But the revenue stream is at risk. Household customers may be buying out of habit, because of family history, or because of a lack of a convenient alternative—not out of attachment. Likewise, business customers may be buying because of automatic reordering systems.

Attitudinal loyalty, on the other hand, reflects deeper trust in or commitment to the company and what it offers. This type of loyalty is revealed in positive thoughts, feelings of affinity, or attachment to the firm and/or its specific products or services. This trust makes customers more likely to rely on the firm for important activities, such as food for their children or key components for their most important products. Trust is even more vital in service settings where the customer must rely on the firm to provide clean sheets, get the package there on time, or fix an ailment on the operating table.

For many price value leaders, trust is based on a promise of low prices. Walmart customers trust that the company will always offer low prices. Walmart's new tagline introduced in 2007, "Save Money, Live Better," also promises customers that the savings will give them an opportunity to lead better lives. For performance value leaders, customers trust that the company will improve its technologies, science, or designs, and they are loyal to the company's stream of new products and services. Customers count on performance leaders to make their lives more interesting or healthier or to make their businesses run faster or longer. For relational value leaders, customers trust that the product, service, or solution will be customized or personalized to their needs.

The Loyalty Funnel

Many firms use the idea of a funnel to depict the customer's progression through a series of stages to the purchase decision. A typical "purchase funnel" is depicted on the left side of Figure 7-1. The process usually follows a sequence like (1) creating awareness, (2) building knowledge about value, (3) getting into the customer's consideration set, (4) generating positive attitudes toward the firm's offerings, (5) gaining trial when possible, and then (6) finalizing purchase. Firms have many variations on this simple funnel to reflect the relative importance of different steps. For example, a pharmaceutical company may be interested in specifying a step in which sales representatives visit a doctor's office to discuss products.

This is a fine model for getting a customer to make a purchase, but purchase is not synonymous with customer loyalty. To build loyalty, customer asset managers take extra steps and move the customer through the loyalty funnel depicted on the right side of Figure 7-1. This involves the following steps.

Satisfy the Customer with an Offering

For a company to have any chance at customer loyalty, its product or service must meet customer expectations after purchase. Robert McDonald, the CEO of Procter & Gamble (P&G), calls this the "second moment of truth" in the company's interaction with customers. If the offering fails here, the prospects for loyalty are bleak. Offerings that perform as promised or exceed expectations breed satisfied customers. Of course, to meet this requirement, companies must identify the proof points the customer uses to make this judgment. For example, if the number of minutes it takes to deplane is the indicator customers use to judge service quality, airlines should invest in this aspect of operations.

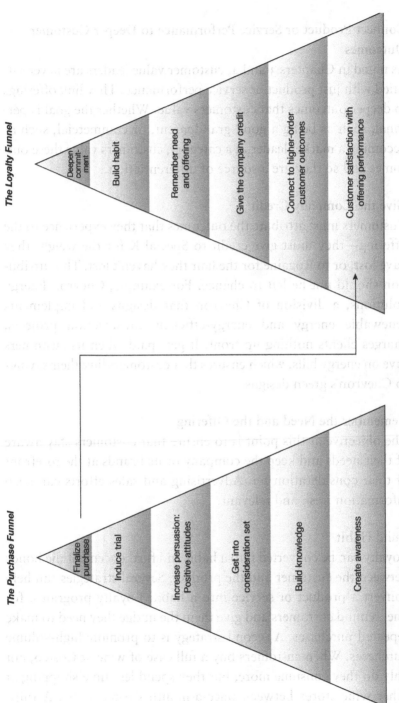

FIGURE 7-1 Moving Customers through Purchase and Loyalty Funnels

Connect Product or Service Performance to Deeper Customer Outcomes

As noted in Chapters 3 and 4, customer value leaders are never satisfied with just product or service performance. They link offerings to deeper outcomes that customers value. Whether the goal is personal, such as being a good grandparent, or commercial, such as becoming a market leader in a category, customers value these outcomes and so they are a source of differentiation.

Give the Company Credit

Customers must attribute the outcomes that they experience to the offering—they must give credit to Special K for the weight they have lost, or to Rogaine for the hair they haven't lost. This attribution should not be left to chance. For example, Chevron Energy Solutions, a division of Chevron that designs and implements renewable energy and energy-efficient construction projects, charges clients nothing up front. It gets paid when its customers save on energy bills, which ensures that customers link their savings to Chevron's green designs.

Remember the Need and the Offering

The objective at this point is to ensure that customers stay aware of their needs and keep the company or its brands at the forefront of their consideration set. Advertising and sales efforts can keep information fresh and relevant.

Build Habit

Loyalty can be converted into a habit and further cement the bonds between the customer and the product. Several strategies can help convert a product or service into a habit. Loyalty programs, for one, remind customers and give them the nudge they need to make repeated purchases. A second strategy is to promote high-volume purchases. When customers buy a full case of wine at Costco, not only do they consume more, but they spend less time shopping at other wine stores between once-a-month Costco visits. A third option is to ask the customer to make investments. Whether this involves installing software or building a specialized ramp to bring a product into a customer's factory, these investments are sunk costs that serve as a reminder of the customer's commitment to the company.

Deepen Commitment

As the customer builds positive experiences with the company, deep affection, trust, and a sense of commitment to the relationship will follow. Success in the long run depends on trust, which is built with transparency and frequent, open communications. Trusted partners face up to deficiencies and never conceal bad news. A dashboard of mutually agreed-upon metrics, so that surprises can be eliminated, facilitates building and maintaining trust.

Sales and service personnel often develop very strong relationships with individual customers. These individual relationships are an important part of building and maintaining trust. However, they are also risky because employee turnover increases customer defection. This problem is common among professional services and financial services firms where as many as 30 percent of their customers have been reported to follow their representatives to a new firm.[7] Hence, companies should build customer loyalty to the firm, not merely to the individual serving the customer.

Furthermore, firms should also require that employees transfer what they have learned about customers to the firm's databases. If turnover does occur, new salespeople will not need to relearn all the things that the departing employee has gathered over the years. This translates into better service and less annoyance for the customer.

From Customer Value to Valuable Customers

Moving customers through the loyalty funnel is just the first step in cultivating valuable customers. The value of the customer asset is quantified as the sum of the discounted long-term profits associated with the customer's purchases and referrals. That potential

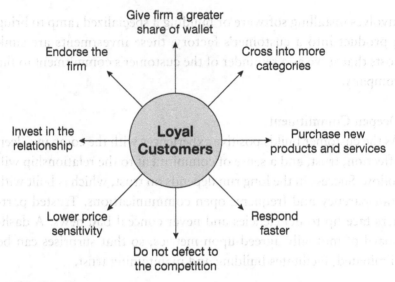

FIGURE 7-2 How Loyal Customers Create Long-Term Firm Profits

sum is greater for loyal customers because loyal customers engage in behaviors that can directly result in increased economic profit for the firm. Most companies never think about the ways in which their customers contribute to their long-term profits, and these firms leave a lot of money on the table. Next, we define the eight behaviors of loyal customers (summarized in Figure 7-2). Companies should systematically engender these behaviors in customers and use these behaviors as metrics for assessing how well they are capitalizing on the customer as an asset.

The Eight Behaviors of Loyal Customers

1. **Give a greater share of wallet.** Out of the 64 ounces of liquid consumed in a day, how much does the average person give the Coca-Cola Company? How much of its logistics budget does The Body Shop give to its longtime partner, The Lane Group? The answer to each question provides the company's "share of wallet"—the percentage of the customer's total expenditure in a category that the company gets. Loyal

customers are more likely to give a greater share, and companies can help by using contact with customers to get a good reading on how the relationship can be extended.

2. **Cross into new categories.** When Disney customers cross from films to the company's theme parks or stores, it's a big win for the company. Compared to new or casual customers, those with multiple connections to the firm are more profitable. Understanding which categories the customer will accept from a company is an important market insight that can drive decisions about this strategy. McDonald's learned this the hard way when it tried to introduce pizza.

3. **Purchase new offerings.** Loyal customers are more open to new offerings from companies within current categories. Customers perceive less risk in new offerings from companies they trust, which increases value. For performance value leaders, customers want and expect these offerings to advance technology, design, or other valued quality features. However, all customer value leaders benefit from this behavior of loyal customers.

4. **Respond faster.** Whether it is to a new product, ad, promotion, sales call, or e-mail, valuable customers respond more quickly. Schering Plough, for example, is 13 percent more likely than the average pharmaceutical firm to complete an appointment with a doctor or nurse during an initial office visit.[8] This means that the company makes profits sooner, thereby increasing the value of profits to the company. Quicker response also means that lower marketing investments are needed to achieve the same result, which also improves profits.

5. **Defect less.** The fiscal rewards of customer retention are on display at USAA. In auto insurance, it has a customer retention rate of 96 percent, compared with 80 percent retention for its average competitor, such as GEICO or Esurance.[9] This means that USAA must replace only 12 percent of its customer base every three years, compared with 49 percent for the

average firm. Profits are also higher, not only because new customers don't need to be recruited, but because current customers need fewer incentives to stay.

High customer retention is also a barrier to entry for new competitors. When prospective entrants look at firms like Netflix, which had 12,268,000 subscribers in 2009, they face a daunting challenge. Netflix subscribers typically have dozens or hundreds of movies in their "queues" waiting to be rented and watched.[10] Knowing that these customers' investments in their Netflix accounts create stickiness, prospective entrants often turn away or seek alternative channels.

6. **Display less price sensitivity.** This behavior is somewhat counterintuitive, since companies across markets often show their appreciation to customers through discounts or loyalty programs. Indeed, in B2B markets, customers will routinely guarantee a greater proportion of their total purchases in return for long-term lower prices. So the issue here is not that valuable customers will pay a premium, but rather that valuable customers are less vulnerable to short-run price promotions or special deals offered by competitors. When customers appreciate the value leaders' overall value position, competitors' temporary price breaks and special concessions lose their appeal.

7. **Invest in the relationship.** Companies benefit when customers make investments on their behalf. Among B2B customers, commitments can be small, such as investing in a joint promotion for the channel. Or they can be substantial, as when customers build specialized equipment, locate the firm's managers on site, train employees to sell a product or service, and even build shared information systems. For example, Walmart has cost-saving partnerships with P&G that focus on increasing the efficiency of order placement, order processing, cross-docking, and inventory holding. The customer's cost of defection increase when it makes investments that are specific to one supplier or distributor and cannot be redeployed.

8. **Endorse the firm.** Customers provide value to companies when they spread positive word of mouth. Three types of advocates can help the firm: early adopters, opinion leaders, and mavens. Early adopters are valued for their expertise in the category. These aficionados have deep knowledge of products in a category and are often the first to try new products. Opinion leaders may not have the depth of knowledge of the early adopters, but these loyal customers are revered for their social standing and drive market acceptance by the sheer force of their recommendations. Mavens know a great deal about what can be purchased, at what price, and where. These social butterflies gain satisfaction from helping others find what they need in the marketplace.[11]

Many top firms, including GE, Philips, and Charles Schwab, use the Net Promoter score to measure the power of these advocacy networks. This score is derived from regular surveys of the firm's current customers. Customers are asked a simple question: "How likely is it that you would recommend [company X] to a friend or colleague?" Customers respond on a 10-point scale, where 10 = "extremely likely" and 1 = "not at all likely." *Promoters* are those who give the firm a 9 or a 10, *detractors* are those who give the firm a score of 0 to 6, and *passively satisfied* customers are those who give the firm a 7 or an 8. Based on these choices, the Net Promoter score is the % promoters – % detractors. Research shows that this score has a strong positive relationship with a firm's three-year growth rate.[12]

How the Eight Loyal Customer Behaviors Drive Long-Term Company Profits

The supportive behaviors of valuable customers directly enhance the stream of profits accruing to the company over the long run.[13] First, cash flows are higher because *revenues are higher.* Higher revenues result from a longer, steadier relationship, a bigger share of wallet, and/or less focus on price by the customer. Second, cash flows are higher when *revenues arrive earlier*. Customers respond faster to company sales calls, ads, or new product introductions. This means that revenues arrive faster and can be reinvested sooner. Positive word of mouth or mouse from existing customers to new customers likewise drives new revenue faster. In addition to increasing revenue levels, longer relationships also *reduce revenue volatility* because defections decline and income streams show less fluctuation.

Longer, stronger relationships also mean *lower costs* for the firm. With fewer customer defections, there is less outlay for new customer acquisition. Costs are also lower when loyal customers respond quickly and consistently, without the need for price promotions or gimmicks. Firms save as well when customers promote the company to others—a recommendation from a trusted peer is always more persuasive than a company sales pitch. Finally, for each dollar spent, firms experience an improved return on investment because of the increased likelihood of response and the faster speed of response.

There are two other ways in which these customer behaviors can improve long-term profits. First, they improve a firm's attractiveness as an alliance partner and its power in alliance negotiations.[14] Second, firms with valuable customers have a lower cost of debt and a lower discount rate applied to determine the present value of future earnings, because their cash flows are less at risk.

The Customer Asset: Profiting over the Long Term

If managing customers as assets is a rich source of long-term profits for companies, why don't more companies act like customer asset managers? The problem is that companies are prone to lapsing into inside-out thinking and making short-term decisions that degrade the value of the customer asset. Here are some common problems that we have observed.

Quantity over Quality

Having more customers does not mean having more profits! Many companies automatically equate success with market share. Success must be based on profits—which can come from focusing on the most valuable customers. Consider the case of Nypro, a provider of integrated plastics solutions. In the 1980s, the firm's then president (now chairman of the board), Gordon Lankton, decided that the firm could be more profitable over the long run if it slashed the number of customers it served from 800 to 30 and retained only its million-dollar accounts. "We decided that if we had a smaller number of big customers we could really concentrate on doing the job right."[15] This focus allowed Nypro to make serious commitments to its best customers, such as Johnson & Johnson, Gillette, and P&G, including building plants next to theirs. Lankton called this the "McDonald's Plan"[16] because these convenient locations reduced customers' cost of moving packaging (from Nypro) to their manufacturing plants. The result was a Corvallis, Oregon, printer plant to serve Hewlett-Packard; a Clinton, Massachusetts, plant to serve Gillette; and a Mebane, North Carolina, plant to serve P&G. This move allowed Nypro to emerge as the "go-to strategic partner" in this fragmented, commodity-like industry. Nypro posted $1 billion in sales in 2008, up from $83 million in 1988.[17] The firm's operating profit increased from $1.7 million in 1988 to $42 million in 2008.[18]

Failure to Learn about Customers

Despite the fact that customers constantly interact with companies, many companies ignore the opportunity to learn from these interactions. Insights about segments of customers, such as how Millennials shop or what kind of pillow a particular customer likes, can be used to manage customer contacts. Whether it's a warm welcome from the cashier at the local grocery store or a reminder of what was purchased last time from an online flower shop, customers value even simple forms of recognition that deepen their involvement with companies. Unfortunately, most companies do not provide this level of service. Instead, they understaff, fail to develop systems to record customer information, and put incentives only on sales, not on learning. While this may improve short-term margins, it dramatically erodes the value of the customer asset, and therefore undermines long-term profitability.

Unwillingness to Spend to Generate Valuable Customers

Valuable customers are the result of strategies that move the customer from transactions to loyalty. Repeat purchase is a start, but there is no natural evolution through which valuable customers automatically emerge. Rather, the firm must manage the transition. For example, in the early 1990s, the Royal Bank of Canada (RBC) had a strong customer base, but it sought ways to become more profitable. RBC used a series of small steps designed to make its most valuable customers more likely to stay with the firm and more likely to give the firm positive word of mouth. For example, instead of applying across-the-board overdraft fees, the company adopted more lenient policies for its high-value customers. Although this meant giving up profits in the short term, RBC managers predicted such policies would produce more loyal and longer-term customers. They were right—the lifetime value of these customers increased by 20 percent![19]

Emphasize Price Discounts Instead of Loyalty

Firms are inevitably tempted to try to improve sales by offering price reductions, sales, or coupons. These actions work in the short term, and the lift over baseline sales can be impressive. However, these gains often come at the expense of profit margins and reflect customer stockpiling, not the acquisition of new customers. Worse, these same actions increase customer sensitivity to price and price promotion activities in the category. For example, analysts studying the beverage industry report a 14 percent increase in price sensitivity from 1994 to 1999 as a result of sales promotions.[20] Such increased price sensitivity may hurt customer retention as customers are tempted by price deals. Furthermore, customers are also more likely to delay purchase in anticipation of a discounted price. Advertising, on the other hand, appears to make customers less price sensitive and more loyal.

Cut Spending on Customers to Improve Short-Term Firm Earnings
Managers often improve their income statements by cutting marketing, service, and R&D expenditures that affect customers. Unfortunately, these decisions have long-term implications. One study examined firms undergoing seasoned equity offerings (SEO), in which the firms issue additional equity to raise capital. A SEO tempts a firm to engage in short-term earnings inflation so that it will look as good as possible prior to the offering. When firms cut customer spending at the time of the SEO, they are indeed overvalued in the short term compared to firms that do not cut marketing spending, the study found. However, over the long run, these cuts have a negative effect on the value of the firm, as the stock price of firms that make such cuts ends up being lower than the price of firms that don't.[21]

Failure to Invest in Customer Recovery Systems
Companies think about the immediate costs of recovering from a product or service failure instead of the long-term income stream that a loyal customer brings to the company. Sure, it might cost $200 to replace the suit lost in the airline bag. But if the customer is won over for life by the airline's generous and empathetic response and shares the positive experience with others, the investment is well spent.

Customer Asset Managers

Customer asset managers skillfully move customers from initial transactions to long-term loyalty. This ensures the progression from providing customer value to profiting from valuable customers.

The value-producing behaviors of these loyal customers are a company asset that improves company cash flows. We build on these ideas in the next chapter by discussing how this asset can be valued, developed, defended, and leveraged to increase company profits.

8

Capitalizing on the Customer as an Asset

In 1990, Pearle Vision was the largest U.S. retailer of eyeglasses and other corrective eyewear, but it served a fragmented, stagnant, and barely profitable market. Competitors followed the same strategy of offering a wide selection of cheap brands at discounted prices and providing lackluster service. Pearle's only advantage was its large number of stores.

Top management found the status quo unacceptable and sought a strategy that would allow Pearle to capture above-average profits.[1] To escape the aptly described "snake pit" of relentless price wars, top management selected a new customer value strategy that repositioned Pearle as a trusted eye-care professional. It did this by following a four-stage customer management process that reflects what customer asset managers do well.

1. **Select valuable customers.** Pearle invested in building relationships with consumers who insisted on consulting a trained, trusted optometrist before purchasing eyeglasses.
2. **Develop valuable customers.** Pearle encouraged independent optometrists to set up shop next to Pearle Vision stores to give customers the convenience of filling their prescriptions at Pearle stores. Pearle also improved service by hiring trained opticians and putting lens grinding labs on-site so that glasses could be made in an hour rather than the usual two weeks.

3. **Defend valuable customers.** Because people replace their glasses only every two years on average, they are easily poached by competitors. To keep in contact with its customers, Pearle built a complete customer database that identified its most valuable customers. These customers received special mail promotions and reminders to replace their glasses. To reinforce this emphasis on relational value, store managers were rewarded for both revenue and customer retention.
4. **Leverage valuable customers for growth.** Pearle leveraged the customer relationship by adding contact lenses to its product portfolio. Because contacts are replaced more frequently than eyeglasses, this increased customer visits to Pearle stores and further cemented the relationship.

Within three years, the strategy started to pay off. Pearle increased the lifetime value of its average customer from $0.73 to $13.45. This was accomplished by increasing the average number of eyeglasses sold per visit (which lifted the contribution margin from $2.00 to $16.68) and increasing customer retention from 30 percent to 50 percent.

Pearle's situation before embarking on this strategy is not uncommon. Many customer value leaders find themselves in a position where they need to make strategic moves to fully capitalize on the customer asset. Chapter 7 introduced key concepts associated with managing the customer as an asset. In this chapter, we'll examine methods for ensuring the correct valuation of customers and for capitalizing on the customer asset by developing, defending, and leveraging the relationship.

Select Customers as Assets

Between 1998 and 2005, Harrah's Entertainment's profits more than tripled from $102 million to $368 million and its share price almost quadrupled from $20 to $74. Most observers consider

Harrah's Total Gold program a turning point in the firm's success. The company's player-card program was designed to identify customers and reward them with incentives to visit Harrah's properties. Behind the program is a massive transactional database that contains information about customer preferences and behaviors. This information is collected when customers insert rewards cards into slot machines or use the cards when checking in at Harrah's hotels and restaurants. Information is collected during the customer's stay and combined with other demographic, geographic, and psychographic information.

Harrah's initially supplemented these data with broader surveys and interviews with customers. This early research uncovered that Harrah's most loyal customers were spending only 36 percent of their annual gaming budgets at Harrah's. Gary Loveman, the firm's new COO, saw this as a massive opportunity. He notes, "Understanding the lifetime value of our customers would be critical to our marketing strategy. Instead of focusing on how much people spent in our casinos during a single visit, it became clear that we needed to focus on their potential worth over time."[2] This meant that Harrah's needed to understand the value of different customers and what motivated these customers to return to Harrah's.

A deep dive into its data uncovered an important initial insight: Harrah's most valuable customers were not gold-cuff-linked high rollers. Instead, they were middle-aged teachers, doctors, bankers, and machinists with modest discretionary incomes. With this insight, Harrah's segmented its current customers into different groups reflecting their value. Total Gold customers have no minimum worth, Total Platinum customers have an annual worth of $1,500, and Total Diamond customers have an annual worth of $5,000. Knowing the value of these customers gave Harrah's a clear idea about how much and in what ways it should spend to get customers to return to its casinos. Harrah's understood whether it was the steak dinner, extra chips, or an invitation to a special event, such as a concert, that was valued by certain customers. Marketing spending was customized to reflect these preferences, resulting in higher ROI.

Customer Lifetime Value: General Approaches

Unfortunately, most firms don't know the actual value of their customers. They are flying blind, with no clear understanding of how much a customer is worth or, as a consequence, any idea how much the firm could profitably spend to attract or retain a customer. Firms that want to capitalize on customers as assets will first need to invest in the capacity to value both current and potential customers. Most of the approaches for doing so utilize customer lifetime value (CLV) models, and they are really not as complicated as many people fear (for some of the technical detail, see the sidebar "Selecting Valuable Customers Using CLV").

Selecting Valuable Customers Using CLV

CLV models take the following factors into account: the customer's gross margin in a specific time period, the customer's retention rate in that time period (the probability of being retained until to the next period), the expected life of the customer (how many years the customer is expected to stay in a relationship with the firm), and the firm's discount rate.

The value of the customer is summed across the expected life, and then the values of those cash flows are discounted to present-day dollars.[3] Lifetime value can be calculated at the individual customer level or for an average customer within a segment. The lifetime value of a customer is:

$$\text{CLV}_c = \sum_{t=1}^{N} M_c \left[\frac{r_c^t}{(1+i)^t} \right] - \text{AC}_c$$

In this equation, M_c is the gross margin for a customer in a given time period t (e.g., a year), net of retention costs such as extra service costs for that customer; i is the firm's discount rate; r_c is the customer's retention rate or likelihood of returning to the firm at time t; AC_c is the acquisition cost, such as the price of a sales call or an e-mail; and N is the period over which the customer is assumed to remain active.

Here's an example of how CLV calculations can expose the true value of a customer. A B2B customer with a gross margin of \$7,000 in year 1 and \$5,000 in years 2 and 3, where the retention rate is 70 percent, the firm's discount rate is 10 percent, and acquisition cost is \$1,000 has a CLV of \$6,768 $= [\text{year 1: } (7,000 \times 0.70)/(1.10)] + [\text{year 2: } (5,000 \times (0.70))^2]/(1.10^2)] + [\text{year 3: } (5,000 \times (0.70))^3]/(1.10^3)]$ $- 1000$. Contrast that with the CLV of a customer that yields a margin of \$7,000 in all three years (CLV = \$8,093) or if the firm could increase its retention rate from 70 percent to 90 percent under the original scenario (CLV = \$10,813).[4]

These simple CLV analyses reveal several important insights. First, acquisition costs should never exceed the lifetime value of a customer. In the example, the firm should spend no more than an additional \$6,768 in the first scenario or \$8,093 and \$10,813 in the second and third scenarios to acquire this customer.

Second, it follows logically that firms should be willing to spend more to acquire and retain customers with a higher lifetime value. If the future profits from a customer are high, then the company can afford to make a bigger investment in today's acquisition costs.

Third, the firm can have a larger impact on the value of the customer by increasing retention than by increasing margin.[5] Research has shown that a 1 percent increase in retention rate has a 4.9 percent increase in customer lifetime value, while a 1 percent increase in margin has only a 1.1 percent increase in customer lifetime value! This is a lesson that no manager should ever forget.

Fourth, if a firm spends according to CLV, it will receive a higher return on investment because every dollar of investment means a greater return.

Challenges in Using CLV Models

Though customer lifetime value models are pretty straightforward calculations that can bring huge value to the business, the following are a few potholes to be wary of in these calculations:

- **Need to account for when money arrives.** The approach we offer assumes that companies have to wait to receive their money from customers until the end of period t. Because this approach is used for all customers, it affects valuation the same way across customers. However, when some customers leave during the first period, these funds are assumed to be lost. This may not be an accurate assumption for companies that receive their money from customers at the beginning of the relationship, such as payments before shipments or health club memberships. If this is the case, the margins, costs, and retention rates from the prior period t should be used in valuing customers to get the most accurate assessment.[6]
- **Missing individual data.** Firms may find that they do not have the data on profits or costs needed to value each individual customer (e.g., many packaged goods companies that do not interface directly with their customers). In these cases, firms can use lifetime value models at the segment level and calculate average profit margins and marketing costs for a "typical customer" in a segment. These are the total profit and total marketing costs divided by the number of customers in a segment.[7]
- **Not sure how long a typical customer is active.** Universities are in the enviable position of knowing that a typical undergraduate takes approximately four or five years to graduate. Most companies don't have such predictable relationship time

frames. A detailed, well-maintained customer database would help address this fundamental question, but in the absence of this resource, some of our colleagues recommend using a three-year period as a good approximation.[8] Another approach is to assume that the life of the customer is infinite. That might sound like an outrageous assumption. However, this approach is quite reasonable mathematically, given that the value of a customer after five years is very small as a result of retention rates and discount rates. Therefore, unless retention rates are very high or discount rates are very low, the infinite CLV approach is a good approximation.[9]

- **Difficulty in assigning marketing costs.** Firms may also find it difficult to assign marketing costs to customers or segments of customers. One way to manage this is to do simple counts of marketing contacts with the customer. Frequency of store visits, warranty claims, customer service calls, and salesperson visits can all be estimated by managers or front-line employees.[10]

Using CLV to Invest in Prospects

In addition to providing information on which current customers to invest in, lifetime value approaches can also guide managers on investments in new customers or prospects. A firm may have strong relationships with customers in a certain segment. Based on that success, the firm may seek to target more customers in that segment. To act on this idea, firms can compute the lifetime value of a prospective customer (PLV) for that segment.[11] PLV shows the expected value per prospect of any acquisition effort.

Once the PLV is determined, managers can use it in several important ways. PLV can be used to guide acquisition spending. To do so, we recommend not including a value for acquisition cost (AC) in the PLV calculation (see the CLV formula given earlier). Instead, since it is a separate term, you can solve for it when calculating PLV. To figure this out, set PLV = $0, and the resulting acquisition cost is the upper limit on what should be spent per prospect. PLV can also be used together with CLV to guide customer selection. Customers scoring high on both CLV and PLV have the greatest value to companies.

Develop Customers as Assets

Having determined which customers the company wants to focus on, several key actions can be taken to develop these customers as assets.

Create a Learning Relationship

Tesco uses its data-collecting loyalty card (the Clubcard) to track which stores customers visit, what they buy, and how they pay. This information has helped Tesco tailor merchandise to local tastes. It also helps the retailer customize offers to individual customers. For example, shoppers who buy diapers at a Tesco store for the first time receive coupons by mail not only for baby wipes and toys, but also for beer, according to the *Wall Street Journal*. Tesco's analysis revealed that new fathers tend to buy more beer at retail because they can't spend as much time at the pub![12]

Ritz-Carlton Hotels records customers' preferences for room types, pillows, newspapers, and other amenities and offers these upon check-in. This means that Ritz-Carlton must have individual-level CRM databases that allow it to capture information, transfer it across time and locations, and share it with all employees who interact with the customer.

Costco, a price value leader, uses special stores as learning labs. These stores are 40 percent larger than most stores, with the extra space devoted to products that Costco is learning about, such as home furnishings. Observing sales outcomes and customer interactions with merchandise allows the company to collect important feedback on new merchandise and concepts. Here the learning is less about developing customized responses such as those we see in relational value leaders like Tesco and the Ritz. Instead, Costco wants to know what will sell big if it rolls out a new product or line to all its stores. These lab stores allow Costco to get a quick reading on what to build into its "treasure hunts." Bought in bulk and sold with heavy discounts, these items are often amazing steals for customers. However, what will be offered is a mystery and it will be gone by the next time the customer shops. Jim Sinegal, Costco's founder and CEO, noted recently: "You're going to come in and find that maybe we have some Lucky jeans that we're selling. You come in the next time and we don't have those jeans but we have some Coach handbags. That's the treasure-hunt aspect. We constantly buy that stuff and intentionally run out of it."[13]

Even performance leaders can benefit from this type of customer learning. If Apple can identify a returning iPod or laptop customer by asking about prior purchases, it can adjust its sales or customer service approach accordingly by offering upgraded features, complementary products, or services. This information is also useful in promoting new features and products to loyal customers over time.

Treat Different Customers Differently

Knowing that not all customers are valuable and knowing what different customers want, customer asset managers invest in their most profitable customers. This means making tough choices and setting unequal budgets, which can ruffle feathers when the firm has a history of dividing budgets equally among different business units. However, unless this strategy is followed, the idea that customers are assets has no meaning.

This does not mean that low-value customers are fired. It simply means that firms direct these customers to lower-cost channels and ways of interacting with the company. For example, a study done by McKinsey shows that a large number of wireless customers go to stores to pay their phone bills.[14] Unfortunately, it is often lower-value customers who initiate these costly face-to-face interactions.

Armed with this insight, wireless firms might migrate these customers to lower-cost channels such as telephone payments or kiosks to pay bills. Taking the time to understand why certain customers are using certain resources, and then finding alternative lower-cost solutions (such as migrating some accounts from a single sales representative to an inside sales team), can free up resources to be devoted to higher-value customers.

A large Fortune 1000 high-tech manufacturer of computer hardware and software offers another example. Using monthly transaction data from January 2000 to April 2007, researchers found that the top 20 percent of customers accounted for 91 percent of total profits, while the bottom 20 percent had a negative lifetime value. Further profiling showed that high-value customers were in the high-tech, aerospace, and financial services industries; had been incorporated for between 15 and 25 years; were multinational; had more than 500 employees; and had yearly revenues exceeding $50 million. In response to these customer insights, the company moved marketing resources to high-CLV customers and directed negative-CLV customers to online channels. It also increased acquisition expenses on prospective customers who matched the profile of high-CLV customers. Profits soared, and its average monthly stock price increased 32.8 percent in the nine months that followed.[15]

Reward Valuable Customer Behaviors

Firms can use a range of incentive and loyalty programs to encourage certain behaviors. Harrah's Total Gold customer reward program encourages repeat visits to casinos and cross-casino visits. Harrah's loyalty card allows it to understand what customers are doing within each casino and across casinos, including whether they won or lost money during their visit. That information is used to tailor rewards to the customer's preferences and offer bigger incentives if the customer lost money.

The Body Shop, the UK-based firm that sells natural body-care products through retail outlets all over the world, set up a novel reward program with The Lane Group, the distribution company responsible for moving products from The Body Shop's distribution center in Little Hampton, Sussex, to stores all over the UK. This program, which is part of the contract between the two businesses, specifies that if The Lane Group delivers better than 99.7 percent of the products to The Body Shop stores within a specified two-hour window of time, it receives a large bonus at the end of each quarter.[16]

Don Pepper and Martha Rogers, CRM gurus, have said, "Give the customer the opportunity to teach you what he wants. Remember it, give it back to him, and keep his business forever."[17] Most well-managed loyalty programs perform this dual role of motivating the customer and providing learning for the firm. In fact, many firms attempt to get customers to identify themselves and their preferences early in the relationship with the promise of more tailored services.

It is essential that rewards build behavioral *and* attitudinal loyalty to the firm and its offerings. If customers get attached to the reward instead, the relationship can be undermined when competitors offer similar rewards. It is also perplexing to us that more firms do not use variable rewards. Most firms use fixed rewards, meaning that customers receive them every time they shop, fly, or buy a cup of coffee. Variable reinforcement would mean irregular rewards, presumably of a higher quality (because they are doled out less frequently). For example, airlines could save one first-class seat (beyond those requested by high-paying customers) on some flights and surprise a coach customer with an announcement to the full cabin that a lucky flyer has been "moved to the front of the plane." For customers that never build enough miles to receive rewards, this strategy would provide a moment of excitement in an otherwise mundane trip. Classic work in psychology shows that variable rewards build stronger habits. We recommend that companies experiment with variable rewards with a small set of customers to gauge the effects on loyalty.

Engage Customers in Communities

Pampers Village is a P&G Internet community dedicated to new parents (www.pampers.com/en_US/home/). The site contains information about parenting, baby care, and new products; a baby-naming service (in the UK); and blogs from new moms and pediatricians. In 2008, P&G used the site to stage a publicity event. The focus was Pampers' ability to provide babies and their parents "Golden Sleep" because the diapers offered 12 hours of dryness or "overnight dryness so babies can sleep." In this publicity event, parents all over China sent in pictures of their sleeping babies. The number of pictures received and posted to the site broke the *Guinness Book of World Records* figure for most baby pictures in a mural.[18] Diapers may not seem all that exciting, but events of this type create loyalty, bond the customer to the firm and to the product, and generate a lot of positive buzz in the marketplace.

Communities can also help firms recover from problems. Dell was suffering from a reputation for offering poor customer service, highlighted by the content of Dell Hell, a blog that became a viral nightmare for Dell. In response to this attack, Michael Dell met with Dell Hell creator Jeff Jarvis, and they co-created Ideastorm, which allows customers to blog and comment on existing products and services. Dell took a public relations nightmare and managed to turn it into a positive opportunity that was co-created with a customer.[19]

Finally, communities can also be used as a way for customers to help each other with technical issues that improve the experience or functionality of products. For example, in Hewlett-Packard's freely accessible technical support forum (h30434.www3.hp.com/psg/), users ask and answer questions; HP engineers often participate in these forums so that they can offer help and learn. The service is delivered through asynchronous online discussion boards organized around subcategories, such as the company's different operating systems products or networking solutions. All exchanges are stored so that customers can use a search engine to review past discussions.

Questioners can award up to 10 points for answers given. Answerers, whether HP employees or other customers, accumulate these points and can reach different levels of "hats," which are clearly visible online next to their nicknames. This level of collaboration fosters loyalty both to the product and to the firm.[20]

Defend Customers as Assets

Given their financial importance to the company, customer relationships need to be protected over time. What actions do customer asset managers take to safeguard customer loyalty from competitors' challenges?

The Best Defense Is a Strong Offense

Before competitors strike, there are several preemptive moves a firm can make to defend customers.

Differentiate Value

When the offering provides exceptional value that is not replicated elsewhere, customers will return. The jeans that fit, the familiar computer setup, the components that are compatible with the aircraft engine design, the consultant who knows the business strategy, and the vacation spot that thrills are not easy for customers to replicate. Differentiation of offerings is the most defensible form of customer lock-in. It is a key to providing value and to maintaining loyalty. Without it, the rest is all smoke and mirrors.

Consider how American Express handles its most elite customers. In its "By Invitation Only" program, American Express might observe that a Cardmember likes to frequent upscale restaurants, and then offer a free dining experience at a new restaurant. The Cardmember wins through a valuable offer from a merchant. The merchant wins because important customers are introduced to the restaurant. And American Express wins by connecting the two and deepening its relationship with its Cardmembers and merchants.[21]

Rebuff Competitors' Challenges

When Walmart bought Asda, Tesco anticipated a price challenge. In a brilliant strategic maneuver reported in the *Wall Street Journal*, "Tesco searched its database and singled out price-shoppers who buy the cheapest available item. Tesco figured they were most likely to be tempted by Asda. Tesco identified 300 items these price-sensitive shoppers bought regularly. One was Tesco Value Brand Margarine. Tesco lowered its price along with other products with similar profiles. Shoppers didn't defect."[22]

Raise Customer Switching Costs

Firms can make it very difficult for customers to walk away from a relationship by raising the switching costs. The classic example is frequent flyer miles. These lock customers into a carrier because of the escalating benefits tied to different levels of miles flown and because miles expire after a certain period of time.

Lock-in can also occur because customers do not want to incur the costs of learning to interact with a new firm. Once customers accumulate enough experience with a retail store so that they can locate items easily or talk to a favorite salesperson who knows their preferences, or with a Web site onto which they have loaded their preferences, they are surprisingly resistant to change. Challengers need to reduce the costs of trial or offer large incentives to induce trial in order to offset these learning curve barriers.

Finally, when a company makes pledges or signs contracts that give a business customer exclusive rights to territories or products, those commitments wed the customer to the company.

Increase Investments in Customers

There are inherent risks associated with making dedicated investments, such as human resources, capital equipment, and information technologies, in customers. As a result, customers are likely to view these investments as a signal that the firm is interested in a long-term relationship. Better yet, when the firm's investments stimulate reciprocal customer investments, partners are in a "mutual hostage" situation. When the incentives are aligned in this way, the relationship is even stronger. Reciprocation is a powerful norm that guides nearly all strong relationships. Most companies forget about this norm when managing customer relationships. When the company exceeds expectations with exceptional service, such as a flight attendant rushing a purse left on an airplane to the unwitting customer waiting at the baggage carousel, customers experience a sense of reciprocity that compels them to return the relationship.

Resolve the Need for Variety
Some customers want a great deal of variety. Regardless of the value that the firm provides, these customers may switch simply to have different experiences. Food and entertainment are areas where customers experience a desire for variety. Many firms defend loyalty against this threat by extending their product lines so that they can offer customers that variety.

Refresh the Relationship
Likewise, customers may also want multiple relationships or a reasonable level of switching in order to ensure that they continue to learn new things. In areas where innovation is important, such as product design, consulting, advertising, and market research, customers may reach out to new relationships in order to overcome the problems of stale knowledge. Companies should manage this problem by systematically infusing new insights into the relationship. Adding new and varied talent to a key account team is one way to bring new ideas to the customer. Regular knowledge sharing, brainstorming, or co-creation efforts with a client can also rejuvenate relationships.

Tighten the Relationship at All Levels
Defense can be accomplished by thinking about actual and potential ways in which the firm can engage the customer. More engagement reduces defection.

Foster Customer Co-creation

If customers co-create products and services with a company, it increases involvement in and commitment to the offering and the company.[23] For example, in B2B co-creation relationships, value-leading suppliers rely on leading-edge customers for help in developing new products. This process can increase customer interest in the success of the new offering, which should translate into higher investments.

The Internet has created an ever-increasing array of ways in which customers can deepen their involvement with companies. Whether they are offering new code for open-source software, rating books, or designing their own sneakers and T-shirts, all of these approaches help to facilitate a stronger relationship between customers and the company. Customers want to know that they matter. Large and small invitations to participate are key ways in which companies can meet this need.

Create Multiple Relationships

It is increasingly common for B2B firms to form multiple relationships with their customers. In 2002, Brocade Communications set up a marketing alliance and a joint venture with HP for manufacturing switches, in addition to selling HP servers, an R&D alliance, and a licensing agreement.[24] Research shows that as the number of interactions increases, the risk of relationship termination decreases. Customers gain a greater sense of shared interest and solidarity with the firm because of the number of relationships. Partners also learn to use the relationships in a compensatory manner, trading benefits and costs so that both parties' interests are served.

Leverage Customers as Assets

Customer asset managers capitalize on opportunities to use what they learn about customers. This knowledge helps them see openings to deepen and widen relationships with existing customers, turning those that are of marginal value into high-value customers. Deeper relationships with these customers, in turn, open more opportunities to learn. There are eight key ways in which firms can leverage their valuable customers for growth.[25]

Activate Customers across Current Categories

Across the array of products and services that a company offers, where are current customers sitting out? American Express looks at expenditures to determine where its customers are *not* using their cards. If a customer does not use his card for everyday expenses, such as groceries or gasoline, the customer may be reminded of a double "Membership Rewards" points promotion for this merchant category.[26]

Tesco does the same thing with its Clubcard and coupons. When quarterly coupon packages are sent to customers, Tesco sends three coupons for products that customers buy regularly and three for goods that Tesco's analytics indicate are bought by similar customers. This approach works well—while for the industry as a whole, only 1 or 2 percent of coupons typically get redeemed, about 15 to 20 percent of all Tesco coupons are used.

Migrate Customers to a Higher-Value Segment

American Express uses customer information to understand the customer's readiness to move along a predefined upgrade path among the different branded cards offered by the company. For example, the first purchase of an upper-class airline ticket on a Gold Card triggers an invitation to upgrade to a Platinum Card.

Bloomberg uses this same migration strategy in B2B markets. Bloomberg's services are delivered through dedicated terminals that provide access to news, stock quotes, and tools that enable analysts to do many things, such as screen stocks based on certain characteristics, build and monitor portfolios, and download data into Excel for report building. Different levels of service offer different levels of functionality. For example, with higher (and more expensive) levels of service, analysts get access to real-time market-maker quotations and can even execute trades over the system. Many users remain unaware of these features and how they can add value to their business. To remedy this and move customers up to these more expensive levels of service, Bloomberg hosts free training sessions at four-star hotels such as the Beverly Hills Hotel and the Los Angeles Biltmore. The day is focused on seminars that emphasize Bloomberg's premium subscription services, networking opportunities for analysts, and even keynote talks from top investment companies.

Create Complementary Sources of Value

A key way in which firms leverage customer relationships is by selling customers items that complement what they have already purchased. A Harley-Davidson motorcycle retails for between $7,000–$38,000, averaging ~$12,900 (in 2010), but fully 25 percent of the company's $5.6 billion in sales is from branded jackets, hats, and glasses carefully selected to complement the riding lifestyle.[27] Harley executives sponsor and participate in Harley Owner's Group (HOG) meetings to gather insight, which they then use to drive these product selection decisions.

Solution selling among B2B companies is a common way to sell complementary sources of value. According to one report, 63 percent of Fortune 100 firms offer solutions, including IBM, GE, and Cisco.[28] Customers also want solution sellers to act as partners after deployment and help them adapt the system as their own offerings and strategies shift. This role points to important growth prospects for consulting opportunities and product sales to meet customers' ongoing needs.

Evolve with the Customer

Many companies forget that their customers are changing over time and that these changes are opportunities for the firm to cultivate a longer and stronger relationship with the customer. The Knot founder David Liu points out, "The Internet has created these watering holes that didn't exist before. You can market against time lines."[29] The Knot was launched as an online wedding-planning resource for brides-to-be, but it has since evolved into a self-described "life stages media brand" that targets 25- to 32-year-old women who are moving into a period of rapid change involving marriage, home, and kids. The Knot collects data when users register on one of its Web sites. Because postwedding life stages tend to follow a predictable pattern, the company can target its customers with event-centric products, services, and resources over time, tied to, for example, home buying (The Nest) and pregnancy and baby gear needs (The Bump).

The Knot strengthens its bonds with customers by partnering with vendors that can fill in gaps. The Knot explicitly mines its customer information and then shares it with these vendors. In its privacy statement, The Knot discloses that it "does share names, postal addresses, and demographic information with other pre-screened organizations that have specific direct mail product and service offers we think may be of interest." Rather than irritating customers who fear being flooded with junk mail, sharing data helps The Knot maintain active, long-term relationships with its customers as their needs change over time. The strategy is paying off, as the business has continued to grow over its 10-year life to the point where 80 percent of would-be brides are clients.

Foster Customer-Created Value

When customers are loyal to a company and love its products and services, they are often willing to help the firm create new sources of value that benefit both the firm and other customers. Internet users post 13 hours of video per minute to YouTube, making it one of the most visited Web sites worldwide. Some media entities took early notice of this trend and figured out how to harness the power of user-generated content for their products. For example, the Cable News Network (CNN) responded with iReport, which allows CNN viewers to submit photos, videos, and stories to news reports.[30]

Some companies are built entirely on the concept of leveraging customer-created value—eBay, Wikipedia, Craigslist, Facebook, Storymash, Flickr, and MySpace, for instance. The T-shirt maker Threadless allows customers to submit T-shirt designs via an online social network. Once the designs are submitted, customers discuss and vote on them, interact with each other, and purchase T-shirts with the most popular designs. Threadless has experienced revenue growth of 500 percent per year without advertising, designers, sales representatives, or retail outlets. Margins on the $15 T-shirts are above 30 percent, costs are low, and nearly every product sells out.[31] Co-creating offers endless possibilities for firms like Threadless to attract new customers, leverage existing relationships, and discover new sources of growth.

Apply Customer Knowledge to Target New Customers

Firms can apply their knowledge of their current customers to attract more customers from the same target market and thus penetrate existing markets more deeply. To do so, companies use information about current customers to develop a profile of a valuable customer. This profile is then applied to the broader population to locate similar customers whom the firm can target.[32] This highly effective, low-risk strategy is often overlooked by many companies. However, if it is deployed, the return on investment for this growth strategy can be very high for two reasons. First, the firm is sticking to its value proposition, so no new investments need to be made. Second, the firm is relying on its deep knowledge of its current customers to go after more of the same.

Transfer Customer Knowledge to Related Markets

Another way in which firms leverage customer relationships is by using what they have learned about existing customers to target customers in related markets. When a firm targeting teenage girls in the United States applies what it has learned to target teenage girls in Japan, it increases the value of the original customer because a new growth opportunity is produced.

The MTN group, a multinational telecommunications company based in South Africa, has emerged as one of the premier mobile networks in Africa and the Middle East through its aggressive and focused growth strategy. It has grown from a meager beginning in 1994 and now serves 21 countries. MTN's strategy was to focus on the business segment in each market it entered. As it did so, MTM leveraged the knowledge and experience it had acquired through previous entries.[33]

Transfer Customer Management Capabilities to New Markets

Sometimes a firm can't transfer customer knowledge to new or related markets. However, companies can transfer the ability to learn about and manage customers. One of Tesco's strengths is its ability to enter new markets successfully. The firm uses a dual strategy that ensures it will optimize in the local environment. First, Tesco uses local managers to run stores, on the assumption that they have important local knowledge. Second, Tesco is very humble about what it knows and what it does not know. As it enters new markets, it studies customer behavior with a passion and openness that is very rare among successful firms. When Tesco entered the United States in the summer of 2007, UK staff lived with 60 local families to learn about their lifestyles, and ideas were pretested in stores with customers. This approach resulted in a store format unique to the U.S. market. This hybrid format, called Fresh & Easy, combines elements of Trader Joe's, Whole Foods, 7-Eleven, and even Tesco stores in Europe.[34] These stores also feature a larger number of prepared meals than those in Europe to reflect American preferences.

Valuable Customers

For Harrah's, Tesco, Nypro, American Express, and other similar firms, customer asset management produces economic profits. This status is not a given, however. Instead, these customer asset managers foster customer loyalty and capabilities in selecting, developing, protecting, and leveraging customers to maximize the long-term contributions of this asset to the firm's bottom line.

9

The Fourth Imperative:
Capitalize on the Brand as an Asset

In 1985, Becton Dickinson, the maker of the color-coded plastic tubes used to collect venous blood samples, was pressured by a large hospital buying group to replace the Vacutainer brand name on its product with the group's brand. Although the customer represented 10 percent of the entire market, Becton Dickinson was prepared, if necessary, to lose the customer in order to protect its brand name. It correctly viewed the brand name as a symbol of the company's quality and innovation. Without it, the firm's products would not be recognized, could not command a price premium, and would ultimately become undifferentiated. In the end, Becton Dickinson did not give in and remains a market leader.[1]

Customer value leaders have value propositions that beat the competition, get the attention of customers, and earn those customers' trust. Fidelity Investments is a trusted provider of lifetime investment solutions and Enterprise Rent-A-Car owns the value proposition "We pick you up." As customers learn to associate a brand with a meaningful benefit, the brand becomes a stake in the ground, claiming territorial rights over the value proposition.[2]

These rights create ripe conditions for companies to capitalize on their brands in powerful and profitable ways. Like customers, brands can become valuable economic assets to the firm. As we will show in this chapter, valuable brands influence both firm revenues and costs. Some of these effects occur through the behaviors of loyal customers observed in Imperative 3. Others occur through independent effects associated with noncustomers and even employees.

Brand and customer assets have much in common, as our discussion of metrics will make clear. Each has a reinforcing effect on the other—a strong brand promise attracts customers, while a series of positive consumption experiences strengthens the brand. In practice, valuable customers and valuable brands usually go hand in hand.

Unfortunately, the C-suite often fails to treat brands as valuable assets. What goes wrong? Managers have a tough time linking a strong brand to the income statement in the same way that they can point to lower costs and smaller inventories. Also, brands do not appear on the firm's balance sheet the way equipment or factories do.[3] As a result, the long-term value of brands is underestimated, and spending on brands is viewed as an expense rather than as an investment. Managers are therefore tempted to cut spending on brands in tough times or to underspend to bolster accounting profits.

A final reason that brands are not treated as assets is that brand value ultimately exists in customers' minds. Any action that a firm takes to manage a brand can build, reinforce, dilute, or damage what the customer thinks. Brand value can be damaged by myopic actions such as short-term price deals, lower-quality raw materials, outsourcing key customer service activities to low-quality providers, or extending the brand into a new category that makes no sense to the customer. Yet these effects are observable in the short term only by the few firms that remain in constant contact with their customers and use market-focused brand metrics. Brands such as Levi Strauss, Kmart, Major League Baseball, Lucent, Palm, and Chrysler have lost relevance by failing to treat their brands as assets, and only rarely have they recovered.

Companies that fully capitalize on their brands—*brand asset managers*—abide by three fundamentals. First and foremost, these companies have achieved the first imperative of customer value leadership. Second, they continue to build, protect, and leverage the brand to generate even greater profits. Third, they support these actions with a comprehensive dashboard of brand metrics.

Metrics for Diagnosing Brand Health

Strong brands have five important effects on customers and employees that can bring significant economic profits to the firm. Given this status, each can be used as a metric for assessing brand value and diagnosing problems.

Strong Brands Yield Customer Recognition and Recall

As customers gain experience through purchasing or learning about a given brand, they learn to *recognize* that brand. This means high scores in response to a list of brand names or logos and a question such as, "Which mobile phone brands on this list do you recognize?" Valuable brands can also be *recalled*, meaning that customers can produce the name without assistance when asked the question, "Which brands of mobile phones can you name?" The best position for a brand to occupy in the customer's mind is at the top—the first mentioned—since this may translate into a top position when customers are beginning a search or when they go to repeat a purchase that they found successful. Both brand recognition and recall can also make salespeople far more effective: they get to see key decision makers, their message has credibility, and they start in the customer's consideration set. A weak, unknown brand faces an uphill battle.[4]

Brands become associated with categories, such as "automobiles," or subcategories, such as "sports cars." As they become more dominant, brands emerge as the best representative or, as psychologists like to say, the "exemplar" of a category. Kleenex is the exemplar for the "tissue" category, TiVo for the "digital video recording" category, and Google for the "information search" category. Firms can assess which brands are exemplars of categories by asking customers to note what brand comes to mind in response to the category name. Knowing whether and how quickly your brand is retrieved is a good outside-in brand metric.

The network of linkages associated with a brand can also help firms understand how effectively they have communicated with customers. When strategy links a brand to a new feature, service, or benefit, ratings of those linkages provide immediate evidence that salespeople and advertising are doing their job communicating what is new about the brand.

Strong Brands Yield Improved Customer Attitudinal Loyalty

Customers often develop *attitudinal loyalty,* or *deep affection, trust, and commitment,* toward brands. This is the critical attitudinal loyalty discussed in Imperative 3. Brand attitudinal loyalty can be measured through direct questions about brand attachment or commitment or through simple experiments. For example, when Clorox was trying to determine the value of using only Green Works, only Clorox, or both brand names, showing customers sample packaging using the different brand names and asking about preferences indicated positive attitudes—even in the absence of product experience.[5]

This type of loyalty will also *buffer the brand against mistakes.* Small failures are more likely to be forgiven, and loyal customers will come to the defense of firms in the event of bigger problems. Loyal JetBlue customers filled up blogs telling the world to "Give JetBlue a chance" after a well-publicized incident in which customers were trapped in a plane for eight hours.[6] When McNeil Consumer Products (a subsidiary of Johnson & Johnson) faced the Tylenol product tamperings that killed seven of its customers in 1982, the company responded with an immediate recall along with packaging and product improvements to reduce the likelihood of future problems. These actions reinforced the "trusted" brand image that McNeil had built over the years and allowed the brand to rebound to its 35 percent market share from a low of 8 percent within one year of the incident.

Why focus on or measure brand knowledge or attitudinal loyalty if the real payoff comes when customers purchase or endorse the brand over and over again? These metrics offer managers two types of insights. First, brand knowledge and loyalty are two important "intermediate states" that customers experience as they move toward repeat purchases and endorsements. The ability to identify changes in these intermediate states can give firms early evidence of a customer's value or the risk of losing a customer so that additional investments can be made.

Second, remember that not all strategies have a direct effect on purchase! Firms can use these intermediate metrics to measure the effectiveness of marketing strategies that create brand awareness or seek to get the brand into the customer's consideration set. For example, the success of a pharmaceutical salesperson's visit may be measured by whether or not the doctor registers and searches on the company's Web site—not directly by prescriptions. If Web site search leads to prescriptions, the visit has been a success. The ability to measure such intermediate states builds confidence that investments in brand knowledge and attitudes are likely to yield additional customer responses.

Strong Brands Yield Ongoing Customer Purchases

We examined a set of purchase behaviors associated with loyal customers in Imperative 3. These behaviors are also associated with valuable brands. Given our coverage in Chapter 7, we'll briefly reintroduce these behaviors and point out any unique features associated with the way they are revealed in brand strategy.

All else being equal, customers are more *likely to purchase* strong brands. This is especially true when they are buying a product that is expensive and infrequently purchased, such as a car, or buying a product in a market in which it is difficult to make comparisons, such as medical services. For example, when visiting the computer monitor aisle, the venerated electronics brand Samsung stands out compared to lesser-known brands. The confidence that the brand brings to the purchase reassures customers who are unwilling to spend more time accumulating information. For the same reason, distributors and retailers are much more disposed to carry a brand that is well known, with built-in demand, than one that is new to the market. We saw this in lower defection rates among loyal customers, and it shows up here as brand-loving customers returning to strong brands over and over again.

Strong brands earn a greater *share of customers' wallets or total requirements.* This market share premium is due to the confidence that customers have in the brand and the relationship that customers have built with it.

A firm may choose not to extract *price premiums* if it is trying to build market share as a price value leader. However, for many strong brands, a firm can charge a higher price for the trust, confidence, or relationship that the customer has in the brand. The average premium is 10.8 percent.[7] Customers who love a brand or value its role in their families or businesses will also be less likely to pay attention to price changes and less likely to switch on the basis of a price change. *Price to switch* is a brand asset metric that uses this idea. It asks how low the price of a competing product has to drop before the customer will switch from the brand name.

When a member of the Cisco sales account team calls a customer, the call is returned quickly. Likewise, when P&G puts a coupon in the *Parade* section of the Sunday paper, it gets clipped and saved for the next shopping trip. And when Apple introduces a device with the newest technology and design, customers who are loyal to that brand are eager to try it. These *fast customer responses* are valuable to the company, not only because the company gets its revenues sooner, but also because less expense is required to generate the customer response.

Customers are more *open to new and complementary products and services* from strong brands. Brands act as a type of warranty that increases customer confidence and lowers customer risk. Knowing that it's a "George Clooney" film or a "Mary Higgins Clark" novel attracts many loyal customers and also lures in others who have heard of the brand and want to give it a try.

Strong Brands Yield Endorsement Behaviors

Strong brands are often endorsed by one person to another. Endorsement can come from three sources. First, regular customers (who purchase the product and who have firsthand experience) can make endorsements, as we saw in Imperative 3. Second, endorsements can come from experts who purchase, rate, and review the product as part of a professional service (e.g., *Consumer Reports*).

Third, endorsements can also come from noncustomers who share what they think and know about brands. This can happen via word of mouth at a dinner party, on Facebook, or through forums. People share both positive and negative information about stores that they have not visited, consultants that they have not hired, books that they have not read, and movies that they have not seen—although bad information often spreads faster. However, when these types of networks endorse, brand knowledge is built, brands enter consideration sets, brands are adopted more quickly, and price premiums may be possible.

The power of these social network effects is evident in the fact that many strong brands, including Starbucks, Chipotle, Zara, and McKinsey, do comparatively less or no media advertising. Chipotle's entry strategy of giving away free burritos on opening day to generate product exposure and buzz in a new market is a testament to what CEO Steve Ellis calls the word-of-mouth power of his "all-volunteer army" (see www.chipotlelovers.com). This type of brand buzz works, and it is also substantially cheaper than traditional advertising. For example, Chipotle spent $4.8 million over the first 11 months of 2006; that's what McDonald's, the company's former parent, spends on advertising in 48 hours![8]

Strong Brands Lead to Talent Attraction and Retention

Just as brands stand out to customers in the market, they also stand out in the labor market. Potential employees often learn about companies by interacting with them as customers or through endorsements in social networks. These reputation effects make employees more likely to join and to stay with companies. From its modest roots in Silicon Valley, Google has been listed among the top 10 firms on *Fortune*'s annual survey of "Best Companies to Work For" since 2007. It is also among the fastest-rising brands valued by Interbrand in *BusinessWeek*'s "Best Global Brands" during this same time period. We aren't surprised that these metrics are moving in the same direction for Google.[9] The Google brand is expressed in its values of innovating and "Don't Be Evil." Externally, this means respecting customers' privacy and needs. Internally, employees are encouraged to use up to 20 percent of their time to improve customer value and to work on new business ideas. The result? Both Google employees and customers are deeply loyal to and huge advocates for the company.

Mapping Brand Asset Metrics

The five ways in which brands create value for companies are summarized in the gray boxes of Figure 9-1. Looking at the figure, we see two key pathways of effects. Along Path 1—what we call the *purchase path* because the impacts are the result of customer purchase—brand knowledge is deepened and attitudinal loyalty increased. These effects, in turn, produce ongoing purchase behavior effects, such as share of wallet and openness to new products. Purchase behavior, in turn, can result in endorsements and talent effects. Endorsements can expose new customers, put brands into consideration sets, and even prompt trial.

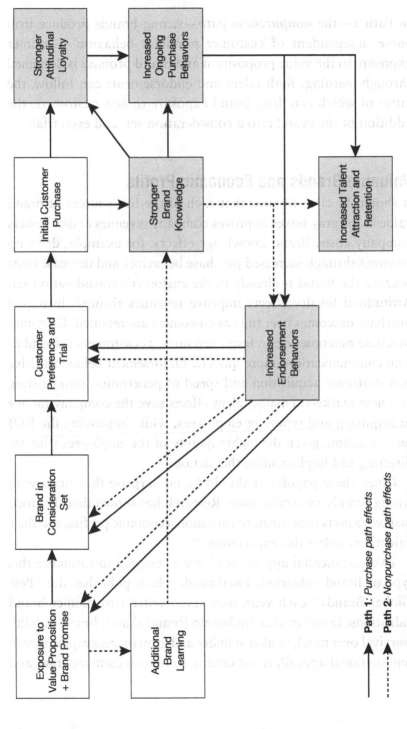

Path 1: *Purchase path effects*
Path 2: *Nonpurchase path effects*

FIGURE 9-1 How Brands Create Value for Companies

In Path 2—the *nonpurchase path*—strong brands produce firm value independent of customer purchase behavior. Customer exposure to the value proposition and brand promise is deepened through learning. Both talent and endorsements can follow, the latter of which can drive brand exposure to new customers, the addition of the brand into a consideration set, and even trial.

Valuable Brands and Economic Profits

It should be clear by now that each of the five sources of brand value in the gray boxes improves company revenues and/or lowers company costs. Brand knowledge effects, for example, drive up revenues through increased purchase behaviors and decrease costs because the brand is already in the customer's consideration set. Attitudinal loyalty effects improve revenues through increased purchase outcomes over time as customers are retained. Customer purchase outcomes mean faster revenues, as customers respond to firm communications more quickly. Endorsement behaviors drive new customer acquisition and speed of penetration into existing and new markets. Finally, talent effects save the company money in acquiring and retaining employees, while improving the ROI on any action, given the higher quality of the employees who are directing and implementing that action.

Given these payoffs, it should be no surprise that firms with strong brands are worth more. Research has shown that the stock market expects these firms to earn more economic profits, and their valuations reflect this expectation.[10]

Two commercial approaches have attempted to formalize this type of brand valuation. Interbrand, which publishes the "Best Global Brands" each year, uses seven criteria to predict brand valuations: brand market leadership (brand share), brand stability (survival over time), market stability and growth, geographic spread (international appeal), trend (ability to remain contemporary and relevant), brand support (level of consistent support), and brand protection (strength of legal protections). Experts rate each brand on these factors, and the ratings are combined using a statistical model to form a "multiple." This factor is multiplied by the operating profit from the most recent period to generate a future-oriented view of each firm's brand value. This approach does not focus on direct customer measures (except for share); instead, it measures firm outcomes (e.g., brand survival), firm behaviors (e.g., legal protections and brand support), or other environmental factors (e.g., market growth) that influence the "health" of the brand.

Another multiple approach, Young & Rubicam's Brand Asset Valuator (BAV), involves a large-scale survey in which consumers rate brands. Consumers rate the *differentiation* or distinctiveness of the brand and the *relevance* or importance of the brand. These measures are thought to reflect "brand vitality" and the future growth potential of a brand. Customers also rate brand *esteem*, or positive regard, and brand *knowledge*, or familiarity with and understanding of the brand, which are combined to form a "brand stature" indicator reflecting a brand's current strength. These dimensions, which are closer to the metrics we advise, have been linked to brand financial health over time.[11] However, BAV only provides the ratings; it does not attempt to predict future brand value.

Contrasting the two approaches, Interbrand's approach uses several customer criteria, but experts make the evaluations. It includes a more comprehensive set of measures that encompass management practices and support for the brand. These are useful because managers can take direct actions in response to getting their scores. BAV, on the other hand, uses direct customer surveys to evaluate brands. Hence the criteria are more limited, but the customer data may be a more valid indicator of brand value. Together, the metrics offer complementary approaches to firm-based brand valuation.

Brand Asset Management Capabilities

Having examined how brands create value for companies, we now consider how this imperative should be managed. Companies that act as brand asset managers focus on three interlocking activities that nurture brands and ensure the company reaps resulting profits:

- **Building the brand** to maximize the impact of the value proposition and strengthen the brand's reputation with coherent investments.
- **Protecting the brand** to anticipate and counter threats.
- **Leveraging the brand** to capture new opportunities and realize the brand's full economic value.

The remainder of Chapter 9 will focus on brand-building and brand-protection activities. Chapter 10 will focus on leveraging the brand.

Building a Strong Brand

Every activity that touches customers, whether or not it is controlled by the firm, is a potential brand builder (or underminer). Therefore, the company must create brand awareness, maintain brand relevance, and make decisions about how to manage all the brands in the company's portfolio.

Creating Brand Awareness

Brand awareness—especially top-of-mind recall—is a necessary condition for success. But many companies waste a lot of money here. Brand asset builders follow two key principles. First, investing in building brand awareness pays off when it ignites the five brand effects previously discussed, namely, improved customer knowledge, increased attitudinal loyalty, repeat purchase behavior, endorsements, and ease of recruiting. Brand asset builders eliminate brand-building activities that don't create these impacts.

Second, brand asset builders understand that strong brands do not need to be universally known and valued. Awareness is essential only among target customers and opinion-leading endorsers. For example, a smart electronics firm will take the inexpensive step of notifying Walter Mossberg about changes to its brand(s) because his column in the *Wall Street Journal* influences the firm's customers more than expensive advertising.

Maintaining Brand Relevance

Valued brands stay relevant. One way to do so is to evolve the brand so that it remains relevant to new customers entering the market. This strategy places a premium on the value of new customers, such as young people entering the market for a first car, or it acknowledges that the brand plays a temporary role in the customer's life. For instance, P&G knows that for Pampers to survive, it must appeal to newly entering customers, as its customers turn over every two to three years.

A second approach is to emphasize existing customers over time and focus on keeping the brand relevant to those customers as they change. This might mean extending the brand to include new services as the customer's business changes or to include new offerings that serve the customer's changing physical or emotional needs. This strategy makes sense when customer acquisition is difficult, when customers are few in number, or when competition is intense.

In reality, most firms have to do both—remain true to their original customers and attract new customers. Brand asset managers manage this paradox of brand dynamism and brand stability.[12]

Successful brands pull off this off by connecting deeply to the evolving social and cultural context and to the "myths" that this context creates. Mountain Dew, one of PepsiCo's carbonated beverages, is a brand that tapped into the larger context in an unorthodox way.[13] Early positioning for the brand focused on resistance to the trapped, urban, organizational, and bureaucratic men of the 1960s and 1970s. Mountain Dew was positioned as primitive, rural, and for the rugged individual. At first this market was southern, Appalachian, and "hillbilly"—which was not derogatory. Instead, it was true, real, and self-determined.

Over time, this theme of resistance morphed into opposition to Wall Street, Yuppies, and the white-collar idea of security. Mountain Dew ads showed young, freewheeling men living on a different frontier. However, as Wall Street lost its glamour in the late 1980s, Pepsi had to come up with a new target of resistance. It chose the idea that "manhood via work is a joke." This was successful because at that time, many young men were unable to find jobs for which they were qualified. Cynicism rose, and these youths stopped investing in their education and careers. These "slackers" understood that they had to find a different way to create excitement and to define themselves.

Later, Mountain Dew encouraged people to "Do the Dew" by showing young men engaged in extreme sports or other impressive physical feats. The physical achievement was not as important as the risk. Mountain Dew promoted itself at events like the X Games and released products like Mountain Dew Code Red that embodied this new, emerging slacker appeal. By staying true to the theme of "resistance" and morphing it to reflect relevant cultural changes, Mountain Dew continued to appeal to its original customers, while also connecting with new consumers who were experiencing their own variation of this theme. The strategy has led Mountain Dew to its status as an iconic brand, solid market share in a competitive category, and long-term survival. In 2009, the Mountain Dew brand was number three behind Coca-Cola and Pepsi in the regular (nondiet) carbonated soft drink market, with a share of 10.1 percent, up from 9 percent in 2005.[14]

As Mountain Dew demonstrates, building a brand is an iterative process in which companies apply what they have learned in the past to build a stronger brand that can survive into the future. Apple faced this scenario in the 1990s. The company had built its reputation on creativity and on breaking the mold set by the major industry players—namely IBM. Apple soared into the collective psyche of America through its iconic *1984* "Orwellian Big Brother" commercial, which featured a runner in vibrant colors smashing the big blue screen and freeing the human worker drones. Apple extended this core brand concept centered on individuality using a marketing campaign that encouraged people to "Think Different." Over time, however, Apple became a less differentiated brand whose value had diminished for all but the most zealous advocates. The reemergence of Apple in recent years has been driven by the introduction of products and services with superior capabilities and design, such as the iPod, iPhone, iTunes, and iPad. All of these offerings stayed true to the creative qualities attributed to Apple and have refreshed and reinforced the original computer brand, as recent sales attest. Apple's iPod held a 54 percent market share among MP3 players in 2008, providing 18 percent of Apple's revenue.[15] Interestingly, Microsoft, which lacks such attributions, has all but failed with Zune, its iPod/iTunes competitor (3 percent market share in 2008). The combination of poor capabilities, lack of design, and Microsoft's questionable hipness have made it a hard sell. As one critic put it, "The Zune is to iPod as Yugo is to a BMW."[16]

Designing Brand Architecture

When a company owns more than one brand, it must decide how to manage the brands relative to one another. The key architecture question that the firm must face is whether its offerings will be in a house of brands (with each offering having its own brand), under one name (a corporate brand), or a mixture of the two. The strategy of building strong individual brands with very little acknowledgment of the larger company behind the brands is followed by Diageo, the luxury spirits manufacturer, which owns the global brands Guinness, Smirnoff, Johnnie Walker, Baileys, J&B, Cuervo, Tanqueray, and Captain Morgan and an array of local brands. Each brand has a distinctive benefit, image, and target market. There is no clear advantage to be gained by linking these brands to Diageo or to one another when approaching the end consumer. Likewise, brands may not be linked to a corporate name because their images are at odds with one another. For example, Axe (a body spray for young men that plays to male stereotypes of women) and Dove (a brand that has taken a stand on a broader definition of beauty and self-esteem, especially among young girls) are managed without acknowledging their common corporate parent. This house of brands strategy is often amended when selling to retailers that benefit from a portfolio of brands from one firm.

Another option is to put all of the firm's brands under one umbrella or corporate brand. While the meanings of individual products tend to converge over time in competitive markets, corporate brands can often maintain distinctive associations.[17] For example, Prudential is "the rock," emphasizing stability; Anheuser Busch reflects American heritage and tradition; and American Express reflects the security of the Federal Reserve and the status of *Vanity Fair*.[18] Many customers are more comfortable placing their trust in corporate brands than in individual product brands.

Finally, sometimes a hybrid approach is needed. For instance, When Marijn Dekkers became the COO of Thermo Electron Corporation in 2000, he inherited a $2 billion company made up of 75 independent firms.[19] All of these firms were scientific-instrument companies, and many of them were targeting the same customer. This meant that although customers were familiar with the individual brands, such as Nicolet and Finnegan, they were not familiar with the parent company, Thermo. It also meant that Thermo companies had multiple personnel selling to and servicing Thermo products at a single customer. For example, 24 salespeople and 24 service people were dedicated to Bristol Myers Squibb. Dekkers, a former GE executive, saw an opportunity to leverage the larger strength of the company and, in his words, "Put all these capabilities together and go to the customer in a more synchronized way."

Dekkers allowed the individual brands to remain, but developed systems to link the brands to a "One Thermo" name over time. At trade shows, the firm placed its brands in one area, and later the firm supported large independent showrooms that featured Thermo products. Salespeople carried cards with the Thermo name (as well as the individual brand's firm name), and they participated in a "lead-sharing program" in which they would ask the customer about its broader needs and then share leads with salespeople for other Thermo brands. Corporate ads presented the larger capability to the customer, and the firm developed services to support all of its brands, creating a whole new business that was not possible with the 75 smaller companies. From 1999 to 2005, Thermo's net income recovered from a loss of $175 million to a profit of $200 million.[20] The strategy steadily improved Thermo's performance over a five-year period, culminating in a merger with Fisher Scientific in 2006 in a transaction valued at nearly $11 billion.

Protecting the Brand

Once built, brands must be defended from challengers and from dilution. This involves both keen strategic moves and effective use of legal tools.

Anticipating Brand Challengers

In 1981, Glaxo introduced Zantac to challenge Tagamet, the leading ulcer drug from SmithKline Beecham. Even though the FDA had given Zantac a C rating because it made "little or no" contribution to existing drug therapies, Glaxo took several bold steps that resulted in Zantac taking over Tagamet's position as the number one pharmaceutical product in the world. These steps included fast worldwide introduction, deep penetration into markets through a large number of sales partnerships, articles published in medical journals about the negative side effects of Tagamet and the potential for improved efficacy with Zantac, and a simplified dosage, reduced from four pills a day to two pills a day. Glaxo also took the bold move of pricing Zantac at a premium over Tagamet. The positioning of the brand focused on "fast, simple, and specific," which doctors interpreted to mean "faster, simpler, and safer." These strategies resulted in sales of $1 billion U.S. dollars by 1989 and a 42 percent global market share.[21]

Why did SmithKline lose so much so fast to a competitor with no real product advantage? It suffered from inside-out thinking. SmithKline believed that Tagamet was unbeatable—it was the "ultimate cure for a bellyache" and impossible to improve upon from a scientific point of view. Therefore, it did not defend itself against Glaxo's criticisms, it established no barriers to entry, and it failed to anticipate that Glaxo would price at a premium, which improved brand quality perceptions.

The key to protecting brands from competitive attacks is to take an outside-in view of the potential competitor's capabilities and intentions and ask how and where it might attack—and how customers are likely to respond. This takes deep market insights to figure out.

One preemptive move that brand asset managers can employ is to extend the brand to occupy positions that would-be challengers might occupy. For example, Tagamet could have been offered in a stronger dose to occupy the ground that Zantac took.

A second approach is to look for market segments that are being treated homogeneously, but that really have heterogeneous needs and could be an entry point for a competitor. Stonyfield Farm, the first mass-marketed organic yogurt in the United States, is an example of a brand filling an unmet need among consumers, who switched from traditional brands such as Dannon or entered the market given the presence of an organic alternative.

Finally, brand asset managers should immediately challenge brands entering the market that play by a completely different set of rules. Newman's Own salad dressings is an example of a novel brand that won loyalty because of the triple threat of great taste, celebrity (Paul Newman), and philanthropy (100 percent of profits are donated to good causes).[22] Whether this challenge takes the form of imitating the challenger's new features or persuading consumers that the changes are not beneficial should be decided using customer-focused criteria—not whether or not the firm has made investments that it may need to cannibalize.

Using Protective Legal and Strategic Moves

While the complexities of the law are worthy of a separate book, a strategist must understand the legal basics of protecting brand assets, and we would be remiss if we did not point out a few here. Managing patents is, of course, the basic form of brand protection. Beyond this, firms can also use other legal tools:

- **Trade secrets**, such as the formula behind Coca-Cola or the recipe for Kentucky Fried Chicken, can be legally protected, and violators of secrecy agreements can be prosecuted. In order to secure this kind of protection from the U.S. Patent and Trademark Office, the firm must make efforts to keep the "trade secret" a secret.
- **Copyrights, trademarks, and service marks** provide additional legal shields for brands by protecting works of authorship, words, names, symbols, or devices used as forms of expression or to distinguish a firm's products or service offerings. The intent of these protections is to reduce confusion in the marketplace by preventing imitation. Companies can be very proactive about these protections. As an example, Disney lobbied for and achieved extensions of copyright protection for Mickey Mouse and other characters by 20 years through passage of the Sonny Bono Act.[23]
- **Trade dress** (any nonfunctional characteristic associated with the appearance of a product or package) has recently become another important legal strategy. In May 2008, Adidas was

awarded $305 million from Collective Brands, Inc., for infringing on its three-stripe design.[24] In September 2008, Glacéau, the maker of Vitaminwater energy drinks, won a suit against Vogue, a hair-care company that used similar rainbow-colored bottles and stated that it included "superfruit ingredients" with beneficial antioxidants.[25]

- Vertical price restrictions can also be used to maintain brands. When Walmart worked out an agreement to carry Burt's Bees products, Burt's Bees management was able to dictate a price minimum to the discount retailer. Historically, suppliers have not been able to negotiate such terms with Walmart. However, the management of Burt's Bees leveraged the firm's brand equity and desirable products to find a way to require certain price points. This move protected other distributors from losing profits and the brand from dilution of its strong position.

- Partner selection can also protect brand equity. This was an issue for Burt's Bees when it went from gift shops and natural food markets to mass merchandisers such as Walmart and Target. Burt's Bees decided that it could maintain brand prestige through price controls in these "nonnatural goods" outlets. However, managers may choose to avoid certain channels and partners if they believe there is a chance that the brand will be negatively affected. Haute couture brands like Prada do not distribute luxury goods in these mass-market channels for obvious reasons.

- Exclusive deals, or contracts with partners to not carry competitors' products, are another approach. These exclusive deals can protect a brand by making it difficult for customers to compare alternatives. A firm with a great deal of market power may face legal challenges when it attempts to make exclusive deals. However, in general, such arrangements are legally acceptable.

Brand Asset Managers

Brands make major contributions to the value of the firm in the form of increased customer knowledge, increased customer attitudinal loyalty, ongoing purchase behaviors, endorsements, and improved talent. Yet most firms fail to fully capitalize on this asset. In this chapter, we have addressed how successful brand asset managers work to build and protect brands. Chapter 10 will cover how successful firms then leverage the brand for additional economic profit.

10

Capitalizing on the Brand as an Asset

A strong brand gives a business permission to enter new markets where its promise is meaningful and credible. This is how Under Armour, the dominant force in the high-performance sports apparel market (78 percent of the $416 million performance apparel category in 2006) was able to enter the athletic footwear market and compete against Nike and Adidas.[1] Like those of other firms, Under Armour's brand promise focused on athletic performance. However, it was viewed as authentic by athletes—the founder created moisture-wicking shirts to address his football teammates' needs.[2] Under Armour's shoes used the best available technology, but they didn't dramatically outperform the competition. What generated retail distribution, buzz, and trial was the strength of the Under Armour name.

Think of a brand as a latent growth asset that gives value to the business when it is fully deployed. The stronger the brand, the greater the potential to leverage it in order to enter or expand into adjacent markets or new geographies. This has to be done with care to protect the brand and to avoid diluting it by entering markets or geographies where the brand promise doesn't fit. Colgate is not going to offer a shampoo! The risks can be contained with creative, outside-in thinking. This chapter looks more deeply at the two major growth pathways, adjacencies and global markets, that are enabled by the brand asset and how the Web can be used to facilitate brand asset management.

Leveraging Brands to Enter Adjacent Markets

Remember the story from Chapter 6 of McDonald's abortive entry into pizza? Its brand promise was simply not relevant in this adjacent market, and customers told it so in no uncertain terms. Had McDonald's persisted, it would have diluted the meaning of its brand and confused its market. A better choice would have been to enter with a different brand (although this is costlier up front)— exactly what McDonald's did with Chipotle, which it later spun off. Another option is to acquire a competitor that is already in the market.

Managers must determine when it is wise to leverage existing brands for growth and when it is better to develop new brands. On the one hand, managers fear that they will dilute their brands by extending them too far. On the other hand, they are wary of leaving money on the table by not using a strong brand to facilitate the entry of a new offering. Given the revenue benefits and cost savings associated with strong brands, as well as the potential to destroy brand value, managers must weigh this decision carefully.

Leveraging Existing Brands across Categories

A 2007 *Wall Street Journal* headline captured the dilemma by asking, "Is Discount a Good Idea for Vera Wang?" Most people answered, "No"—that Wang's reputation as a high-end designer of $2,800 gowns should not be used in this way. Critics focused on the problem of brand dilution, arguing that Wang's high-end customers would interpret these forays as a loss of cachet for the brand, and that its high price tags might no longer be justified. And yet the designer introduced a line of dresses starting at $68 and handbags starting at $49 for the discount chain Kohl's under the brand name "Simply Vera Vera Wang." Does this strategy of leveraging the "Vera Wang" brand make sense?

The study of brand management has been dominated by the belief that new offerings should "fit" the image, benefits, and customer type associated with the original brand. Without such consistency, new offerings will dilute the value of the original brand. This finding is hard to argue with when the offerings are targeting the same customers with similar products that serve similar needs.

But what if the brand is leveraged for different products serving different needs? This is what Wang is doing with her line. In her view, "The Kohl's line is about being comfortable, edgy. . . . It could be for my teenage daughter, a young working professional woman, or a young mother. Even a middle-age mother . . . it's not about age. Kohl's is about ease, and comfort, and you can throw it on. It can be put together; you can make it part of your own wardrobe."[3]

Contrast this statement with the characteristics of Vera Wang's high-end line—gowns and accessories that are all about appearance and elegance. These gowns are never "thrown on" or easily integrated with the rest of a woman's wardrobe. Instead, these gowns are planned and worn on very special occasions, often with a unique set of accessories. This contrast might signal lack of "fit" to critics focused on brand dilution. However, for Wang and other designers who have adopted the strategy, this separation is a safety net against consumer confusion.

These considerations are relevant not just to luxury goods. We think there are important lessons that can be used by any firm with strong brands that it wants to leverage. The old-school dilution view of brands is being replaced by an emerging growth view that is much more outside-in in nature. In this view, managers must identify and communicate unique customer benefits to distinct customers and customer needs. If they do, firms can leverage valuable brands to expand the firm's presence into new categories by offering more products to a wider range of customers. The Simply Vera Vera Wang line focused on a distinct customer, filled a distinct customer need, and offered distinct customer benefits. Wang is betting that customers will not be confused.

This "high-low" strategy of featuring high-end designers in discount retailers at low prices has also been used in other stores. Take Target's partnership with Isaac Mizrahi, which featured $13 T-shirts and $29.99 dresses. This entry by one of the world's trendiest designers has grown to annual sales of $300 million. Here is an even bigger surprise—upon this entry into Target, sales for Mizrahi's haute couture line increased at other retailers, including high-end outfits at Bergdorf Goodman that cost $12,000 to $15,000.[4] Instead of diluting the brand, leveraging the brand increased exposure for the higher-end offerings. Because the offerings were clearly separated, customers were not confused, and the brands complemented each other instead of competing. If the line had been focused on department stores that sell midrange-priced products, there might have been more dilution.

Procter & Gamble offered a very different example of this growth view of branding when it entered the Chinese oral care market with two different versions of Crest. One brand, Ku Bai, is a premium brand that targets urban consumers who are interested in teeth whitening and breath freshening. The brand was promoted in ads and on Crest's Chinese Web site by featuring Li Yuchun, a popular singer voted "Super Girl" in an *American Idol*–type contest in 2007. This toothpaste sold for 95 cents for 5 ounces (19 cents per ounce). Ken Zhang, director of P&G's Crest Dental Research Institute in Beijing, explains that if you are one of Ku Bai's customers, "You're thinking you are more sophisticated. You're looking for toothpaste with science and with sophistication."

This brand is contrasted with Crest's offering for consumers who are interested in a more natural product. Cha Shuang, a green-tea toothpaste, retailed for 88 cents for 5.8 ounces (15 cents per ounce). Ken Zhang stresses that this product is for rural consumers. If you are one of these consumers, "You're looking for herbal, natural, green or Chinese herbs, some kind of regimen to help your oral health," and, "It's not only tea flavor. It's also a signal of the culture behind that. It's kitchen logic, it's grandmothers' stories. Chinese people think tea keeps your mouth fresh."[5]

A strict dilution view might insist that the urban product could not command a price premium when the same brand name is extended to a product targeting lower-status, traditional, rural consumers. However, the separation of these products is clear in consumers' minds, so P&G has been able to leverage the Crest brand across the two market segments. P&G has found this strategy useful even when the products are sold in the same online and retail stores.

Consider Clorox's entry into the natural home cleaning market to understand a different leveraging principle. Clorox is most strongly associated with the bleach category, where consumers ascribe to it strong efficacy and trust, as well as a heavy dose of chemicals. This perception was a strike against leveraging the Clorox name into a new natural line. However, Clorox had other insights about its target: mainstream customers. These consumers did not want to shop at separate stores for natural cleaning products, and there were few alternatives available to them within their normal stores. They were also skeptical of the cleaning ability of most natural products and did not want to work harder at housework in order to be environmentally sensitive. Clorox entered the category in January 2008 with a line of products called Green Works, which are used to clean kitchens and bathrooms. The cleaners are sold in supermarkets, drugstores, and mass merchandisers like Walmart and Target. On the front of the package, consumers can see the prominent display of both the "natural" label *and* the Clorox logo.

Does using the Clorox brand for this entry make sense? On the one hand, Clorox epitomizes harsh chemicals through its strong association with bleach. On the other hand, the Clorox name also reassures consumers that they will *not* have to sacrifice cleaning power when they cut out the chemicals. By including the Clorox logo on the Green Works packaging, the company leveraged its brand to target customers who want to be mindful of the environment, but do not want to sacrifice cleanliness or ease. The Sierra Club gave the product line a stamp of approval with a first-ever endorsement. Eleven months into the launch, Green Works sales were five times what Clorox had expected.[6]

Leveraging New Brands Intelligently

While Clorox successfully leveraged its brand to break into the natural cleaning market, the brand would not have provided the same permission to compete in the personal-care products category. A brand that reminds consumers of powerful bleach does not sell lip balm. So, when Clorox sought to extend its environmental sustainability strategy to include products that were not only "around me," but also "on me," the firm acquired an established brand that granted it immediate permission to operate in that category. Burt's Bees, which Clorox acquired in 2007 for $913 million, was the fastest-growing brand (30 percent per year) in the fastest-growing segment of the personal care industry: the natural personal-care industry. As a brand, Clorox had nothing to contribute to the all-natural, quirky Burt's Bees brand. It was likely to do more harm than good.

Firms that manage their brands as assets know that there are times when leveraging brands can yield a high return in a fresh space and times when it is better to acquire brands that already have a strong reputation in the category. The Burt's Bees brand was purchased and folded into Clorox's portfolio with little awareness of the change in ownership by the end consumer.

In other situations, companies acquire another firm and/or its brands, but then eliminate the existing brand immediately or over time. When Federal Express Corporation (FedEx) acquired Kinko's in February 2004 in order to reach a broader customer base, the stores were quickly renamed FedEx Kinko's to reflect the range of services that the customer could get in these centrally located stores. Over time, FedEx decided not to continue to use the Kinko's name, but instead moved the brand to FedEx Office to underscore the types of services available and to distinguish office services from shipping and freight services. During the transition, the Web site read, "FedEx Kinko's is now FedEx Office" and reminded customers that they could "Print, Assemble, and Ship" at these store locations. With this strategy, FedEx took customers through a learning process.

The most common strategy, however, is for firms to eliminate the purchased brand immediately and fold the acquired customers under the firm's existing brand.[7] When UPS purchased Mail Boxes Etc., it renamed the retail stores "The UPS Store." When DHL acquired Airborne Express in 2003, it introduced an array of DHL Express services.

What about branding choices following mergers? Depending on the connection to the customer, the correct answer may be to combine names, to adopt the stronger firm name of the two firms, or to create a completely new name. When the Frito Company and H. W. Lay & Company merged in 1961, they combined their popular brand names to become Frito-Lay, Inc. By combining well-recognized names, Frito-Lay was positioned to bring its customers together and maintain its market leadership position.[8] However, when Frito-Lay, Inc., merged with Pepsi-Cola, both maintained independent brand names in order to continue to capitalize on decades of consumer loyalty. The newly created company was named PepsiCo, Inc. However, to the end customer, the original brands stayed intact.

For the remaining cases, the stronger of the two brand names, which is often that of the firm initiating the merger, is used for the merged firm. When Dow Chemical merged with Union Carbide in 1999, Dow let Union Carbide's brand fall by the wayside because of its devastating associations with the chemical poisoning of thousands of people in Bhopal, India. However, in a small percentage of cases, the firm being acquired has a stronger reputation. When Allied Signal acquired Honeywell, management decided to abandon Allied Signal's brand. Similarly, Manulife Financial acquired and adopted the brand of John Hancock Financial, and First Union exchanged its brand for Wachovia's.

Leveraging Brands in Global Markets

In 1983, Ted Levitt, a *Harvard Business Review* editor and Harvard Business School professor, took a controversial stand: "The globalization of markets is at hand." He went on to forecast:

> *With [globalization], the multinational commercial world nears its*
> *end, and so does the multinational corporation. The multinational*
> *corporation and the global corporation are not the same thing. The*
> *multinational corporation operates in a number of countries, and*
> *adjusts its products and practices in each—at high relative cost. The*
> *global corporation operates with resolute constancy—at low rela-*
> *tive cost—as if the entire world (or major regions of it) were a*
> *single entity: it sells things in the same way everywhere.*[9]

Implicit in Levitt's vision was the eventual dominance of global brands. These are brands with consistent names, identities, positioning, and target markets across countries. Today, 27 years later, global brands can be found in nearly every industry. Not all companies have chosen to develop their brands on a global scale, however. Instead, there is a lot of variety.

Coca-Cola and Nike standardize their products and positioning in every country in which they operate. Procter & Gamble offers different brands that are unique to specific countries or regions, with only a handful of global brands. Other companies, such as Campbell's Soup, have well-known brands that are unique to specific markets. Campbell's belief is that eating habits are geography-specific and require local brands. At the other end of the spectrum is Godiva chocolate, a global food brand that perhaps is successful because chocolate is a fairly universal taste.

Brand strategies for global markets can be divided into three general groups. The firm can use the same brand and target similar customers with the same marketing strategy (i.e., distribution, communication, and pricing strategies) in all markets. This is a *global brand strategy*. Alternatively, the firm can use a new brand, target new customers, and deploy a different marketing strategy when entering new geographies. This is a *local brand strategy* involving strategy adaptation. Finally, the firm can use elements of global and local strategies, with a range of *hybrid brand strategies* depending on what can and cannot be leveraged across markets.

Extreme global or local strategies are increasingly seen as important outliers—exceptions to a general pattern of convergence toward a hybrid approach. We resist calling this a compromise position, for that implies vacillation and uncertainty. Think instead of an informed balancing of forces that favor some aspects of global branding with countervailing forces that favor other aspects of local identity and adaptation.

Forces Favoring Global Brands

- **Increasing homogenization of customer requirements.** This is the driving force that is singled out most often as the reason that markets are behaving globally. Homogenization is due to many forces, especially the ubiquity of media and entertainment. This homogenization is most evident in the preference for up-market consumer goods, such as Prada, Montblanc, and Burberry, among consumers who are better educated, have higher discretionary incomes, and enjoy wider global travel and communication with international social groups with comparable lifestyles. On the other end of the spectrum, products with purely functional benefits, such as diapers, also seem to travel easily across borders. This is probably because that most consumers experience the same need and easily understand the product benefits.
- **Globalizing competitors.** Many firms with diverse local brands and autonomous country operations have been forced toward greater standardization because of competitors' moves. One trigger is the realization that a globally coordinated competitor is using the financial resources from one part of the world to cross-subsidize a competitive battle in another.
- **Improving global marketing effectiveness.** When a brand promise works in most markets, it can achieve cost efficiencies and higher impact. A single campaign for IBM, even when

translated into different languages, costs much less than creating separate campaigns for each market. As firms learn to develop successful global campaigns, there will be increasing incentives and pressures to go with global brands.

Forces Favoring Local Brands

- **Inherent customer differences.** Critics of global brands charge that "most often the need for global brands is in the mind of the producer, not the mind of the consumer."[10] The argument is that consumers are not actually converging toward common tastes, needs, and values. Evidence for sustained differences across markets comes from the experience of KFC, which now has 5,000 U.S. restaurants and another 6,000 restaurants abroad in 80 countries. It has learned that it cannot open restaurants based on the U.S. model, and has become adept at understanding and satisfying local tastes. In Japan, for instance, KFC sells tempura crispy strips, but in the Netherlands, it features potato-and-onion croquettes. In France, pastries are sold alongside the chicken. In China, where KFC has more than 600 restaurants, the chicken gets progressively spicier farther inland to reflect local preferences.
- **Entrenched local brands.** Global firms eventually hit a ceiling on the size of the segment in any geography that is willing to buy global brands rather than local brands. This segment size varies considerably by country and product category, but it is usually well short of the total market. The ceiling depends on both consumer resistance to paying a price premium for global brands and the strength of the local brands.
- **Market practices and conditions.** Traditional ways of doing business can also inhibit the entry of global brands. If advertising is less important than word of mouth, for exam-

ple, a global attacker will find it difficult to change loyalty patterns or to gain distribution by outspending local brands. The existence of a fragmented market in which buyers prefer to work with local operators also makes entry expensive and challenging for global brands. Finally, if the market is both small and localized, companies will experience few economies of scale in marketing, manufacturing, or sourcing, so the cost advantage of global firms is narrowed.

Using Market Insights to Guide Global Branding Decisions

The choice between the global and local options is often tipped by cost considerations or by ethnocentric bravado about the inherent superiority of a particular product formulation or ad campaign. Among firms that manage brands as valuable assets, however, there is more humility. Instead of using internal criteria to drive the decision, these firms use an outside-in approach. They accurately reason that standardization reduces costs only if the product sells well. This is why Tesco spent six weeks living with American families when it entered the U.S. market in the summer of 2007. Deep insights into how families eat, cook, and store grocery products have allowed Tesco to enter 15 new markets worldwide. This customer focus is paying off not only in entry but in market success, as Tesco is one of the top five firms by market share in Hungary (#1), Thailand (#1), Ireland (#2), South Korea (#2), Malaysia (#2), Slovakia (#3), Poland (#4), and the Czech Republic (#4).[11]

We recommend that companies address 10 questions (see sidebar) in conjunction with deep immersion in the new market. The answers will give the firm a market profile that will be useful in driving decisions about the most effective level of global and local strategies.

Managing Brands in Global Markets

1. What are customers' needs for the product or service? In what situations and for what purposes is the product or service used?
2. How much knowledge or experience do customers have in this category or area of behavior?
3. Can customers pronounce the firm's brand name? Does it have any negative associations (e.g., Chevy Nova = Chevy No Go), and can customers be taught positive associations for the name? It's surprising how many firms overlook this simple question and end up in the annals of brand-name blunders.
4. How do customers perceive the benefits, costs, and risks associated with alternative ways of meeting a need?
5. How do customers acquire, use, and dispose of the product or service?
6. What are customers doing now to meet their needs for this product or service?
7. How strong are customers' loyalties to existing providers of alternative methods of meeting this need?
8. What are competing firms' and potential entrant firms' current strategies, strengths, and weaknesses?
9. Can the firm reach customers with information about and distribution of the product or service?
10. What is the nature and importance of channel partners in reaching customers?

We have found it useful to ask companies to compare the answers to these questions for the new market geography with the answers for its current markets. This yields insight into how the new market relates to one or more of the firm's existing markets. Because many firms are in different markets, it can also be useful to compare answers across these markets, as the firm may be able to leverage different aspects of branding strategies from different market profiles.

Managing "Central Control–Local Touch" in Global Markets
Companies need an outside-in view to find the best balance of global reach and local presence—for both existing and new brands. This does not mean that they should ignore internal factors, but that the internal factors should be judged in light of how they serve current or future customers. Here are several principles for gaining the benefits of central control and local touch.[12]

Adapt in Areas That Are Important to Local Customers
This point is at the heart of an outside-in view. While it still uses a common brand around the world, Walmart allows local stores to adapt their product assortments to better match the markets that they are serving. So while the positioning remains the same—a hypermarket with national brands and low prices—the inventory within the different stores may vary.

Identify "Clusters of Similarity" to Drive Down Costs[13]
American Eagle Outfitters stores in western Florida share preferences and price elasticities with those in communities in California and Texas. Female customers in the United States respond the same way to Unilever's "campaign for real beauty" as customers in the UK, Germany, and the Netherlands. This idea of seeking "clusters of similarity" was first applied by Bain in supermarkets in the mid-1990s as a way to ensure sensitivity to local markets without giving up all the scale advantages that are regained by the "clusters." Programs such as Walmart's "Retail Link" program allow suppliers and buyers to direct the most effective mix of products to groups of stores that share important characteristics. The result is lower inventories and higher revenues as more targeted products are purchased faster by more customers.

Allow Adaptation on Nonproduct Marketing Decisions

One problem that can arise in truly global branding strategies is that local managers become disenfranchised because local market insights are dismissed in favor of central control. Allowing local managers to adapt nonproduct marketing decisions is one solution. Pricing and distribution decisions can also benefit from local insights. One common approach is to allow local managers to adjust promotional activities within a set of guidelines set by the firm. This ensures both consistency and productive adaptation. For example, Smirnoff, a leading brand of vodka, allowed local managers to develop their own ads around a theme of "Pure Thrill." Lilly's global launch of Cialis, an erectile dysfunction drug, ensured consistency around a set of principles involving the use of couples (not just men) and color choices for lettering and backgrounds. Both of these strategies offered the company a chance to benefit from local variation in the look and interaction of the couple and the ad scene chosen, while maintaining important consistency across markets.

Access Global Managers' Knowledge[14]

Companies must also create a culture that maximizes what can be learned from local and corporate offices. Success comes when managers openly share best practices and insights throughout the entire company. Firms with global brand strategies often use knowledge management systems to facilitate regular communication around the world. For example, P&G picked up the highly successful Pantene slogan, "Hair so healthy it shines," from a Taiwanese subsidiary. The ads, showing women with long, shiny hair that flows off their shoulders as it is lifted by their hands, helped turn Pantene into one of P&G's early global megabrands, topping $1 billion in sales. Other times, the company may benefit from global brand councils, teams with representatives from around the world, competitions among regions or countries for brand ideas, or letting a country that has been successful with a certain brand take the leadership role in a global effort.

Balance Market Access with Attention to Ensuring Quality and Building Trust
Glaxo completed the worldwide introduction of Zantac in a record time of three years by partnering with independent sales forces all over the world.[15] The strategy worked in part because the product was tightly controlled and regulated, but also because Glaxo was able to capitalize on existing relationships between salespeople and doctors.

When the product is actually created in the partnership, stricter controls may be necessary to ensure quality. Starbucks had to develop training, operations, and product standards to ensure that contract vendors, such as Host Marriott, were offering the same high-quality cup of coffee at the airport stores they operated for Starbucks as would be offered at a Starbucks-operated store.

www.Branding.com

Brand building, defense, and leverage have been dramatically altered by the advent of Internet-enabled search marketing, mobile marketing, and social media. The territory of social media has expanded to include social networking, video and photo sharing, and online communities and forums. Financial investments in these strategies are expected to take off over the next five years.[16] The CMO Survey reports that current marketing budget spending on social media averaged 6 percent in February 2010, and that this is expected to grow to 10 percent by February 2011 and to a total of 18 percent by 2015! Importantly, this increase is occurring across all sectors—not just in B2C firms.

The biggest implication of the Internet is that customer relationships in all markets are becoming increasingly interactive. Connected customers are empowered customers, able to shape the brand with their opinions, ratings, and feedback. This challenges the management of the brand asset in three ways.[17] First, any pretense of tight control over the brand message (which is still possible with traditional media) gives way when the customer shares ownership of the brand. Second, one-way communication gives way to two-way engagement and participation. H&R Block uses Facebook, MySpace, Twitter, and YouTube to make tax preparation accessible and to engage its customers at times other than tax preparation season. Finally, global brand builders can aim precisely at markets that they could never find before with smarter paid search routines that accelerate entry. These transitions are being driven by customers' comfort with social media and by firms' increasing use of the Web to reach and interact with customers.

Managing Your Brand on the Internet

Using the Internet to manage brands has both perils and exciting possibilities for firms that manage their brands as assets. We offer several guiding principles that firms should consider in order to maximize the upside of such activities and minimize the downside risks.

Listen and Learn, Learn, Learn

There is a lot of talk on the Internet. Some of it is valuable to company strategy, and some is not. However, companies must listen well in order to uncover opportunities to act on and shape the dialogue about their brands.

Establish a Community

The need to learn drives many firms to establish communities or forums. Few companies merely watch these forums anymore. Instead, most participate by (1) creating categories of information, such as "the ABCs of touring" or "pins and patches" on the Harley Owner's Group site, (2) encouraging employees to blog or tweet on topics on which they are experts, (3) running small experiments to test different ideas, and (4) asking customers for solutions, ideas, or their involvement in product development and marketing activities.

Don't Sweat the Negative Opinions If Your Product Is Good
On the Web, everyone has an opinion, but not every opinion matters. We discussed the Pampers Village "Golden Sleep" campaign earlier in the book. Despite its breaking a record in the *Guinness Book of World Records*, there were still naysayers. From one blog: "So what is Golden Sleep exactly? It isn't anything—it's meaningless, a bit of brandspeak made up to make buying Pampers products seem more important, and there's a bit of a hint in the campaign that your kids will grow up better if you shell out for some Golden Sleep for them." This comment was countered on other sites, such as this one by a breast-feeding mom blogger: "Sleep is worth its weight in gold—my positive experience with Pampers: I think Pampers are doing a fantastic job of raising awareness of how detrimental lack of sleep can be to parents."

Take Unified and Swift Actions in Response to Negative Evidence
While some opinions can be ignored, hard evidence about the quality of the company's products or services or any part of its operations or strategy must be taken seriously. Consider the YouTube postings of Domino's Pizza employees littering pizzas with phlegm and mucus.[18] While the offending employees claimed that these were a "hoax," Domino's took swift action to deal with the more than two million views of the offensive video. Patrick Doyle, president of Domino's USA, appeared in his own YouTube video, in blogs, and in traditional media apologizing (this is key) and describing the specific steps that the company was taking to rectify the situation. This included firing and prosecuting the employees; sanitizing the Conover, North Carolina, franchise; reviewing hiring practices to ensure high-quality employees; and using auditors to perform surprise sanitation checks. Mr. Doyle also did something else that was useful: he reminded YouTube viewers that Domino's customers came to the company's rescue with information about the pranks, and that the other 125,000 Domino's employees running small businesses wanted and deserved customers' continued loyalty.

Monitor

The Domino's incident makes it clear that companies must keep their fingers on the Web's pulse. Although we recommend that the firm go further and look for deep market insights that can be used to manage the brand and the other imperatives, monitoring is a minimum defensive strategy that all firms must employ.

Truth and Transparency

Company statements about the brand on the Web, like all communications, must be truthful. If they are not, deceptive advertising charges can be brought. It is equally important that the firm be transparent about what it is doing on the Web. This includes identifying employees as employees and not allowing them to pose as customers. As of December 1, 2009, the Federal Trade Commission requires customers and commentators writing about a company or its products to disclose whether they have received free products or payments from the company. We predict that this rule will help, not hurt, firms as consumers get renewed confidence in Web communications.

Identify Connectors in Your Market

Tremor, a P&G social networking site launched in 2001, enlists teens to pitch brands to their friends. Tremor now has an army of 250,000 "connector" teens. Vocalpoint, a social network involving moms, performs the same function for P&G, with 450,000 "connector" moms participating. Chapter 7 references several tools for identifying opinion leaders and mavens.

In the B2B realm, firms are jockeying for status as thought leader "connectors." Take IBM's Institute for Business Value, which states on its Web site that it is "comprised of more than 50 consultants who conduct research and analysis across multiple industries and functional disciplines. The Institute has a worldwide presence, drawing on consultants in eleven countries to identify issues of global interest and to develop practical recommendations with local relevance."

The consultants develop new knowledge in key areas such as customer relationship management, business analytics, human capital management, and supply-chain management. This knowledge is published in white papers on the Web and in regular blogs by consultants. Such efforts drive business into IBM consulting operations and help traditional IBM consultants deliver more value to customers.

Engagement
The Web is a terrific venue for involving customers with the brand in ongoing ways. Walmart's Facebook page has 858,373 fans as of April 2010! Many friends are also employees, reinforcing the brand's role in attracting and retaining customers and employees described earlier. Charlene Li and Josh Bernoff's *Groundswell* coverage of Jim Cahill (www.emersonprocessxperts.com), the Emerson blogger who tells war stories "from the front lines of process automation," is also very instructive. As Jim found, blogging is not just a way to blow smoke. His effort generates important sales leads for the company week after week.

Finally, when Chanel determined that its powerhouse No. 5 brand was "aging," it used the Web to take steps to reengage the customer. The campaign used a younger celebrity model, French actress Audrey Tautou, and a series of teaser ads pointing to "the journey begins on 05/05," which was the day of the launch. E-mail invitations were also sent out to consumers describing a short "film" shown on a redesigned Web site on launch day.

Reaping Brand Dividends

Because brands are a critically valuable asset to companies, they deserve to be managed as a strategic imperative, with sustained top team attention to three issues: *building* the brand by adopting a long-run investment perspective, *protecting* the brand against competitive attacks and loss of relevance in the market, and then optimizing the value of the asset by *leveraging* it prudently.

Careful use of metrics will allow the company to assess whether brands are paying off in profits.

The customer comes to know the brand by interacting with the entire company—the innovation and design of R&D, the speed and service of the supply chain, the quality of manufacturing, and the financial requirements established by accounting and finance. This means all members of the C-suite are critical to this imperative. The CMO or his counterpart can earn the right to coordinate management of the brand asset across these activities to ensure large dividends for the firm.

Part Three

Living Outside In:
Bringing It All Together

11

Market Insights and the Customer Value Imperatives

In the last ten chapters, we've delved deeply into how outside-in companies create customer value and capture superior profits. However, the four customer value imperatives work only when they are built on a solid foundation. That foundation is where we turn our attention in the next three chapters. In this chapter, we'll examine the critical role of deep market insights. In Chapter 12, we'll discuss organizational culture, structure, and capabilities. Finally, in Chapter 13 we'll look at leadership—specifically, how CMOs can earn the trust and provide the leadership necessary for executing the four customer value imperatives.

Deep market insights are the fuel of the outside-in approach to strategy and the catalyst for the four imperatives. Many firms, though, fail to appreciate the value of market insights. Because insights are foundational and often "obvious" once someone has done the hard work to unearth them, their strategic role can be overlooked. However, without market insights, neither outside-in thinking nor the customer value imperatives can deliver superior customer value or profits.

The Dutch company Eneco Energie was able to break away from competing on price in the natural gas industry by gaining better insight into what its largest and most important customers really needed. These customers, operators of the Netherlands' famous flower-producing greenhouses, needed more than just energy—they wanted a way to track and control the temperature in each greenhouse. Eneco was able to provide such a system in addition to providing natural gas. This broader insight into its customers' deeper needs allowed Eneco to move from acting as the provider of fuel to offering a full set of services to its customers. The payoff has been increased loyalty and the ability to charge premium prices.[1]

Despite the compelling benefits from using market insights to inform and shape strategy, most firms are ineffective at consistently gathering market intelligence, making sense of it, and then acting on it. It is useful to look at some of the main problems that afflict the market insights capability in order to see how to create an effective capability.

First, inside-out companies often lack a disciplined market insights capability because it is not a priority for them, or because they are confident that they know their market well enough that they no longer need to learn from their customers. Technology companies are especially prone to agree with an opinion that Ted Levitt originally attributed to engineers: "Consumers are unpredictable, varied, fickle, stupid, short-sighted, stubborn and generally bothersome."[2] This is surely an overstatement, but it underscores the reality that markets are complex and that sustained hard work is needed to comprehend them.

The second impediment is that key market insights activities are either outsourced or pushed into a support function. This virtually guarantees a lack of influence and squanders the potential of engaging the entire organization in listening and responding to customers. Outside-in companies mobilize every employee as a "listening post" whose insights are valued.

Third, inside-out companies keep what customer information they do gather in silos. As a result, it is impossible to "connect the dots" and arrive at a 360-degree view of the customer experience. Instead, the portrait of the customer is splintered into tactical-level fragmentary pictures.

Outside-in companies, on the other hand, invest in and profit from market insights. They understand that developing a strategy without deep market insights is like shooting at a target without aiming. Outside-in companies invest in a disciplined market insights capability, and learn to ask and answer insightful questions about customers, competitors, channel partners, and market forces.

Asking Insightful Questions

Powerful insights tend to come from addressing one or more guiding questions—who, what, where, when, how, and why. These questions are useful because the answers can be translated into the customer value strategy and value innovation. As we'll show, these questions are useful for analyzing both customers and competitors—two key targets of a firm's market insights.

Customer Insight Questions

Here are a few of the questions that customer insight might address: *who* may be a good customer (i.e., what segments to target); *what* customers think, feel, prefer, or do; *where* and *when* customers use products and services; *how* customers engage in these internal activities (e.g., draw inferences about quality) or external actions (e.g., how customers search on the Internet); and *why* customers have these needs. For Campbell's entry into the Russian market (see sidebar), the insight that the soup must have "soul" underscores *why* soup was so important and that chunks of meat, fat medallions, and aroma are *what* the customer uses as signals of that soulful status.

Customer Insights: Understanding the Soul of Soup

Customer insight is not customer data or information, although it can be derived from both. Customer insight builds on data and information to generate a novel understanding of the customer. Take the experience of Bob Woodard, director of customer insights for Campbell's Soup, who was asked to help the company enter the Russian soup market in 2007. What he discovered was that soup played a deep and complex role in the hearts and stomachs of Russian men.[3] Campbell's researchers found that it was very common for a pot of meat bones to be boiling on the kitchen stove in a typical Russian home. Russian wives would spend several days nurturing the rich broth and recovering large chunks of meat and savory fats. This process puts the *dousha*[4] (soul) into the soup. Given this context, bringing ready-made soup into this market was not going to be easy. Campbell's duly noted that competitors had tried to enter with Western European bagged and premixed soups. Russian women scoffed, and Russian men considered the use of such products sacrilegious. These ready-to-serve soups "had no soul."[5]

As the purveyors of this *dousha*, however, Russian women were in a bind. Since they worked full-time, they could not tend to the soup that had such importance in the Russian household. This was the customer's problem and Campbell's opportunity. Through a process of ethnographic work involving deep interactions with Russian families, Campbell's developed a product that could offer Russian women a way to solve the problem of preparing homemade soup with packaged ingredients. The *Domashnaya Klassika* ("Home Classics") line of soups contains chunks of real meat and visible fat medallions, both of which build consumer confidence that the soup has been prepared with care. Brand images reinforced the message to both women and men. All ads feature either the *domovoi*, an elflike "protector" spirit that "lives" in the kitchen cabinets of all Russian homes, or the family gathered around the table. These customer insights paid off, and Campbell's expects the line of soups to be profitable in Russia by 2013.[6] Larry McWilliams, president of Campbell's International, noted, "Customer reaction to the initiative has been strong, and several of our Russian customers are actively extending [the] distribution ... ahead of our expansion plans, based on their very positive experience in the Moscow lead market."[7]

Campbell's insight work went well beyond information. Instead, it delivered the key ideas that drove all of the firm's subsequent strategies. First, it uncovered an unmet need for "soup with soul" among Russian families that were too busy to stay at the stove for several days. Second, it exposed what product features Russian consumers were using to judge that "soulful status" (e.g., visible fat medallions and chunks of meat). Third, it revealed what consumer behaviors could not be sacrificed. In this case, the soup pot needed to be on the stove for more than a few hours. This meant that Campbell's could play a role as a soup starter, not as a soup substitute. Fourth, key symbols such as the *domovoi* and the family gathered around the table were established for use in packaging, in ads, and on the Web site.

The power of simply understanding *what* customers are thinking, feeling, or doing is also evident in a novel approach taken by John Sculley when he was vice president of marketing for PepsiCo back in the 1970s (before going on to serve as president of Apple, Inc.). Sculley, facing the challenge of catching Coca-Cola, kicked off a study in which 350 families came to a PepsiCo warehouse and took as many soft drinks and packages of snack foods as they wanted. During the week, families would record in diaries what and when they ate. At the end of the week, they would turn in their diaries and pick up more food. Sculley's staff analyzed the data and uncovered one very interesting observation: families ate everything they took! This *what* observation led to the insight that if PepsiCo could get more soda and snacks into the customers' homes, they would be consumed. The two-liter bottle was born.[8]

Another example comes from Cisco. Back in the 1990s, Cisco uncovered that its customers wanted faster and simpler access to technical support information, including tips and documentation. This *how* insight led the company to put technical problems and solutions on its Web site. CEO John Chambers later noted, "That became standard practice in our industry many years later, but back in the early 1990s it was risky and radical. By the late 1990s, well over 85% of our customer troubleshooting was handled directly on the web."[9]

Figure 11-1 describes an approach to generating useful insights. For example, companies may generate insight into internal customer drivers, such as who is loyal, what are they loyal to, how they became loyal, and why they remain loyal. Likewise, external customer behaviors, such as who searches, what they search for, how they search, and why they search, will help companies facilitate customer information acquisition about their products and services.

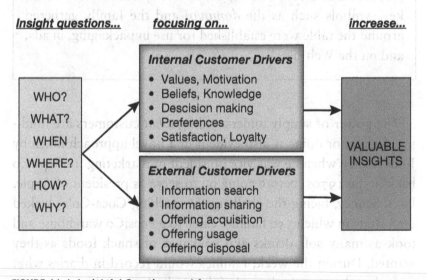

FIGURE 11-1 Insightful Questions and Answers

Competitor Insight Questions

Most firms routinely do teardown analyses of their competitors' products and monitor news sources and company documents for unusual competitive activity. Often the outcome of these efforts is an undigested mass of news clippings and some comparisons of the price and performance of their own products with those of competitors' products. Meanwhile, the most important information may never come to the attention of those who can act on it. Thus, the first step in improving competitor analysis is to direct employee attention to key questions about competitors that are likely to produce valuable insights. This is especially important for employees who serve in boundary-spanning functions that have a great deal of contact with customers and partners that interact with competitors. We recommend these questions, which mirror those that we asked for customer insight.

- **Who are the firm's competitors?** Most firms don't know who their real competitors are. Industry classifications used by economists can tell managers which firms sell similar products or services, such as telecommunications equipment. Publicly available data can also tell managers which firms are similar in terms of size, revenues, profits, or geographic or industry scope. However, these data rarely address the question of competition. Market insights can identify competitors by providing an assessment of which current and future firms inside and outside the industry can offer the same benefits to customers.

  The range of these offerings is broadening, and firms are increasingly being threatened by competitors from distant product and geographic markets who are targeting their customers. The COO of a local credit union in Durham, North Carolina, recently commented that his biggest threat was not from traditional banks, but from Walmart entering retail banking. In the 1970s, U.S. Steel's greatest threats and ultimate death came at the hands of Japanese and Korean steel companies—not the competitors in Europe and the United States that the company was focused on. Marketers must widen their vision to ensure that these competitors are not missed.

- **What are competitors' value propositions?** This may be the easiest aspect of competitive insights. Most firms reveal who their customers are and the nature of their offerings when they launch into markets. Reviewing products, promotional materials, Web sites, and packaging and talking to salespeople will often yield remarkable insights into what the competitors' value propositions are.

- **How do competitors create and capture value?** This deeper question about a firm's business model is harder to answer. Competitors sometimes reveal *how* knowledge by announcing partnerships or opening a new channel. However, other capabilities, such as how advertising is developed, prices are set, and segmentation is determined, are more difficult for firms to understand. Benchmarking takes competitor analysis somewhat further by comparing the firm's costs and performance against that of its best rivals at every step in its value chain. This reveals advantages in capabilities and processes that can be used to increase a competitive lead or provide a warning that improvements are needed. Firms like Xerox often use the outcomes of these benchmarking studies to shake up complacent manufacturing and service groups with the news that they are slipping behind.

- **Why are competitors taking actions?** This deeper motivational question is likely to be associated with the firm's history, current leaders, board composition, or financial pressures. For example, under Jack Welch, GE made public statements about the rationale for choices in the firm's product portfolio—brands (or lines of business) had to be larger than $1 billion in sales, or they would be dropped. Public statements to shareholders and press releases can often convey the firm's strategic rationale, but they may be shrouded in secrecy or intentionally vague.

- What are the moves of our competitors? How will competitors respond to our moves? It is not enough to answer these questions with a focus on what competitors are doing now. Companies must anticipate both competitors' next moves and their countermoves. This is a high-level game of chess played under conditions of considerable uncertainty. A "Red Team" exercise is an effective way to gain a point of view on likely competitive moves (this term is adapted from war gaming, where the opposing force in a simulated military conflict is the red team).[10] In these exercises, teams of managers role-play a specific competitor and make key strategic choices for the firms they represent, using whatever information on the competitor they have on hand.

The key to anticipating how a competitor will react is to think like its management team, given its resources and market positions.[11] Thus, McDonald's and Burger King had different responses to the negative publicity about obesity and fast foods. As the dominant and most visible player, McDonald's couldn't ignore these concerns and introduced a variety of healthier options. Burger King, on the other hand, saw a chance to cherry-pick customers in the less health-conscious market segment and introduced high-fat, high-calorie sandwiches supported by in-your-face ads parodying healthy choices. Burger King also knew that there was no way that McDonald's could respond to this attack.[12]

A Market Insight Capability

Firms shouldn't count on insights emerging organically. Instead, insights must be actively sought, shared, and acted on with a disciplined market insight capability. This capability is realized through a process of market sensing, sense making and sharing, acting, and evaluation. This is a learning process, in which continuous exercise builds new layers of insight.[13]

Key Steps in the Capability

Market Sensing

The process is often triggered by an impending decision or strategy review, an emerging problem, or a belief that an innovation initiative requires deep insights into customer needs. This spark begins the active search and acquisition phase to acquire relevant and actionable information—including what is already stored in a firm's knowledge system and what managers throughout the company know. When this is done well, the company has the information it needs to anticipate where its markets are going and get there before its competitors. This "skate to where the puck is going" mentality gives a robust market insight the ability to shape the customer value strategy.

Sense Making and Sharing

If findings are to be useful, they must be distilled to find coherent patterns and converted into usable insights. Many errors are made during this sense-making stage, as managers misinterpret what they see in favor of what they *want* to see. Worse, they may dismiss results that don't confirm their expectations.

Insights need to be shared with relevant decision makers and stored in the firm's knowledge management system. In both cases, transfer makes the information available for use, alone or in combination with other stored knowledge.

Insights may be lost or rejected when they challenge the prevailing wisdom. When one detergent maker decided to look for growth in the market of noncommitted users, it formed a diverse team to study these users (mostly women). The aim was to understand the pressures of their lives, their needs and wants, and their relationship with their clothes. From these deep observations, the team came up with a new way to appeal to these customers' feminine sensibility. This ran counter to the senior managers' beliefs about how the brand should be positioned. To overcome these beliefs, the team dramatized its findings in a one-hour "play" with scripts derived from the verbatim recordings of the consumer immersion sessions.

Taking Action

This stage in the market insights process can happen close to the time when the insight was created, or much later if the firm has to dip into its knowledge stores to act on newly emerging opportunities. The longer the lag, the harder the firm needs to work to ensure the retrieval and application of old knowledge to new problems. This can be very fruitful for firms with a vast number of patents, for example. Considering an existing patent in the light of emerging science, policies, or customer preferences can often generate new products. For example, Cognis, the large chemical manufacturer, developed a plant-based fabric softener (most softeners are based on animal fats), but it did not work well in water and hence could not be used effectively in washing machines. However, while working with a developer of moist dryer sheets, Cognis saw the opportunity to apply its existing technology. In partnership with Arm & Hammer, the ultimate product was introduced as a breakthrough entry into the category in 2009. Branded under the name Total 2-in-1 Dryer Cloths, it combines a liquid fabric softener and an antistatic agent in one dryer sheet.

Application also happens when market insights change managers' thinking. The occurs when managers get new ideas to add to their mental models of customers or competitors. LG Chem expanded its mental models in the window category by gaining insights into a segment of customers that saw windows as a form of art for their homes. The result was the development of a new product that combined the functionality of a window with the aesthetic of a piece of art. Likewise, Flor, a flooring company, offers customers the opportunity to create a piece of art under their feet by mixing and matching fun and colorful combinations of carpet squares that are sold individually, not as a roll. In both cases, managers had to move from a narrow mental model of what these customers wanted to a new understanding that they valued the artistic qualities of their products.

Feedback and Learning

Once actions are taken, additional learning comes from feedback about what actually happened. Did the market respond as expected, and if not, why not? Were judgments confirmed or repudiated? Undertaking a postmortem of the strategic action and market insights is important. Improvements to any aspect of the market insights process can be captured. Likewise, focusing on the strategy, firms should store reflections about what happened, why it happened, and how the firm might have improved its performance in accessible knowledge bases. Was the strategy good, but the implementation poor? Was the insight good, but the strategy poor? Answers are useful in refining the market insights capability and improving its contribution to the customer value imperatives.

Improving the Capability

Maintain Direct Contact with Your Customer

Companies make two common mistakes in designing market insights capabilities. First, they outsource insights work to agencies or to a small staff group within the company. Second, they rely solely on secondhand information about customers and competitors, such as purchased reports from vendors or quantitative reports such as monthly customer satisfaction reports. The problem with these approaches is that managers do not have direct contact with customers and treat them as abstractions.

Companies can use several strategies to solve this problem. Many companies refuse to outsource their sales function because it is a key opportunity to interact directly with customers.

Others use the Web to go directly to customers. P&G has recently opened up its own online store to learn directly from customers. As reported in the press, "P&G officials don't expect the eStore to boost the manufacturer's revenue or profit very much very soon. They're more interested in the data it will produce about their shoppers and what works for them—whether it's product pairings, social media links, environmentally friendly pitches, packaging options, and even the web standby of banner ads."[14] Other companies use online forums and newsgroups to spend time with customers, as we have discussed several times in the book.

Companies such as Hewlett-Packard have successfully used customer visit programs to gain direct customer insights. In these programs, managers can visit customers either individually or as members of a cross-functional team. There are important benefits to team visits. When both marketing and R&D hear the same thing at the same time, the information may be more likely to be dissected for insight and acted upon in subsequent strategy. This is an effective way to overcome the conflicts, implicit assumptions, and poor communications that too often afflict the marketing/R&D/manufacturing interface.

Another way to get a deep understanding of the market is to "be your customer." Netflix gives its employees a subscription, Smith & Hawken asks employees to work in company gardens with the tools it sells, and P&G employees live on a low-income consumer's budget—all in the interests of understanding how and what their customers are thinking, feeling, and doing. This emphasis on customer empathy is beginning to gain ground, and even retailers are sending executives into the field with gloves and dark glasses to understand the challenges that elderly customers encounter when shopping in their stores.[15]

Keep an Open Mind
Managers inevitably suffer from systematic blind spots. It's a result of the way our brains work—we use what are known as heuristics, or mental shortcuts, to process information. While this enables us to function while we are inundated in information, it also means that we get locked into certain ways of seeing the world. In managerial terms, this often means getting stuck focusing only on current customers and current competitors, especially those competitors that are most similar or geographically proximate. Another form of myopia is defining the business in terms of features and not benefits. When this happens, managers miss competitors coming from

other product categories that meet the same need. Finally, most managers have weak peripheral vision, which means that they miss signals associated with change that is on the horizon, but has not yet happened.[16]

Open-minded and bias-free collection and processing of information is often difficult to find in companies. Market information is often collected to answer a specific question. The results are interpreted only in reference to that question, and because of this, other opportunities buried in the information may be overlooked. Worse, managers may "reinterpret" results or dismiss results that do not confirm their expectations. Psychologists call this *confirmation bias*. Again, our human tendency is to interpret information in a way that confirms rather than challenges our existing beliefs.

In other words, our brains can conspire against attempts to find breakthrough insights. This highlights the necessity of having a disciplined market insight and analysis process. We simply cannot trust our brains to do it by themselves. Market insight processes must have checks to ensure that new insights are excavated from old questions or that managers hold to a reasonable set of standards for data manipulation and interpretation.

Triangulate with Multiple Methods
Firms tend to use a single method for understanding the market. It is far better to use multiple methods with different biases and limitations. For example, price elasticities may shed light on who the firm's competitors in the current category are, but they are unlikely to produce insights into unmet customer needs. There is a tendency among managers to get absorbed with quantitative tools, such as conjoint analysis (which can help in understanding what is driving preferences) or surveys. These tools are essential, but usually they are helpful only once the company has deeper insights, which require direct contact with customers *and* a big dose of creativity. For instance, Robert Drane, vice president of innovation for Kraft Foods/Oscar Mayer Division, was traveling in Japan in the 1980s

when he noticed people eating out of bento boxes. He had the insight that Oscar Mayer products could be sold to U.S. consumers in similar convenient packages—an insight that could never have come from quantitative analysis or customer surveys. The company's successful Lunchables line was created in 1988.

We think IDEO's qualitative techniques for gaining a deep understanding of the customer are among the best we have seen. Whether the advice is "spend a day in the life of your customer" or "be a fly on the wall," these techniques are relatively easy and cheap for all kinds of firms to use.[17]

Take the case of Kimberly-Clark, which uncovered a profitable niche in the diaper market by observing an unsatisfied customer motivation. Charged with taking market share from P&G's Pampers brand in the 1980s, Kimberly-Clark's Huggies managers, armed with notebooks and tape recorders, headed into homes where there were babies and toddlers. Listening deeply, they discovered that parents judged the success of a child's development and their job as parents by the child's ability to progress from diapers through toilet training to underpants. Parents worried about helping their child navigate this process. They didn't want to push the child to the next stage, but they clearly wanted to make it happen "on time," if at all possible. Huggies had no solution in its product portfolio. However, based on this insight, Kimberly-Clark developed a line of products called Pull-Ups that had all the protection of a diaper, but were pulled on and off like a pair of underpants. Pull-Ups gave parents confidence that the child was progressing and were a sign of that progress to the outside world.[18]

Experiment Continuously
True learning organizations are serious about continuous experimentation. This process of active, ongoing experimentation to address persistent issues is where original insights into the market are developed. Walmart's intelligence-action cycle encourages quick experimentation, and whatever doesn't work is never in place for

more than a week. Using a different learning strategy, Frito-Lay made a four-year commitment to an in-market test of TV advertising for its main brands. It learned, for example, to always advertise when there is brand "news" and that ad spending on big brands in the absence of such "news" is unlikely to drive sales volume increases.[19]

Field experiments are done in the market with some parts of the firm trying something new (the "treatment" group) and comparing outcomes to similar units that retained old strategies (the "control" group). Many firms don't like to use field experiments, in part because they take time, but also because field studies reveal the firm's strategies to competitors ahead of rollout. Managers also have to choose which units or geographies receive the "treatment" and which don't, a process that can be politically charged and lead to disgruntled employees. Yet field studies are often the best way to learn what does and does not work.

Create a Common Picture of the Customer

The best insights won't come from a single study or a single data point, and so managers need to look across studies or databases. This means that knowledge management systems must be engineered to allow such cross-referencing. For example, by integrating customer data to capture all the products and services that the customer purchases, a firm can understand the true value of that customer, and also determine how best to approach and reward the customer.

For example, when customers show up at a Harrah's casino or phone into Capital One, these firms are able to provide better customer service because they understand the customer's current behavior in light of her history with the company. No one piece of the customer's history tells the whole story. These systems can also enable firms to track the value of a customer, to understand what motivates customers, and to form and test predictions, which are fundamental analytic aspects of a firm's sense-making skills.[20]

Share Customer Insights and Best Practices

The most effective insight systems are active hubs of give-and-take. Knowledge must be available to everyone who interacts with customers, and everyone must be encouraged to add what he thinks. Therefore, the costs of accessing the system, in terms of time or money, must be low. This ensures that the firm is leveraging all that it knows to compete on customer value and that effective strategies are being scaled out across the organization.

Knowledge sharing and knowledge transfer can be undermined in several ways. Sometimes managers don't want to share what they have learned because they are using it to outperform other managers who are involved in similar tasks. In other cases, there is no time to record what managers learn. In still other cases, the manager does not fully appreciate what has been learned because the insights are tacit or because the manager lacks experience. By the same token, other managers who are in need of information don't look in shared archives because they don't want to give credence to an internal competitor's ideas, because they don't make the time to search for solutions, or because they are overconfident.

In global organizations, transfer can be impeded by power differences between the home country and its subsidiaries. When local managers unearth an important insight that they believe may have applicability to other units, there needs to be a mechanism and an incentive for sharing it. There are many stories of insights that came from outside the home country and were effective when adopted globally, including the Coca-Cola Company (the black Coke Zero package from Australia), McDonald's ("I'm loving it!" from Germany), and Unilever (Dove facial cleanser from Japan).[21]

Market Insight Metrics

Firms that excel in the generation and use of market insights put a dashboard of simple metrics in place to gauge how well the organization is carrying out various aspects of the capability. Three types of metrics can be used: input, process, and outcome metrics. The Web and computer networks make these metrics increasingly easy to collect and share.

- **Insight input metrics** include the quantity and quality of customer and competitor reports the firm has available, the number of reports downloaded, the number of posts to shared knowledge management repositories, and inquires from operating units to market and competitor intelligence units internal and external to the firm.
- **Insight process measures** include any aspect of the sense-making and learning process beyond inputs and outcomes. This might involve asking users to comment on the quality of reports or to comment on ideas that others share. Likewise, users may be rated on the quality and quantity of the market insights they contribute. A company's insight users must trust the providers of those insights, and so a measure of trust in these providers is also a useful process metric.[22]
- **Insight outcome metrics** should include measures of the impact of insights on how the managers think about key market-related issues, such as who the firm's competitors are or the nature of customer needs. One way to do this is to collect data on what managers think before and after insights are provided.[23] The best insights also affect the decisions made and the effectiveness and speed of strategy actions, including those related to the customer value imperatives. Postmortems can be used to capture the role of insights or evaluations of insights at key steps in the process. Postmortems may also require managers to report the number of hours or days of insight work during the project. Likewise, postmortems could cite market research reports that were instrumental in strategy development and execution. Frequency of these citations is one measure of impact.

Driving Attention to the Outside

Without market insight and a sustainable insight capability, management of the customer value imperatives will yield limited returns. Market insight drives managers' attention toward what matters and helps ensure that customer and competitor insights play a role throughout the strategy-making and implementation process. This investment pays off in profits from current strategies and new growth activities, as well as in valuable brand and customer assets. These payoffs are sustainable because competitors cannot easily understand or imitate market insight capabilities.

12

Organizing to Compete on the Customer Value Imperatives

Executing on the four customer value imperatives requires considerable management acumen. Customer value leadership, value innovation, and the effective management of customer and brand assets can result in optimal profitability, but it takes companies years of planning and execution to be successful. Some companies get it right for a while, but then lose their way.

There are many factors that separate the firms that are able to build and execute a strategy from the outside in based on the customer value imperatives. Two general and pervasive factors that we address here at the end of the book—the organization and its leaders—underlie many specific differences that show up in the press, in case studies, in our classrooms, and in our work with organizations of all sizes.

No organization can continue to make decisions from the outside in without the strong guidance of outside-in-minded leaders. Leaders communicate a compelling vision, provide resources to support an outside-in strategy, and are willing to override silos. They send innumerable signals that encourage outside-in thinking, such as an insistence on comparing the business against the "best of breed" and, during strategy reviews, an emphasis on deep consideration of customers' needs rather than the details of financial forecasts. The leader is critical, and her role in guiding the four imperatives gets its due attention in Chapter 13.

In this chapter, we address the organizational attributes required to allow companies to get full economic value from the four customer value imperatives. From a base of strong leadership, the customer value imperatives can thrive only when three fundamental organizational factors are in place: an outside-in *culture, alignment* with the market, and *capabilities* for competing on customer value.

First, there are no outside-in organizations in which the *culture* isn't immediately recognizable as being outside in. These companies are held together by pervasive, externally oriented activities that emphasize providing superior value on the customer's own terms. At Tesco, the mission is "creating value for customers, to earn their lifetime loyalty." This statement both reflects and continually points Tesco back to a focus on the customer.

Second, there must be an *alignment of the organization* with the market. Alignment involves structure, metrics, and incentives. The aim is to ensure that customers have a seamless interaction with all parts of the business and that there is clear accountability for the customer. This was a challenge to General Electric's Aircraft Engine Business Group when it found, to its surprise, that its jet engine customers were not happy with the service component of the offering. The company's inside-out (Six Sigma quality) metrics had shown the opposite! In response, the group undertook an in-depth study to find out what customers really wanted in terms of responsiveness, reliability, and help in improving their productivity. The project led to wholesale organizational changes. A corporate vice president was assigned to each of the top 50 customers to build the relationship and to ensure that each customer had a clear channel to the top of the organization. The last step was to incorporate customer service metrics into employee evaluations and to create employee rewards for superior service.

The third requirement for outside-in organizations is *capabilities for competing on customer value*. These capabilities are the organizational processes that allow the firm to implement the four imperatives on a continual basis. We'll see that these companies have systematized procedures—in other words, real skill—for performing the steps we have outlined for each imperative. Given that we've noted the danger of the capabilities-based view in terms of encouraging inside-out thinking and behavior, there is a valuable distinction between cultivating customer-focused capabilities and driving strategy based on existing capabilities. No firm can consistently drive superior customer value without investing in and managing the capabilities to do so. On the other hand, if the capabilities themselves become the focus, rather than being viewed simply as useful tools for accomplishing the goal of customer value, then the firm is in danger.

These organizational factors can form the foundation for managing by the customer value imperatives. As such, they point to and enable the strategy that we have recommended. Likewise, these organizational elements can also be built by the day-to-day strategic and operational focus of managing by the customer value imperatives. When this happens, the organization mirrors what is in the minds and plans of its leaders and employees as they enact an outside-in strategy.

From Market-Oriented to Outside-In

These two concepts of organizations, both focused on making decisions from the market back, are fundamentally joined at the hip. They have the same genesis and motivation, arrive at similar organizational prescriptions, and are endorsed by the same extensive body of research on the performance rewards.[1]

The genesis of both concepts comes from Peter Drucker, who insisted, "There is only one valid definition of business purpose: to create a customer. . . . [Marketing] is the whole business seen from the point of view of its final result, that is, from the customer's point of view. Concern and responsibility for marketing must therefore permeate all areas of the enterprise."[2]

Today, 56 years later, market orientation has evolved to mean identifying and satisfying customer needs better than the competition. This orientation is implemented through a *market-driven organization*, which has a "superior ability to understand, attract and keep valuable customers."[3] This definition also incorporates Drucker's dictum that the purpose of a business is to attract and satisfy customers at a profit. But satisfaction is not sufficient because customer acquisition is costly. Real profitability comes from keeping valuable customers by building deep loyalty.

The *outside-in organization* is a natural evolution and broadening of a market orientation. There are three notable differences.

1. First, everything that these organizations do is about achieving and sustaining superior customer value. In market-oriented thinking, this connection is often not made. Instead, there is a jump from the organization's attributes and processes to performance, without the enabling mechanism of customer value.

2. Second, winning outside-in strategies take account of both income statement and balance sheet effects through the economic profit model. Advocates of market orientation often limit themselves to beneficial consequences for revenue and earnings, without regard to the productive use of assets or the capitalization of the brand and customer assets.

3. Finally, a truly outside-in strategy is forward-looking and is paranoid about the possibility that hard-won customer value advantages will erode and disappear under competitive pressure. The antidote is a long-term emphasis on innovation that creates new value that customers will pay for.

Outside-In Organizational Cultures

Culture is expressed in generally accepted beliefs and norms that guide the organization's day-to-day activities and show "how things are done around here." Culture is not dictated formally by leaders. Rather, it is felt at all levels of the company and is reflected in what employees believe about the company and their roles within it, and how they behave when they are doing their jobs. We have observed three sets of company beliefs that allow the customer value imperatives to provide the basis for how the firm competes.

Beliefs about the Market

How the organization and its employees view the market is essential to building an outside-in culture. The importance of defining the business and making decisions from the customer's point of view as well as having direct contact with customers and worrying deeply about how competitors are serving customers are at the heart of these beliefs.

The Customer-Defined Business

When A. G. Lafley, the former CEO of Procter & Gamble from 2000–2009, said, "The customer is boss,"[4] employees knew that the customer was the firm's key priority. They realized that without customer value, there is no company value. And because there has to be a customer before firm value can be captured, it follows that the firm's top priority is the delivery of customer value.

Similarly, when Amazon's CEO Jeff Bezos said, "We're a consumer company, not a book company," employees understood their mission. It is not about products, technologies, services, or Web sites. These are all key parts of the firm's strategy, but the customer remains the focus.

The Mayo Clinic's mission to "empower people to manage their health" and eBay's mission to "help people trade practically anything on earth" are vivid illustrations of defining the business from the outside in. Ted Levitt's insight that "The organization must learn to think of itself not as producing goods or services but as buying customers, as doing the things that will make people want to do business with it"[5] is exactly the point.

Customer-Based Decision Criteria
Customer benefits define the business and should permeate the way firms create and improve customer value over time. With customer benefits as the criterion against which decisions are made, there is less chance that important market signals will be missed, even by aggressive outside-in companies. One such company, Johnson & Johnson (J&J), fell prey to overlooking customer benefits when it pioneered the stent, a device inserted to support failed arteries or veins of the heart. After creating the market in 1994, within two years the firm had a 91 percent market share. Three years later, it had only an 8 percent share! What happened? The initial product was offered in only one size and could not be seen in an X-ray machine. Both of these issues were problematic for heart surgeons. J&J was so busy meeting the strong demand for the stents that it lost its outside-in focus and was too slow responding with improved versions that satisfied doctors' concerns.[6] Competitors who were more receptive to customers' needs stepped in.

Direct Contact with Customers
A defining feature of these cultures is the insistence that everyone spend time with actual customers. Bill George, the ex-CEO of Medtronic, a medical device maker, required all engineers and designers to attend at least one surgical procedure a year to get face-to-face customer feedback from surgeons while they were using Medtronic's products.[7] This mindset made it difficult for the company to stray too far from what customers valued. Direct contact deepens relationships with customers and helps everyone identify potential innovations.

Paranoia about Competitors
Effective outside-in firms also watch competitors closely, calibrate their own performance against the best in class, and celebrate wins against competitors. They take the customer's point of view to understand why they are winning or losing within each segment. By studying their rivals, outside-in companies are able to anticipate and influence those rivals' actions. They send signals to discourage competitors from attacking their core markets. They monitor innovation activity so that they can anticipate new offerings and quickly work to neutralize the competitor's advantage.

Paranoia about competitors does not mean that the company loses sight of its core customer value proposition, however. Many firms make the mistake of gathering competitor intelligence and responding to every move by a competitor without considering what makes that competitor's products and services special from the customer's point of view. Paranoia about competitors is therefore not an invitation to blindly copy competing moves. Rather, it is a way to stay aware of long-term market changes and innovations and to develop a plan for delivering superior customer value into the future.

Beliefs about Managing the Market
In addition to all the advice we have given throughout the book about managing the market, two key beliefs are often housed in the cultures of successful outside-in companies.

Everyone Is Responsible
The firm will not be successful unless all of its functions and employees perceive the connection between their work and customer value. For example, at the American Girl book and doll division of Mattel, buyers and inspectors are asked to focus on the joyful reaction of each young customer opening a gift, rather than on inside-out criteria such as acceptable defect rate per thousand. As David Packard pointed out, "Marketing is too important to be

left to the marketing department." His statement is not a condemnation of marketing, but rather a reminder to all employees about the connection between their work and what the customer experiences.

Expense versus Investment Mindset
In many firms, a short-term, expense-oriented approach is used to evaluate decisions such as whether to create a special sales force to open up a new market segment, launch a new brand-building campaign, or change the pricing model. The fallacy of a short-term, expense-oriented mindset is that it leads to a "pay as you go" requirement that confuses cause and effect. Budgets for the sales force or advertising are set according to what the company can afford given next year's sales forecast. In an investment mindset, budgets are set against the criteria of whether heavier expenditures will spur future sales and profits. This mindset also tends to bring a longer-term view to evaluate outcomes. Successful outside-in firms tend to manage the imperatives as long-run investment strategies.

Beliefs about Talent
The culture guides and enables employees as they work to make an outside-in view a company reality. Two key beliefs help ensure the connection between employees and customers.

Satisfied Employees Lead to Satisfied Customers
Research shows that employee satisfaction and customer satisfaction are closely linked.[8] If employees are unhappy with the way the firm treats them, it is nearly impossible to get them to focus on serving customers. Managers must compete on talent if they are to have a chance at competing on customer value. A central part of Marriott Hotels' value proposition is consistency of operations, so that customers are not surprised. Marriott achieves this largely through its oft-stated goal to "treat its people right."[9] As founder Bill Marriott

says, "If the employees are well taken care of, they'll take care of the customer, and the customer will come back. . . . That's basically the core value of the company."[10]

Empowered Employees

Problems arise when employees are not empowered to take responsibility for ensuring that the customer is successful or for helping the customer solve problems. "I just work here" and "That's another department's problem" are common phrases heard in firms with an inside-out culture. A culture that tolerates passing the buck on customer problems will not get very far trying to live by the customer value imperatives.

Some of these problems can be dealt with by selecting employees who have a proactive and problem-solving style. In truth, however, even the most motivated employees cannot make a difference within companies whose policies preclude them from doing anything but giving such responses. Therefore, it is important that company policies make the correct employee behaviors clear and easy to implement. The company must also ensure that employees know that they are part of a larger system that serves the customer and that they are responsible for detecting and solving customer problems. At Ritz-Carlton, for example, the manager on duty has a $2,000 expense account each day dedicated to resolving customer issues. This money might be spent to offer a gift, such as a bottle of wine, a free meal, or an upgraded room, to customers who have experienced problems.

Outside-In Organizational Structures

Structures That Align the Organization to the Market

There has been a steady evolution toward organizational designs in which there is clear accountability for customers, not just products or profits.[11] The aim is to overcome the inside-out myopia of functional or product-dominant designs. These old and familiar structures often fail to know who the customer is, comprehend the customer's total experience, assess the competitive situation, and solve cross-functional problems. The customer falls through the cracks. No one is looking at the company through the customer's eyes and asking how processes can be improved to reduce customer frustrations or what new customer requirements can be satisfied with an augmented offering. Likewise, without clear accountability, no one may be responsible for tracking customer profitability or changes in the customer defection rate.

A key factor in determining the right structure for a particular company is the customer value leadership position. If, for example, the emphasis is on relational value and the best customers see great value in buying integrated solutions from one source, the firm may find it optimal to create a structure with dedicated account teams. Conversely, price value strategies can be served with simpler key account structures. We discuss a range of approaches firms can use to get good alignment with the market.

Key Account Managers

This is often the first step that organizations take to overcome the deficiencies of product or functional silos.[12] Key account managers coordinate the firm's cross-functional activities with a customer. This makes interactions more effective and efficient for the customer and, if managed well, more profitable for the firm.

Front-Back Hybrid Designs

IBM adopted this approach with its "Client-Centric Model." It involves, first, a strong customer-focused "front end" that markets products and solutions to particular market segments. This requires seamless integration of different groups to present a unified front end. Behind this is a back end that builds products and provides services. IBM's original business units for personal computers, servers, software, and technical service were the "back-end" suppliers to the solution sellers who helped customers assemble complete computing systems.

Cummins India is another case in point. It created three front-end subsidiaries, each of which focused on providing customers with a particular solution. The subsidiaries were "product agnostic," which helped them serve customers better. For example, customers whose businesses required uninterrupted power were better served with diesel engines—products that had to be procured outside the company!

Cross-Functional Segment or Account Teams
Rohm and Haas (R&H), the specialty chemical giant purchased by Dow Chemical, used this approach and integrated a variety of functions, including new product development, technical support, supply chain, marketing activities, and communication channels, into customer account teams. A senior manager was assigned to each team as well. In conjunction with this move, R&H segmented its customers into one of three tiers. The bottom tier was turned over to R&H's national distributors so that the new customer account teams could focus on customers in the top tiers. The product line was optimized to focus on the products that were most important to the firm's most important customers. The customer-focused team and product line helped Rohm and Haas capitalize on customers by building deeper relationships that were then leveraged for growth.

Customer Managers and a Customer Department
The most dramatic and yet to be fully realized change may be the creation of a "customer department."[13] In this new customer department, customer and segment managers identify customers' product needs. Under the customer managers' direction, brand or product managers then supply the products that fulfill customers' needs. This requires shifting resources—principally people and budgets—and authority from product managers to customer managers. This structure is common in the B2B world. Unilever, for instance, has key account managers for major retailers like Walmart. They are given incentives to maximize the value of the total relationship over the long term rather than to sell any particular product. Some B2C

companies use this structure as well; foremost among them are retail financial institutions that put managers in charge of segments (wealthy customers, college kids, retirees, and so forth) rather than products.

In a company that is organized this way, a consumer-goods segment manager might offer customers incentives to switch from less profitable Brand A to more profitable Brand B. This wouldn't happen in the conventional system, where brand and product managers call the shots. Brand A's manager isn't going to encourage customers to switch, even if that would benefit the company, because he's rewarded for brand performance, not for improving customer lifetime value or some other long-term customer metric. This is no small change: it means that product managers must stop focusing on maximizing their products' or brands' profits and instead be responsible for helping customer and segment managers maximize theirs.

A more extreme approach eliminates the product management structure completely. This works well when the firm does not have its own branded products, only customers. Nypro, the plastics molder, puts product experts on teams with others that serve the customer. Best Buy, the mega-electronics retailer, has taken this path with a customer-centric initiative that started by segmenting customers into lifestyle groups and gave them human faces, such as Buzz (young technology buff), Jill (soccer mom), and Barry (wealthy male professional). The company then linked these segments to specific product and consumption needs, making it possible for store staff members to tailor product presentations to the specific client, not focus on any one product line or brand. Staff members were supplied with questions to help them identify which type of customer they were interacting with. If a salesperson identified a customer who was interested in digital cameras as Jill, the salesperson would focus more on benefits that are important to the family, such as ease of use, long battery life, easy to print, and so on, rather than technical details such as resolution and megapixels. Best Buy also selects merchandise for individual stores that reflects the lifestyles of customers in the area. Since this structure was introduced, Best Buy has seen a 3.6 percent increase in store sales compared to stores and salespeople operating under the old regime.[14]

Tightening the Marketing-Sales Alignment

The benefits of structural changes that infuse outside-in thinking into every corner of the organization can be magnified further by supporting efforts that break down silo barriers. A key place to begin is with the sales-marketing interface. Both groups should be working together to bring the market realities into the rest of the organization. More often, their influence is diluted because they behave like feuding family members, with scant respect for each other and conflicting views of customer needs and requirements.

Workable ways to align sales and marketing include dedicated team liaisons; mechanisms for sharing problems and information, such as common customer databases; and the alignment of incentives to recognize collective behavior.[15] For example, marketing could be rewarded for the number of qualified leads that are converted into new customers. At the same time, sales incentives could be shifted from revenue to the profitability of the account.

Managing Implementation Pitfalls in an Outside-In Structure

Managers who are attempting to reorganize their function- or product-dominant organizations around customers must understand the potential risks. We offer three lessons to help ease the transition.[16]

Lesson 1: Keep Everyone Focused on the Customer's Total Experience

Function- and product-dominant structures are notably weak at comprehending the total customer experience and solving cross-functional problems. No one looks at the company through the customer's eyes and asks how processes can be improved, how products can be integrated across units, or what other requirements might be met with an augmented offering. Without clear accountability, no one is responsible for tracking customer defections or trying to win customers back.

Improving accountability requires a combination of system changes, customer-focused metrics, and employee incentives tied to customer-segment performance. To implement these changes, companies must have unified customer information that can be filtered through linked customer activity and cost databases. Companies with fragmented information systems have great difficulty coordinating their offerings. Consolidating information at the point of customer contact makes it easier to separate the front-end customer solution from the back-end product infrastructure.

Lesson 2: Adjust the Pace of the Alignment Process to Address the Obstacles

Restructuring invariably takes longer than expected. Many people have unrealistic expectations about how quickly plans can be carried out. At Fidelity Investments, for example, managers estimate that it took the firm at least three years to accomplish 60 percent of its reorganization goals. The main constraint was the time it took to make information system changes and upgrades.

A company's culture can either make it easier for the organization to realign around markets or make it harder. Nokia Corporation, for example, benefited from a flexible culture that encouraged information networking and task forces composed of people from different business units. That made it easier for the employees to accept the idea of separate businesses serving distinct markets with bundled products.

Even though one of the strongest arguments in favor of realignment is that it helps managers differentiate product and service levels based on customer value, long-standing customers who are costly to serve usually resent being relegated to a lower status, and they often work hard to circumvent the rules. Companies need to design strategies for dealing with these issues to avoid jeopardizing the whole program.

Lesson 3: Use Continuous Realignment to Stay Ahead of Market Changes

Markets are always changing, so organizations inevitably slip out of alignment. Companies that are seeking to stay aligned with the market need to respond to both customer opportunities and competitive cost considerations. For example, when Philips Semiconductors Company established global account teams to handle its bigger customers, it encountered a number of problems. Some of these problems were a consequence of managing teams across multiple time zones; others were related to the cultural complexities of having employees report to managers located in another country. Management also found that some customers didn't really want a closely linked, collaborative relationship that functioned like a joint venture. In response, Philips evolved to a more hybrid organization, with global teams involved with only the biggest customers. The rest it served on a more regional basis.

In tough economic times, competitor cost pressures may also prompt a shift to a mixed structure. During most of the 1990s, Square D Company, part of Schneider Electric SA and maker of industrial control and distribution systems, was organized around its main markets to serve global customers that sought integrated solutions. This customer-focused structure worked well for many years, but it ran into difficulty when the economy slowed and customers started to move production overseas. In response, Square D shifted to a hybrid structure, with the front end of the organization aligned around markets and the rest structured around products.

Cisco approached cost pressures differently. Until the technology slump of 2001, Cisco had done well with a highly integrated structure selling three separate, semiautonomous lines of business. Each line developed, manufactured, and sold its own customized networking solutions to distinct customer segments: Internet service providers, large companies, and small to midsize businesses. But the market slump in 2001 exposed problems with the structure—in particular, the high costs of redundant engineering and innovation needs across the three segments. Meanwhile, the technological sophistication and requirements of the segment were also converging. To make matters worse, tough competitors, such as Huawei Technologies Co. Ltd. of China, were offering competitive products at lower prices. To reduce redundancies, Cisco centralized all related technologies into 11 different technology groups. Solutions engineering teams, which were assigned to the central marketing function, mixed and matched from the various technologies. This allowed Cisco to share technology across multiple customer segments. Within two years, the benefits of the cost efficiencies were visible. Customer satisfaction remained high, and in 2003, net income rose to $3.6 billion.

Outside-In Organizational Metrics and Incentives

Companies must use a dashboard or portfolio of metrics to ensure that employees at all levels (1) understand how to manage the customer value imperatives, (2) know whether they have accomplished these outcomes, and can diagnose the problem if they have not, and (3) get excited about the promised results because incentives are directly tied to these results. Our discussion of each imperative in Chapters 3 through 10 includes a set of recommended metrics to track a company's progress on the four customer value imperatives. In this section, we offer additional advice regarding how companies can approach the issue of designing a dashboard of metrics and aligning organizational incentives accordingly.

Pick the Right Metrics

There is no shortage of possible metrics. The title of one recent book is *Measuring Marketing: 103 Key Metrics Every Marketer Needs!*[17] Most of these are highly relevant to measuring the four customer value imperatives. But that's the problem—if everything matters, then nothing matters. What is needed is a focused, valid, and limited dashboard of metrics.[18]

The automobile dashboard metaphor is apt because there are many possible metrics for assessing the health of an automobile. The key is to select a reduced set of the most vital measures to display on the dashboard. Like the driver of an auto, a leadership team is unlikely to be able to give sustained attention to more than five to eight metrics at a time (while having a background roster of diagnostic metrics and triangulation to confirm the diagnosis).

While most automobiles have similar dashboards, each business needs a customer value dashboard specifically tailored to its strategy and market situation. For example, British Sky Broadcasting (better known as BSkyB), the satellite broadcaster of pay TV programs to the UK market, was able to distill its dashboard down to four key metrics: (1) customers' perceived value for money paid, (2) net subscriber growth (new customers minus churn), (3) viewing share of pay TV channels, and (4) gross margin growth (after programming costs). Taken together, these revealed the firm's ability to compete profitably against pay TV channels, and to attract and keep customers with a relational value strategy.

How should companies decide which metrics to include in their dashboards? First, and perhaps most obvious, *metrics must be valid.* Valid means that the metric measures what you think it measures. For example, customer satisfaction is not a measure of purchase intention, and brand reputation is not a measure of customer satisfaction. This is a simple point, but one that many companies overlook.

Second, *metrics must reflect the company's value leadership strategy.* Some metrics, such as diagnosing customer endorsements through the Net Promoter Score, will be shared across the value leaders. However, other metrics are likely to be specific to a particular customer value leadership strategy. Tesco's metrics as a relational value leader should not be the same as Walmart's metrics as a price value leader. Metrics must follow the value strategy. In Chapter 4, we offered metrics for assessing customer value and the business models associated with each customer value strategy (see Table 4-1). This is a good start.

Third, *metrics should be nested within a particular industry and make sense for that industry's customers.* This means that metrics that are helpful to Zappos are not necessarily going to be helpful to Medtronic or Roche. This is a no-brainer criterion, but we have found it remarkable how frequently managers imitate metrics that have no relevance to their business! Even metrics derived from the same industry need to be translated into the company context. Unfortunately, companies seem to find it easier to copy than to think hard about their business. Better to invest in what matters for your business than to jump on the bandwagon.

Fourth, some *metrics should be leading indicators that give the company a competitive jump.* Harrah's found that if a customer visited more than one casino, it was an important early signal that the value of that customer would increase over time. Cross-visits revealed that the customer had begun to perceive casinos as a "vacation destination" and valued staying at a casino in different locations. Harrah's could then profitably spend more to provide these customers with service excellence.

Playing with this example, one natural step would then be to look at the customer behaviors at the originating casino or at other individual demographic, geographic, or psychographic customer characteristics to determine if Harrah's could predict which customer behaviors or characteristics were related to cross-visits. If such indicators could be determined, Harrah's would clearly want to reward customers who exhibit those behaviors or characteristics in the hope of improving the likelihood or speed of their decision to cross-visit.

Fifth, *metrics should diagnose root causes.* If a physician routinely ordered eye exams for patients who came in complaining of, say, indigestion, the insurance companies and the patients would be upset. Yet managers in other industries routinely collect information about customers that is not value-relevant. For example, it is not helpful to know that customer loyalty is decreasing unless additional questions are asked about the causes, such as poor service or the introduction of a competitive product. The problem is that many metrics have little *diagnostic value*, so managers never get to the root cause of problems, and they waste money fixing strategies by attacking the wrong cause.

Finally, some *metrics should capture important intermediate states*. Companies should think of their metrics as part of a process map that connects the firm's actions to its economic profits. Understanding that a firm's actions may not have an immediate effect on economic profit is valuable because managers who know that their actions are influencing intermediate states, such as customers' beliefs or buzz, will know that they are on the right track. Of course, the intermediate states need to pay off for the company in terms of behavior and ultimately profits. Such process metrics are often severely lacking in firms that direct managers to improve outcomes, such as sales or profits, without providing supporting steps that can be taken and monitored along the way.

Align Incentives

If the firm wants to compete on customer value, then incentives for all employees have to be structured to encourage achievement of the four imperatives. There are several challenges that firms have to manage in order to get incentives aligned:

- **Shifting incentives.** Competing on customer value should not be viewed as another managerial fad or bandwagon. People must know that these rewards are permanent; otherwise, they will not expend the time and cost to learn new skills and behaviors.
- **Training and support.** Competing on customer value will require major shifts in the way the firm does business and

employees operate. If the firm wants to minimize unintended negative consequences, it should offer training and other types of support so that sound procedures, not shortcuts, are adopted to reach the appropriate outcomes.

- **Incentives across levels.** All levels and areas of the firm must live and die by the same incentive structure. If they do not, those who get the short end of the stick will sabotage the effort.

- **Mixed messages.** Incentives should be aligned, or eliminated if they cannot be aligned. Firms run into trouble when they ask employees to perform well on dual criteria, such as customer satisfaction and cost reduction or even market share and customer satisfaction.[19] When this happens, employees may make trade-offs that compromise customer value.

Organizational Capabilities for Competing on the Customer Value Imperatives

Culture, structure, metrics, and incentives are vital to competing on the imperatives. To maximize the full profit potential of the customer value imperatives, however, companies must build capabilities for each imperative. Capabilities are organizational-level processes involving a set of sequenced activities for acting on the imperative. The steps are not owned by an individual manager and are not a function of which side of the bed the CEO wakes up on. They reflect strategy and are collectively enacted and valued.

Throughout the book, we have addressed the specific steps that companies need to take in building these capabilities for each imperative—whether it is acting like a customer value leader, a customer value innovator, a customer asset manager, or a brand asset manager. For example, a customer asset management capability resides in the ability to value, select, develop, defend, and leverage customers.

For these capabilities to become a permanent feature of the firm, they must share a set of common features:

- **Viewed as fundamental.** For the capability to take root and become distinctive, there must be a shared belief that it is a "must do," not a "nice to do."
- **Coordinated across functions.** When capabilities are working well, they dominate functions. The focus must be on what is best for the customer, not on turf.
- **Reflected in formal and informal routines.** When capabilities show up in the company's day-to-day steps and procedures, a natural learning curve takes over. The result is increased efficiency and effectiveness in managing the customer value imperatives.
- **Nested within a supporting structure and incentive system.** This makes enacting the right sequence of behaviors logical and seamless for employees. Indicators are pointing in the same direction, and there is no confusion or arguments about what should be done or why it's important.
- **Tough for competitors to imitate.** When capabilities become entrenched in the company in these ways, they drive—often in an invisible way—the employees' mental models and behaviors, which in turn drive the day-to-day operations of the company. Competitors may look, but they cannot easily learn how to copy what is happening. Even effective employees may not be able to make explicit what glue is holding things together, and so copying or trying to "hire away" these capability recipes is not easily accomplished.

In addition to capabilities for competing on the four customer value imperatives, it is also essential that the firm develop a market-insight capability, as discussed in Chapter 11. We have made it clear throughout the book that acting on the imperatives in the absence of market insight is an empty exercise. To stay with our recipe metaphor, the core ingredient is missing. Together, capabilities for competing on the customer value imperatives and market insight are a powerful complement of capabilities that the most effective companies exhibit and competitors find challenging to imitate.

Walk the Talk

Many companies talk about managing from the outside in, but few orient themselves around delivering against the idea. A complete alignment of the firm, from culture to incentives to capabilities, is the only way to "walk the talk." Further, if marketing is too important to be left to the marketing department, then outside-in thinking is too important to be left to the C-suite alone. It is the responsibility of the leaders of the firm to make sure that every part of the organization is aligned and onboard to create an outside-in reality.

Chapter 13 now considers the vital role of CMOs as part of the leadership necessary to create and maintain an outside-in posture. For CMOs to be able to fulfill that role, however, they must earn the trust of their C-suite colleagues. We'll share the inspiring examples of two companies whose CMOs who earned that trust and are using it to relentlessly drive customer value—and profit from it.

13

Leading for Customer Value

ho is going to drive the four customer value imperatives into
the organization? Because the customer value imperatives are
such important contributors to economic profit, the entire C-suite
must be responsible if the company is going to be successful. Moreover, in order to sustain an outside-in approach to strategy, it is
essential that all leaders in the firm are committed to and focused
on this way of operating.

Yet responsibility is not the same thing as accepting accountability for actually getting things done and being answerable for these
actions. Given that deep market insights are the driving force of an
outside-in approach to strategy and the basis for all actions that
respond to the customer value imperatives, ultimate accountability
may lie best in the company's marketing leader. In some companies, this will be a chief marketing officer (CMO), but the exact
title is likely to vary by company and industry.

This advice is less obvious than it may appear. In many
businesses, there is a problem with making the CMO the focal
point for orchestrating the imperatives: a pervasive credibility gap.
The obstacle is that "CEO's already see that their most important
challenges are marketing ones—they just don't believe that marketers themselves can confront them."[1] To overcome this obstacle, CMOs have to *earn* their strategic role as the champion of the
four imperatives.

What exactly is a marketer to do if she is to earn this important role? Having watched many top marketers—CMOs, senior vice presidents, executive vice presidents, and vice presidents—fail, we see a number of key factors at play in their successes (and failures). In this chapter, we discuss the key organizational strategies and individual traits that top marketing leaders use to earn their seats. No one factor is sufficient—they all contribute. Here we'll look at the examples of two companies in which CMOs have successfully earned both the title of CMO *and* the responsibility for managing the customer value imperatives: Andrea Ragnetti and Geert van Kuyck, CMOs of Philips, and Stephen Quinn, CMO of Walmart. We follow their stories with a more detailed analysis of what made a difference in their success. We begin, however, with a general discussion of the different types of roles that marketing leaders can play within companies.

Marketing Leadership

The roles of marketing leaders are as diverse as the firms they serve. The job of the CFO is well understood and accepted, but the job of the top marketer is more ambiguous and depends on the type of industry, the role of sales, and the importance of information technology to the business. The possible roles for the head of marketing function can be grouped into four categories.[2]

Marketer as Top-Line Leader

In this role, marketing has a central strategic guidance function that directs all customer-facing activities and is accountable for the brand strategy, driving the organic growth agenda, and positioning the business for the future. It has ownership of the customer value proposition. In many organizations, the CMO will have shared P&L responsibility and will be accountable for the return on marketing investments. He may have direct oversight of sales. This emerging model of a CMO flourishes in companies with big global brands, such as Diageo or American Express. The balance of activities and accountability depends on the realities of the competitive strategy and the relationship with sales.

Marketer as Market Advocate

Like top-line leaders, these CMOs are advocates for the customer and are responsible for bringing longer-term market and brand-building considerations into C-suite deliberations. They lead teams that monitor the market setting, scan for shifts in the media and consumer environment, and then interpret these consumer insights to guide new product development. They differ from top-line leaders in that they have only a limited role in the broader strategic dialogue. They seldom have direct oversight of sales, strategy development, or product development. While their role may be broad, they are primarily coordinators and communicators. Market advocates are especially prevalent in sales-driven organizations.

Marketer as a Service Resource

This is the least influential type of CMO. Indeed, the leaders of these marketing organizations are rarely given the label of CMO, but usually have a title such as vice president of marketing services. They manage a group of marketing professionals that operates as a cost center, overseeing central marketing research and coordinating relationships with key marketing partners, such as advertising agencies, market research firms, direct-mail houses, and new media outlets. Business unit managers with profit and loss responsibility are not compelled to use these marketers if they think they can find better capability outside the firm. Service resource marketers also have sundry administrative responsibilities, such as monitoring compliance with brand, logo, or trademark guidelines and coordinating shared customer databases.

This model of a strictly supportive marketing function is found at science-based and high-technology firms, such as pharmaceutical makers like Amgen or Merck. These firms have strong R&D

cultures in which product managers have complete P&L responsibility and business development is often housed in a corporate strategy or finance group.

Marketing as Sales Support

In this model, marketing plays a subordinate and supportive role to sales, and many marketing activities have been folded into the sales group. This model is particularly prevalent in smaller B2B firms that are reliant on intermediaries.[3] In these situations, sales usually wins the battle over budget allocations.[4] Sales gains a further edge when the CEO is on a short-run earnings quest or when the economy turns bad. In the absence of agreed-upon metrics and credible data, the contribution of the sales group is easier to judge than the long-run investments in brand building, advertising, or new segment prospecting proposed by the marketing team.

The relative power of the sales group is further enhanced if powerful customers and distributors expect to be served by large multifunction teams, coordinated by sales. A Tesco, BMW, or Apple may be served by a colocated team of 50 to 200 people from a major, tier-one supplier. These teams of logistics, manufacturing, packaging, IT, and other specialists are expected to take a long view of their relationships with customers, and they have a growing influence on the marketing strategy dialogue.

Summary

A firm's marketing leadership model tends to fall into one of these modes based on the product and market, company culture, and dominance of the CEO. In any company and in any role, nonetheless, the lead marketer should help understand, create, and defend how an outside-in strategy becomes an operational approach to managing the customer. What are the qualities and approaches of some effective persuaders? We next take a look Philips' Andrea Ragnetti and Geert van Kuyck to see two powerful examples.

Philips' Move to Outside-In Strategy

At the start of the decade, Philips Electronics was widely seen as a trusted but dull global company. While it had a history of technology leadership, it also had a well-entrenched culture with an inside-out "factory mindset" that focused on reducing costs while improving current product performance.[5] The company was underperforming relative to its potential—sales had flat-lined, and net income was negative. One analyst criticized, "Philips is a company that consistently destroys shareholder value."[6] This occurred for several key reasons.

First, the company was organized into six loosely related product divisions (including lighting, consumer electronics, appliances, and medical systems) with a legacy of entrepreneurial country operations that impeded global coordination. Second, there was a costly welter of hundreds of different brand names, with no tie to Philips and without a meaningful umbrella positioning theme. Third, there was no unifying thrust to what strategic marketing should or should not do. Fourth, marketing capabilities at the corporate and business levels were weak—even though each product division had its own CMO.

The transformation to an outside-in, market-driven organization was orchestrated by the CEO, Gerald Kleisterlee. One of his first moves in 2002 was to establish a corporate CMO function. This alarmed the divisional presidents, since it signaled a greater level of centralization and the loss of some of their power.

Following a worldwide search, the position of corporate CMO was awarded to Andrea Ragnetti, a former P&G manager who was heading Telecom Italia's efforts to become more market-driven. Two of his early moves at Philips reflected a strategic decision that becoming market-driven did not require the centralization of marketing expertise. The first move was to set up a strong and committed marketing board made up of the CMOs from each product division to share best practices and coordinate activities. The second move was to start a Philips Marketing Academy to enhance marketing capabilities throughout the organization. These two moves were designed to work in tandem to help nurture common projects, showcase best practices, and facilitate networking across divisions.

Meanwhile, the existing global brand management group that reported to Ragnetti began to invest heavily in gathering customer insights. The research program engaged more than 1,650 consumers and 180 customers in 120 in-depth interviews, 24 focus groups, and 1,439 quantitative interviews.[7] That work revealed, among other insights, some deep customer frustration with the difficulty of using technology and the complexity of buying from Philips.

Both consumers and customers wanted simplicity in their lives and technology that got the job done. They also wanted an easier way of doing business with Philips. Philips' current umbrella positioning of "Let's Make Things Better" lacked coherence, especially when compared to major competitors like GE, Siemens, Sony, and LG, and this added pressure to find a new positioning.

After much debate, a new umbrella positioning called "Sense and Simplicity" was chosen. It was based on three brand pillars:[8]

- **Designed around you.** "This means all our activities must be driven by insights into how our customers experience technology."
- **Easy to use.** "People should be able to enjoy the benefits of technology without any hassle or frustrations."
- **Advanced.** "The central idea is progress . . . something is only truly advanced when it improves the lives of people."

The product divisions liked the idea that the new positioning differentiated Philips from its competitors and that it was achievable. Some products already met the standards. For example, the new Senseo coffeemaker used innovative steaming technology and a simple one-button design to deliver café-quality coffee with no complications.

The adoption and implementation of the new positioning theme was not smooth, however. Some opponents were worried about the fate of products that contradicted the brand promise, while others did not want to pay the € 80 million cost of the initial campaign. At this point, the CEO stepped in and forcefully decided to proceed.

The implementation of the new value proposition had a huge impact on the traditionally technology-driven company. All new product development projects had to go through a rigorous process called the "Value Proposition House and Marketing Funnel" that demonstrated how well the offering fit the three brand pillars. The process also ensured that there was a clear connection between customer insights, what Philips was offering in the value proposition, and how this was unique relative to the competition. In 2006, for example, 25 percent of the projects in development were "sent back" for further work, and 15 percent were terminated.

The new market-driven initiatives touched all the other functions and processes within the company—from the hiring and review criteria used by HR to the key performance indicators for core processes. This meant that the incentives to employees and the customer value proposition were now aligned. The brand pillars were also used to introduce improvements to the sales organizations within each product division. New, more collaborative sales models that focused on bringing simplicity to these customers were piloted and rolled out. Results indicated that the new systems were working as Philips began to rack up awards in this area.

One of Ragnetti's key hires during this time was Geert van Kuyck as senior vice president of global marketing management in the fall of 2005. van Kuyck, also a former P&Ger, was the vice president of marketing for Starbucks when hired. He was charged with, in his words, "bolting the brand promise to the company."[9] In 2006, van Kuyck began piloting a program that used the Net Promoter Score (NPS) measure to evaluate Philips' performance with the customer in three product units: oral care, MRI, and TVs. NPS was chosen because it connected the customer and the product or service offerings, and it was simple enough to be used across all the units. The pilot study showed that it predicted customer behavior. Specifically, a high NPS predicted Philips' ability to drive revenue, retain margin, and improve share of wallet. Based on this success, the program was then rolled out to other units, using a variety of approaches such as digital strategies, warranty cards, and a survey of business partners. The company evaluated Philips' NPS performance relative to competitors and relative to its goals. This singular focus helped drive attention.

van Kuyck said that this was when "we made the outside-in, an inside-the-board-room conversation." The CFO began thinking about investing with customers for whom high NPS could be achieved, and the chief strategy officer began thinking about product portfolio decisions from the customers' point of view. Even R&D adopted a "beta NPS" in which it used NPS to evaluate customers' response to early products. These types of changes inside the boardroom and throughout the company made it clear that managers understood, in van Kuyck's words, "Profits don't get made in the factory anymore."

Philips took the idea of customer focus from a company focus to a set of compelling value propositions and ultimately into the heart of the customer's experience. With a single-minded focus on the customer, Philips has seen improvement in the company's consumer and professional businesses, from its power base in Europe to highly competitive emerging markets like China and India. By 2007, revenue from substantially new products introduced within the previous two years had increased from 25 percent to 53 percent of the total. Interbrand estimated that the value of the Philips brand had risen from $4.4 billion in 2004 to $7.7 billion in 2008, mainly because of improved earnings.

Throughout the recession, Philips has been remarkably resilient. Brand value has grown, NPS scores are the highest the company has seen, with 60 percent of revenue coming from business where Philips is the NPS leader. Even in markets such as construction in

Spain, where competitors have seen a 40 percent drop in business, Philips has held its performance levels for the year.

As a postscript, and apropos of Philips' deep commitment to customer focus, in January 2008, Philips implemented a new organizational structure focused on market sectors—Philips Healthcare, Philips Lighting, and Philips Consumer Lifestyle. The product divisions disappeared, and the company began to use solution or customer managers. At that time, Ragnetti was appointed CEO of Consumer Lifestyle, and Geert van Kuyck was appointed CMO.

Walmart: Regaining a Customer Focus

Stephen Quinn was named Walmart's chief marketing officer in January 2007. The two prior years had been tough on the world's largest retailer—same-store sales had declined, and the number of new store openings had slowed considerably. The press characterized this period as one of "marketing missteps and a need to lift anemic sales growth."[10]

Quinn came to Walmart as a 13-year veteran of PepsiCo, most recently the executive vice president and chief marketing officer for the Frito-Lay division. Prior to that, Quinn had held consumer marketing positions at Procter & Gamble, Johnson & Johnson, and Quaker Oats.

Quinn worried that in the early part of the decade Walmart had lost its historical concentration on the customer.[11] Walmart, the world's largest retailer, had begun to fall prey to many of the inside-out forces, including the power of its supply-chain operation, that we discussed in Chapter 1. New store openings were driving out attention on maximizing the profitability of existing stores. A decentralized and entrepreneurial culture, which was a boost in many regards, interfered with a unified view of the customer and the brand. As Quinn noted, "We lost a focus on the customer and the brand."[12]

Quinn understood that his job was to regain that outside-in focus and to stay true to Sam Walton's famous quote, "There is only one boss: The customer. And he can fire everybody in the company, from the chairman on down, simply by spending his money somewhere else." Quinn understood that this focus needed to be shared across the different areas of the company. Quinn notes, "While retailers generally, and Walmart specifically, long have needed to focus on store operations and supply-chain issues, marketers need to take the lead [among those other disciplines and steer] in a consumer-focused direction."[13]

Quinn found a strong customer advocate and brand champion in Eduardo Castro-Wright, the president of Walmart's U.S. unit. This leadership made Quinn's job much easier. If he was going to ask everyone in the company to think about the customer, it was essential that his boss be a living example.

But first Quinn had to nail down exactly what the brand should stand for, what that meant operationally in the store, and how it would influence communications. Quinn started with a powerful combination of market insights and a strong customer intuition. Under his leadership, Walmart invested heavily in market research, polling more than a million customers monthly. Quinn states very clearly, "At Walmart marketing, we never guess."[14] This careful and exhaustive research and analytical work drove a number of important changes.

Quinn spent time figuring out who Walmart's customers were and who they were not. It was clear that not all customers were going to find value at Walmart; for example, customers who were interested in performance value (e.g., top-of-the-line electronics) or relational value (e.g., the highly personal service at Nordstrom) would not.[15] A new segmentation scheme based on this research sought to penetrate existing markets more effectively and to drive efforts at leveraging existing customers to purchase from more categories across the store.

Research clarified what these customers really valued. Labeled "Project Impact," this effort focused on the key factors that would improve customer satisfaction—cleaner stores with wider, less-cluttered aisles, better merchandise, and more visible and appealing store branding.

Quinn sought out internal partners that wanted deeper insight into how their categories could be revitalized. Electronics was an early partner. With better insight into how customers viewed Walmart's electronics offerings, Quinn's team was able to help develop and execute a strategy that has been very successful for the company. During a period in which Walmart's sales in the category increased, Best Buy's were flat and Circuit City went out of business.

External forces were also molding the brand in important ways. Quinn concluded that Walmart was losing the battle by letting others define the brand. Market research revealed that consumers needed to be reminded *why* lower prices should be viewed positively—with the answer being that lower prices can help consumers lead better lives. In response, Walmart shifted its brand message from a focus solely on low prices in the form of "Always Low Prices. Always." to "Save Money. Live Better." This was a big change for Walmart, as it connected to the deeper benefits—"Live Better"—that customers really wanted. Quinn also understood that the former slogan, focused only on lower price, was too easy to imitate. It was also important that the new brand message be played out in everything that Walmart did and said. This meant solving problems like Walmart's unwillingness to pay for employee health care because customers felt bad if they saved money at someone's expense.

Even more fundamentally, it meant that Quinn had to ensure that everyone in the company understood that "You are the brand," and this became his mantra to the company. He notes, "In retail, you have to manage the whole interaction with customers and vendors. In-store media and media in general are important because I have to go tell the Walmart story, but at the same time, I've got a bunch of people who are telling their story through the stores, and how you pull all that together is challenging."[16] Quinn used Sam Walton's famous Saturday morning meetings to show employees videos about what Walmart stands for and how each and every one of them was important to the customer's experience. He understood that he could accomplish his job only through the rest of the organization.

The "Live Better" tagline described earlier had to be socialized internally as well. Physical assets, such as signs, truck logos, and so on, were tied to the old tagline and were expensive to change. There was also resistance because it seemed to deviate from the company's legacy. However, Quinn took the focus off himself and the marketing function and instead noted that "Save Money. Live Better" could be attributed to Sam Walton himself, who said: *"If we work together, we'll lower the cost of living for everyone . . . we'll give the world the opportunity to see what it's like to save and have a better life."* Quinn used this information to sell the tagline internally and, more important, to have it adopted as the company's mission, not just an advertising concept.

Bringing the customer's perspective and experience into the company's operations took hold. Discussions about the customer's experience became common at C-level staff meetings, in meetings for all company officers, and even at the company's legendary Saturday morning meetings. Customer metrics were added not only to the marketing area's goals, but also to the goals of merchants and store operators. In this way, the individual store became responsible not only for sales, but also for the customer's experience in that store. This caused a strong alignment between merchandising, operations, and marketing in identifying, solving, and implementing solutions to customer problems.

Reflecting on his process, Quinn noted, "I'm proud of the story here, because I think it's showing how marketing is making a really big difference to a company that maybe didn't take it as seriously as they do today. . . . I do think marketing has a seat at the table. . . . This company had a strong merchant and operations culture, and now we've added this third leg of the stool."[17] The first full year following the introduction of all of these changes was 2008. In that year, Walmart grew $27 billion, with $16 billion of that growth coming from the United States. Comparative store sales rebounded by a factor of three versus the prior year, market share growth accelerated, and Walmart outgrew its major competitor in all six of its business units.

Earning a Seat at the Table

Whether marketing plays a lead role or a supportive role in managing the customer value imperatives depends on many factors. The stories of Ragnetti, van Kuyck, and Quinn, and our experience with many successful CMOs, offer lessons on how to earn this leadership role.

Gain Credibility and Buy-In

Unless the CEO believes that marketing is a priority, and is willing to visibly act on that belief by supporting the CMO with authority and resources, the game is over before it starts. This means making an organizational commitment that won't falter at the first stress point. As Ragnetti said, "Mr. Kleisterlee [the CEO] may not be a marketing expert but he is someone who believes that Philips, for all its 100,000 technology patents, must become market-led rather than a technology-led organization."[18] At Walmart, in Eduardo Castro-Wright, Quinn had a CEO who was willing to champion marketing and the brand. Both CEOs knew that marketing leadership was important.

The CEO's support increases when the CMO's job is aligned with the firm's objectives. Both Quinn and Ragnetti were hired to help their firms grow by managing customers more effectively. Press reports at the time of Quinn's appointment noted that the company and Castro-Wright were under pressure to show results after changes to field operations and store upgrades had failed to deliver improvements. Ragnetti was charged by Kleisterlee with turning Philips into the "P&G of its space," which meant new growth driven by customer insights.

While the CEO's support is crucial, broader buy-in from the rest of the C-suite is essential. Because the work of marketing had to happen through the technologies at Philips and through the stores at Walmart, both leaders knew that successful marketing meant managing cross-functional relationships. As he built internal relationships, Quinn would "say yes to any meeting" and work hard to convey to people, including his equals, how important it was for them to work together to do what the company needed. "Certainly it's not a marketing-led company in the way a lot of packaged-goods companies would consider themselves to be. So I have to be careful not to overstep what it really is."[19] Quinn found willing partners in his C-suite peers who shared his strong desire to make Walmart better and to work together to make it a reality.

Ragnetti spent his first year at Philips' home base in Amsterdam focusing on raising marketing's profile with Philips management. He needed to change the attitude of company scientists and engineers so they would take an interest in developing popular consumer products.[20] Likewise, Quinn knew there was a lot of skepticism about marketing at Walmart. Initially, he focused on the people internally who thought marketing could help them. He also didn't try to do too much, which would have spread his resources too thin.

Be the Expert on the Market

Raoul Pinnell, chairman of Shell Brands, summarized this lesson when noting: "Marketing cannot demand a voice. Marketing has to earn its place at the table of strategy. It has to prove and to deliver. It has to challenge internal 'perceived wisdoms,' but it must do this through rigorous research."[21] Both Quinn and Ragnetti drove strategy with rigorous market insights.

At Philips, both market-driven and technology-driven innovation was based on market insights. This was a big shift for a company that in the past had relied on strong science, but a weak understanding of the customer. Ragnetti started with major investments in market insight. He also formed the "Simplicity Advisory Board," made up of health-care, fashion, design, and architecture specialists from outside Philips. Ragnetti said, "Philips was too inward-looking . . . and to really embed simplicity into the company's DNA, it needed an element of vision." The board was created to help Philips rethink what its customers wanted. It pushed Philips to get deep market insights, and van Kuyck brought market insights and operational customer accountability, in the form of the NPS metric, to all divisions and all areas of the company.

At Walmart, Quinn faced a strong merchandising culture that believed that "what worked in the store" was a good customer insight. Quinn invested in a more programmatic approach to insights as a means of getting the customer to cross into more aisles when visiting Walmart. This involved deep observation and interaction with customers as well as large-scale surveys performed on a regular basis to understand trends. Walmart employed a broad range of metrics, including concept appeal, copy effectiveness, ROI from marketing mix models, and brand equity and image improvement measures. These complemented the things with which the CEO was most concerned—sales, returns, and customer loyalty.

Keep the Focus on the Customer (to Help the Company)

Scott Cook, founder and former CEO of Intuit, built his company on the belief that it was being trusted with customer's financial lives and that it was essential that it "do right by the customer."[22] Likewise, both Quinn and Ragnetti advocated making the customer the essential focus of strategy. Preferences were driven by what was right for the customer, not what was expeditious or easy. Quinn noted, "We lost our way and it was as simple as focusing on our customers to get us back on track."[23] Ragnetti understood that growth efforts had to be customer-centric. He noted, "In the past, [Philips] just developed the technology and hoped someone would buy it. Now we are starting from the point of discovering what exactly customers want a product to do."[24]

Quinn took heat for many things—the new company position, the new logo—and he had an uphill climb to prove the value of marketing at Walmart. However, he never made it about what he wanted—only what was right for the customer, and therefore right for the company. Quinn noted, "I didn't want to make Walmart into Target; just a better Walmart. Walmart doesn't need to attract a different customer to succeed—we just need to do a better job selling to and maintaining the loyalty of existing customers."[25] These kinds of statements and a laser focus on the customer quieted fears that Quinn was out for personal glory. Ragnetti likewise faced enormous resistance from scientists and engineers who were entrenched in technologies. By keeping his personal needs or any focus other than the customer off the table, he gained credibility for his ability to find successful applications for good science within Philips. Then van Kuyck continued with this same company-first viewpoint. He said, "Earning it [respect for marketing, in this case] has a lot to do with not wanting to own it."

Obsess about Talent

Because employees are the agents of a firm's strategy to compete on customer value, they will be the reason that it succeeds or fails. This means that marketing's contributions will need to come, in part, from wisely selecting, training, and retaining employees and managers who can flourish within this strategy. Marketers need to work with human resource professionals to identify the critical skill sets and develop a spotting, hiring, and development process for talent to ensure that the best people are in place.

In an organization dominated by merchandising and operations, Quinn had to build a marketing organization for Walmart. He did so, in part, by hiring a group of people from Frito-Lay. The key aspect of these hires was that Quinn screened heavily on "culture" fit. He knew that it was not a matter of pure talent—although he wanted that, too. He needed people who would fit into Walmart and be able to cooperate across the organization.

Ragnetti took a different approach, but with the same effect. One of Ragnetti's key hires was Geert van Kuyck as senior vice president of global marketing management. Together, Ragnetti and van Kuyck focused on talent that would adopt a strong customer vantage point. The reorganization and restructuring within Philips is not quite finished as of the writing of this book, but the focus is on moving forward with "talent that is trainable."

Accept Accountability and Advocate for Metrics

There is no foreseeable future in which marketing won't be expected to demonstrate acceptable returns on marketing investments. At every turn, marketers will have to combat short-termism, which focuses on immediate share and revenue possibilities, at the expense of long-run enhancements of the customer and brand assets that drive economic profit. Both Quinn and Ragnetti knew that they had been hired to produce profits for their companies. As a result, both men were willing to have their efforts measured and deeply scrutinized. Quinn believes that many marketing leaders have an aversion to measuring their performance through metrics and that most just don't want to be evaluated. He said that metrics are important for making sure that, "Getting it right is more important than looking good."

The focus on NPS at Philips helped make an outside-in approach to managing the company a reality. Although other metrics were also used, such as brand value and revenue from new products introduced within the last two years, NPS played a key role in the cultural transformation of the company. Ragnetti was the visionary who brought a customer focus to the Philips brand, and van Kuyck, the mastermind, then "bolted" this focus to the rest of the company.

Partner with Sales

Too often, there is an adversarial Mars and Venus coloration to the relationship of marketing and sales that is rooted in mutual incomprehension of the other's role and in divergent goals and incentives. In reality, both win if they work together to craft the value proposition and deliver it to the customer in the selling process. Marketing needs to provide sales with better selling tools to help it be more successful, tools that are based on a deeper understanding of segments, a robust storehouse of information about the customer relationship, and the identification of cross-selling opportunities that make sales look good.

At Philips, Ragnetti took the new brand messaging to sales with great success. Customers were also tired of the complexity of working with the company and rewarded Philips' new approach to managing the relationship. Ongoing evaluation of NPS also gave sales a clear incentive to adopt a customer focus. The sales team was able to see the value of promoters and detractors for its sales levels on a daily basis. Hence, NPS was an easy sell to sales, as the salespeople saw the direct connection between a customer focus and their work. At Walmart, marketing was able to give merchandising, including Web sales, a better understanding of the needs and opportunities of customers, including new segment insights.

Show Relevance to the C-suite

All of these marketing leaders understood that for the outside-in approach to become the basis for day-to-day company operations, the customer had to play a fundamental role in interactions in the C-suite and in the operational plans and ideas of all the top leaders in the firm. At Philips, the customer's experience and rating scores entered boardroom conversations. The heads of strategy and finance began to use these ideas and approaches to drive their decisions and as this happened, van Kuyck found these factors were "close to the CEO's hip." As a result, he saw "marketing becoming a true business partner."

The same thing has happened at Walmart, but through different means. The currency of conversations in the C-suite focuses on what Walmart is doing for its customers and how to do better. Metrics on these issues drove the way in which stores are evaluated and merchandising is rewarded. This brought a singular and shared view back to the customer and put marketing in a position where it can contribute to the company's strategic dialogue.

In the Driver's Seat

At Philips, changes were made so that the marketing organization at the corporate and business level "owned" the four customer value imperatives. Creating more value for customers by improving product design and functionality meant that Philips could emerge as a performance value leader. The brand was built and leveraged as a guide to product development and as a way to attract and retain customers. Because organic growth cuts across so many parts of the organization, ownership meant being the core facilitator and coordinator. At Walmart, marketing was also in the driver's seat on the imperatives. The use of market insights to drive customer value in the selection of store merchandise, store environment, and a focus on "better living" meant that Walmart's price value leadership position soared. Marketing also contributed to innovation within stores, across stores, and across markets. There was a clear focus on building loyal customers and strong brands, which were then leveraged for deeper profits through increased share of wallet, purchases from new and complementary categories, and less defection.

As Ragnetti, van Kuyck, and Quinn show, when CMOs are empowered to drive the four customer value imperatives across the firm, the results can be truly impressive. They also demonstrate that the trust required must be earned—and must be re-earned constantly, even daily. CMOs and marketing organizations are as susceptible as any other executive or organization to succumbing to the temptations of inside-out thinking. Earning and retaining the right to lead the customer value imperatives means that they have to, first and foremost, be the primary advocates, defenders, and implementers of outside-in thinking.

Conclusion

We began this book by noting how common it is for companies to be seduced into inside-out thinking despite the common-sense and verifiable benefits of driving strategy from the outside in. One highly successful company built on unique market insights that was unable to avoid the trap of inside-out thinking is Liz Claiborne.

Liz Claiborne was founded in 1976 as a fashion design company that sold professional women's clothing through high-end department stores.[1] The company identified a new market segment—women who needed clothes to wear to offices as they entered the workforce. As Claiborne noted, "The goal was to clothe the working American woman. I was working myself, I wanted to look good, and I didn't think you should have to spend a fortune to do it. Only a couple of companies were catering to that emerging woman. . . . I felt we could do it better."[2] Liz Claiborne made clothes that actually fit the shape of women's bodies, designed clothes as collections that made for easy mixing and matching, and offered "breakfast clinics" for women to attend before going to the office. Retailers were required to buy entire collections and display them in prescribed ways, essentially creating a store within a store.

The company was also aggressive on price, using low-cost overseas production facilities, so that customers could be confident they didn't need to "shop around." This strategy allowed Liz Claiborne to build a trusted brand among career women who didn't have time to shop. By 1991, sales had reached $2 billion, net income hit $218.8 million, and the stock price was at an all-time high.

Like so many others, the company did not retain its outside-in focus, however. By the end of 1994, it was in trouble. The early 1990s saw an increased trend toward casual work attire that the company completely underestimated. Retailers were suffering under the weight of liquidity problems during this time, and so staff was cut to the bone—staff that knew how to display and sell Liz Claiborne's products. Pressure on prices and inventories, along with competitors' improvements in reordering systems, put the firm at a disadvantage. Liz Claiborne did not shift its strategies, and it suffered. Sales stagnated at just over $2 billion, and net income dipped (to $82.9 million), resulting in a drop in market cap from $3.5 billion to $1.3 billion.

But Liz Claiborne has more lessons than just being another company that succumbed to inside-out thinking. Showing that an inside-out company can change its stripes, Liz Claiborne reclaimed an outside-in strategic posture. First, the company returned to designs based on insights into how its target market was evolving—women were playing more roles throughout the day, so they needed clothes that were more versatile. Second, the company implemented a new sales strategy, including in-store merchandising personnel that installed in-store fixtures (called LizView shops). Third, the company used national brand advertising to boost the relevance of its stale image. Finally, the company reduced the number of its suppliers and shifted half of its production to the Western Hemisphere. This gave the firm buying power and logistics to speed up cycle times, which enabled it to bring new designs to market faster. By the end of 1997, the company had regrown its sales to $2.4 billion and its net income to $184.6 million.[3]

The Liz Claiborne roller-coaster ride is a fitting epilogue to our book because it epitomizes the experience of many of the companies that we have worked with and studied—an outside-in approach to delivering customer value brings a firm success. But eventually that success leads to complacency and the replacement of outside in with inside out. Only a few companies manage to reverse this trend or prevent it in the first place. What can you do to be one of them?

Seizing the Initiative

Superior customer value is the "true north" of an outside-in strategy. It is a centering concept that keeps the whole organization focused on what matters. If the firm's focus is not on superior customer value—as defined by the customer, not by product development executives or competitive intelligence analysts—then that is the place to start.

Successful execution of an outside-in strategy is also essential because its achievement drives the firm's economic profit and shareholder value. Managing the customer value imperatives using deep market insights is the pathway to ensure that an outside-in organization is, in fact, profitable.

With superior customer value as the guiding star and the customer value imperatives as the operational guide, your firm will be well on its way to creating value for customers *and* shareholders. Based on our study of the various firms we've profiled throughout the book, here are a few more pieces of advice to help you on your way. These are behaviors that have helped firms execute from the outside in consistently.

Stay Focused on the Market

Strategy is a living, breathing, and ever-changing game. Winning requires a clear vision of how to gain, sustain, and renew the customer value imperatives. It also means resisting the temptation to try to be all things to all customers and so lose distinctiveness and relevance to target customers. This demands tough decisions on where to make investments and where not to—both decisions that should be made explicitly by leaders.

Stay Vigilant

An outside-in approach keeps a business ahead of market changes. Ironically, the more successful a company becomes, the more likely it is to succumb to inside-out thinking. When the vital connection with the market is lost and early signals of change are ignored, as happened with Liz Claiborne, the customer value advantage will soon erode.

While inside-out thinking is crippling, it can be reversed by a vigilant top leadership team that is armed with market insights and tools for managing the customer value imperatives. The vigilant leaders featured in this book are notable for (1) an external, active, and inquisitive orientation, (2) listening to a wide array of sources, (3) a willingness to challenge prevailing assumptions about their markets, and (4) a long-run perspective on customer value.

Master an Ambidextrous Strategy

All outside-in strategies evolve from two interlocking strategy processes. A deliberate or intended strategy process is based on rigorous analyses of customer requirements, forces of competition, drivers of growth, and so forth. This very structured approach is balanced with an emergent strategy process of trial-and-error experimentation that learns quickly and tests frequently. In this process, experiments that succeed are quickly recognized, and the failures are abandoned. Outside-in firms excel at both processes. Leaders are constantly taking the temperature of their market, and using the insights to decide which projects to fund and which to kill. They let resources follow the best opportunities within the firm's overall strategic thrust.

Mobilize Everyone

Implementing a strategy based on the customer value imperatives will take time. Top leaders must never forget that this strategy must be sold—not just communicated—to every employee. Delivering superior customer value requires the entire organization, and every part of the firm must be asked to play its part. At Liz Claiborne, the turnaround involved sales, marketing, product development, finance, HR, logistics, and procurement making complementary changes.

When all the pieces of an outside-in strategy come together, every employee at every level sees how her ideas and activities can directly contribute to the creation of value that customers will pay for. By mobilizing everyone to create, keep, and leverage customers, the business can indeed profit from customer value.

turnaround involved sales, marketing, product development, finance, HR, logistics, and procurement making complementary changes.

When all the pieces of an outside-in strategy come together, every employee at every level sees how her ideas and activities can directly contribute to the creation of value that customers will pay for. By mobilizing everyone to create, keep, and leverage customers, the business can indeed profit from customer value.

Notes

Chapter 1

1. Kathleen Kerwin, "Remaking Ford," *Business Week*, October 11, 1999, pp. 132–142.
2. Daniel Lyons, "The Customer Is Always Right," *Newsweek*, January 4, 2010, pp. 85–86.
3. Rajiv Lal and Catherine Ross, "HP: The Computer Is Personal Again," Harvard Business School Case 9–509–010 (Boston: Harvard Business School, 2009).
4. news.cnet.com/Where-Dell-went-wrong/2010–1006_3–6155242.html; accessed on January 7, 2009.
5. A representative study is Neil A. Morgan, Douglas Vorhies, and Charlotte Mason, "Market Orientation, Marketing Capabilities and Firm Performance," *Strategic Management Journal*, August 2009, pp. 909–920. A recent meta-analysis of many studies that supports a positive and robust relationship between a market orientation and firm performance is Ahmet H. Kirca, Satish Jayachandran, and William Bearden, "Market Orientation: A Meta-Analytic Review and Assessment of Its Antecedents and Impact on Performance," *Journal of Marketing*, April 2005, pp. 24–41.
6. W. Chan Kim and Renee Mauborgne, *Blue Ocean Strategy* (Boston: Harvard Business School Press, 2005).
7. Case based on a presentation made by Brian Crean at the Marketing Science Institute Spring 2009 Board of Trustees Meeting and Conference on Leveraging Customer Insights, Boston, April 2–3, 2009.
8. Extracts from a speech by Anne Mulcahy, "Getting Heard in a Sea of Information," at Navigating the New Marketsphere, MPlanet American Marketing Association Conference, January 26, 2009.

9. Thomas H. Davenport and Jeanne G. Harris, *Competing on Analytics: The New Science of Winning* (Boston: Harvard Business School Press, 2007).

10. Hugh Courtney, John T. Horn, and Jayanti Kar, "Getting into Your Competitor's Head," *McKinsey Quarterly*, February 12, 2009, pp. 1–9.

11. Yoram (Jerry) Wind, "A Plan to Invent the Marketing We Need Today," *MIT Sloan Management Review*, Summer 2008, pp. 21–28.

12. Christopher Vollmer, "Digital Darwinism," *Strategy+Business*, Spring 2009, pp. 58–69.

13. We are grateful to Paddy Barwise and Sean Meehan for sharing their analyses of the Scion launch, "How Toyota Grabbed a Piece of Generation Y," January 9, 2007.

Chapter 2

1. Net profits have increased by a factor of 6 in the most recent five years. Meanwhile, nearly half of Tesco's GB £50 billion sales came from outside the UK, and it was entering the United States with a convenience store called Fresh & Easy that defied conventional wisdom. Sources include David E. Bell, "TESCO Plc," Harvard Business School Case 9-503-036 (Boston: Harvard Business School, 16, 2006); en.wikipedia.org/wiki/Tesco; Matthew Boyle and Michael V. Copeland, "Tesco Reinvents the 7-Eleven," *Fortune*, November 26, 2007, p. 34; and Darrell Rigby and Paul Rogers, "A Retail Revolution," *Wall Street Journal*, February 15, 2006, p. 12.

2. Sources include Bell, "TESCO Plc"; analysts' reports; en.wikipedia .org/wiki/Tesco; accessed on January 9, 2010; and Clive Humby, Terry Hunt, and Tim Phillips, *Scoring Points: How Tesco Continues to Win Customer Loyalty* (London: Kagan Page, 2008).

3. There are many ways to measure the three different aspects of *customer value* in this simple model. One way is to ask customers directly to rate how a set of competing offerings perform on benefits and costs. These beliefs are often captured on a scale ranging from 1 (not at all) to 7 (very well). Perceived risk can be measured on a scale from 0 to 1, where 1 is the highest risk. When risk is 0, it eliminates any benefit-cost advantage. The model can also be elaborated to reflect *customer preferences* for certain aspects of customer value. For example, a customer may rate a toothpaste as breath freshening but not value this benefit as much as cavity fighting. To include these

preferences, the belief scores can be multiplied by the preference scores. The resulting score can be summed up over the benefits to get a preference-weighted belief score. The same can be done for costs. Seasoned researchers will know this model as the multiattribute model used to assess consumer attitudes (see Icek Ajzen and Martin Fishbein, *Understanding Attitudes and Predicting Social Behavior* [Englewood Cliffs, N.J.: Prentice Hall, 1980]; and Martin Fishbein and Icek Ajzen, *Belief, Attitude, Intention, and Behavior: An Introduction to Theory and Research* [Reading, Mass.: Addison-Wesley, 1975]).

4. Based on internal documents prepared by a leading accounting firm.
5. This section benefited greatly from Roger Martin, "The Age of Customer Capitalism," *Harvard Business Review*, January-February 2010, pp. 58–65.
6. Peter Drucker, *The Practice of Management* (New York: Harper & Brothers, 1954).
7. A. G. Lafley and Ram Charan, *The Game Changer: How You Can Drive Revenue and Profit Growth with Innovation* (New York: Crown Business, 2008).
8. These examples were adapted from descriptions of the 50 most innovative companies in "The World's Most Innovative Companies," *Fast Company*, March 2009, pp. 52–97; and Suzanne Kapner, "The Mighty Dollar," *Fortune*, April 27, 2009, pp. 65–66.
9. Andrea Felsted and Patrick Jenkins, "Cash and Carry," *Financial Times*, July 20, 2009, p. 5.
10. David Welch, "Lessons from Saturn's Fall," *BusinessWeek*, March 2, 2009, p. 25.
11. Tesco, Annual Report, 2009, p. 20.
12. The purpose of economic profit is to ensure that strategic decisions take into account the impact on fixed assets and working capital. Sales growth almost always requires additional investment in fixed assets, receivables, and inventories. These factors are considered as follows: Economic profit = NOPAT (net operating profit after taxes) minus WACC (fixed assets and working capital), where WACC is the weighted-average cost of capital (debt and equity). We don't explicitly account for the fact that successful customer value strategies have a long-run effect on reducing the risk premium in WACC. For more details, see Alfred Rappaport, *Creating Shareholder Value* (New York: Free Press, 1986).

Chapter 3

1. This framework was introduced in George S. Day and Robin Wensley, "Assessing Advantage: A Framework for Diagnosing Competitive Superiority," *Journal of Marketing*, April 1988, pp. 1–20.

2. Leander Kahney, *The Cult of iPod* (Toronto: No Starch Press, 2005); Goldman Sachs research report on Apple Computer Inc., September 7, 2005.

3. Richard Normann and Rafael Ramirez, "From Value Chain to Value Constellation: Designing Interactive Strategy," *Harvard Business Review*, July-August 1993, pp. 65–77.

4. Youngme Moon, "Break Free from the Product Lifecycle," *Harvard Business Review*, May-June 2005, pp. 86–94.

5. Tom Murphy, "Intel's Window Closing in Portable Device Market," *Electronic News*, May 27, 2002, findarticles.com/p/articles/mi_mo EKF/is_22_48/ai_86875517/; accesssed on January 23, 2010.

6. Damon Darlin, "Cashing In Its Chips: Texas Instruments on the Rebound," *New York Times*, July 9, 2006; Coreen Bailor, "Texas Instruments Takes a Walk," *CRM Magazine*, August 2, 2004, www.activapr.com/news.detail.php?articleID=13; accessed on January 24, 2010.

7. This section benefited from Patrick Barwise and Sean Meehan, "Don't Be Unique, Be Better," *MIT Sloan Management Review*, Summer 2004, pp. 23–26.

8. Kevin Lane Keller, Brian Sternthal, and Alice Tybout, "Three Questions You Need to Ask About Your Brand," *Harvard Business Review*, September 2002, pp. 81–86.

9. David S. Landes, *Revolution in Time: Clocks and the Making of a Modern World* (Boston: Harvard University Press, 2000).

10. There are many variations on the standard life cycle model. See: Geoffrey A. Moore, *Crossing the Chasm* (New York: HarperBusiness, 1991), and *Dealing with Darwin: How Great Companies Innovate at Every Phase of Their Evolution* (New York: Portfolio, 2005).

11. Adapted from Hugh Courtney, *20/20 Foresight* (Boston: Harvard Business School Press, 2001); and Paul J. H. Schoemaker, *Profiting from Uncertainty* (New York: Free Press, 2002).

12. "Apple's Most Significant Creations: 30 Products for 30 years," *MacWorld*, June 2006.

13. Examples of the possibilities are Harold L. Sirkin, "Globality: Challenger Companies and Radically Defining the Competitive Landscape," *Strategy & Leadership*, 2008, pp. 36–41; and Pankaj Ghemawat and Thomas Hout, "Tomorrow's Global Giants: Not the Usual Suspects," *Harvard Business Review*, November 2006, pp. 80–88.

14. "Healthy Snacking—US—June 2009," from Mintel Report, (academic .mintel.com); accessed on February 10, 2010.

15. See Clayton Christensen, *The Innovator's Dilemma* (New York: HarperCollins, 2003) and Clayton Christensen and Michael Raynor, *The Innovator's Solution: Creating and Sustaining Successful Growth* (Boston: Harvard Business School Press, 2003). See pp. 152–155 for a description of how this process works in markets that were initially served with an integrated supply chain that evolved toward a modular architecture.

16. One ironic effect of this escalation is that, in some industries, the absolute value of performance on a vector goes down even as more firms advance to parity. In retail, for example, pressures to compete on price, quality, and service have meant that while more firms are average on service, the absolute level of service has actually remained fairly flat over the last three to four years (see the American Customer Satisfaction Index, www.theacsi.org).

17. Michael E. Porter, "What Is Strategy?" *Harvard Business Review*, December 2006, pp. 1–9.

18. Sources include "Commerce Bank," Harvard Business School Case 9–603–080 (Boston: Harvard Business School, 2003); Kimberly Healy, John White, Cormac Petit dit de la Roche, and Sunny Banerjea, "Banking 2015: A Classic Strategy Battle of Scale vs. Focus," *Strategy & Leadership*, 2006, pp. 51–58; Youngme Moon, "Break Free From the Product Lifecycle," *Harvard Business Review*, May 2005, pp. 86–94; and www.commerce-online.com. Commerce Bank was acquired by Toronto Dominion Bank in late 2007, and has been rebranded as TD Bank, as the rights to the Commerce name were not obtained in all markets.

19. Joseph Urbany, David B. Montgomery, and Marianne Moore, "Competitive Reactions and Modes of Competitive Reasoning: Downplaying the Unpredictable?" *Marketing Science Institute Report No. 01–121* (Boston: Marketing Science Institute, 2001).

20. "Canadian Sugar Industry," Canadian Sugar Institute Web site, www.sugar.ca/english/canadiansugarindustry/sugarmarket.cfm, accessed on January 23, 2010.

Chapter 4

1. Larry Light and Joan Kiddon, *Six Rules for Brand Revitalization* (Upper Saddle River, N.J.: Wharton School Publishing, 2009). McDonald's 2003 Annual Report indicates that net income peaked at $1.98 billion in 2000 and slid to $893 million in 2002 and returned back to $1.47 billion in 2003. "Simple, easy enjoyment" was the slogan of the campaign developed by Interbrand, www.interbrand.com/case_study.aspx?caseid=1066& langid=1000; accessed on January 26, 2010.
2. Louis V. Gerstner, *Who Says Elephants Can't Dance? Leading a Great Enterprise through Dramatic Change* (New York: HarperCollins, 2002).
3. Good overviews of what constitutes a strategy can be found in Donald C. Hambrick and James U. Frederickson, "Are You Sure You Have a Strategy?" *Academy of Management Executive*, November 2001, pp. 51–62; Constantinos Markides, "Strategy as Balance: From 'Either-or' to 'And,'" *Business Strategy Review*, Autumn 2001, pp. 1–10; and David J. Collis and Michael G. Rukstad, "Can You Say What Your Strategy Is?" *Harvard Business Review*, April 2008, pp. 82–90.
4. Formulating these objectives is not the focus of this book. Interested readers can find plenty of advice on the formation of objectives from more traditional strategy texts.
5. James C. Anderson, James A. Narus, and Wouter van Rossum, "Customer Value Propositions in Business Markets," *Harvard Business Review*, March 2006, pp. 91–99.
6. Adapted from Collis and Rukstad, "Can You Say?"
7. Traveler Review section of www.tripadvisor.com and customer blog section of the hotel Web site, www.gingerhotels.com; accessed on February 2, 2010.
8. Sometimes a business model is treated as interchangeable with strategy by including the customer value proposition. See Henry Chesbrough, *Open Business Models: How to Thrive in the New Innovation Landscape* (Boston: Harvard Business School Press, 2006), and Mark W. Johnson, Clayton M. Christensen, and Henning Kagerman, "Reinventing Your Business Model," *Harvard Business Review*, December 2008, pp. 58–59. For other definitions, see Constantinos Markides, *Game Changing Strategies* (San Francisco: Jossey-Bass, 2008).
9. Christoph Zott and Amit Raphael, "The Fit Between Product Market Strategy and Business Model: Implications for Firm Performance," *Strategic Management Journal* (August 2007), pp. 1–26, provides empirical support for a clean separation. They find that product-market

strategy and business model are distinct constructs that separately affect firm performance.

10. Nirmalya Kumar and Sophie Linguri "Zara: Responsive, High Speed, Affordable Fashion," ECCH Case Ref 305–308–1 (London: London Business School, 2005).

11. Youngme Moon, "Electronic Arts Introduces the Sims Online," Harvard Business School Case 9–503–008 (Boston: Harvard Business School, 2003).

12. "Briefing Rolls-Royce: Britain's Lonely High Flier," *The Economist* (January 10, 2009), p. 63.

13. Case based on Fidelity Investments interviews and George S. Day, "Aligning the Organization with the Market," *Sloan Management Review*, Fall 2006, pp. 41–49.

14. This distinction is made by Geoffrey Moore, *Dealing with Darwin: How Great Companies Innovate at Every Phase in Their Evolution* (New York: Penguin Portfolio, 2006).

15. Similar criteria are proposed by Devon Sharma, Chuck Lucier, and Richard Molloy, "From Solutions to Symbiosis: Blending with Your Customers," *Strategy+Business*, second quarter 2002, pp. 38–43. For empirical support, see Kapil R. Tuli, Ajay K. Kohli, and Sundar G. Bharadwaj, "Rethinking Customer Solutions: From Product Bundles to Relational Processes," *Journal of Marketing*, July 2007, pp. 1–17.

16. A very insightful source of answers is Adrian Ryans, *Beating Low Cost Competition: How Premium Brands Can Respond to Cut-Price Rivals* (Chichester, England: John Wiley & Sons, 2008).

17. Thomas Baumgartner, Roland H. John, and Tomas Naucler, "Transforming Sales and Service," *McKinsey Quarterly*, 2005, pp. 81–91.

Chapter 5

1. Bronwyn Fryer and Thomas A. Stewart, interviewing John Chambers, "Cisco Sees the Future," *Harvard Business Review*, November 2008, p. 75.

2. Innovation has recently been defined by the Measuring Innovation in the 21st Century Economy Advisory Committee as "the design, invention, development and/or implementation of new or altered products, services, systems or business models for the purpose of creating new value for customers and financial returns for the firm."

3. There is a vast literature on the challenges of managing and motivating innovation. Representative examples are Vijay Govindarajan and

Chris Trimble, *Ten Rules for Strategic Innovators: From Idea to Execution* (Boston: Harvard Business School Press, 2005); Scott D. Anthony, Mark W. Johnson, Joseph V. Sinfield, and Elizabeth J. Altman, *The Innovator's Guide to Growth* (Boston: Harvard Business School Press, 2008); Michael L. Tushman and Charles A. O'Reilly, *Winning through Innovation* (Boston: Harvard Business School Press, 1997); and Clayton M. Christensen and Michael Raynor, *The Innovator's Solution: Creating and Sustaining Successful Growth* (Boston: Harvard Business School Press, 2003).

4. Edward D. Hess, *The Road to Organic Growth: How Great Companies Consistently Grow Market Share from Within* (New York: McGraw-Hill, 2007).

5. David Meer, "Enter the 'Chief Growth Officer': Searching for Organic Growth," *Journal of Business Strategy*, January-February 2005, pp. 13–17.

6. W. Chan Kim and Renee Mauborgne, *Blue Ocean Strategy* (Boston: Harvard Business School Press, 2005).

7. See Clayton M. Christensen, *The Innovator's Dilemma: When New Technologies Cause Great Firms to Fail* (Boston: Harvard Business School Press, 1997); and Gerard J. Tellis, Jaideep C. Prabhu, and Rajesh K. Chandy, "Radical Innovation across Nations: The Preeminence of Corporate Culture," *Journal of Marketing*, January 2009, pp. 3–23.

8. Robert G. Cooper, "Your NPD Portfolio May Be Harmful to Your Business Health," *PDMA Visions*, April 2005, pp. 22–26.

9. Projects are plotted by asking managers to answer key questions about the relationship of the innovation project to the company's current markets and current products/technologies. A complete description of these questions and the entire methodology can be found at George S. Day, "Is It Real? Can We Win? Is It Worth Doing?" *Harvard Business Review*, December 2007, pp. 110–120.

10. These estimates of risk are similar to those reported by George C. Hartmann and Mark B. Myers, "Technical Risk, Product Specifications, and Market Risk," in Lewis M. Branscomb and Philip E. Auerswald, *Taking Technical Risks* (Cambridge, Mass.: MIT Press, 2002). See also C. R. Davis, "Calculated Risk: A Framework for Evaluating Product Development," *MIT Sloan Management Review*, Summer 2002, pp. 71–75. The ranges of probabilities in the "shaded bands" are mainly due to differences in the ability of firms to manage risk and avoid unnecessary failures.

11. Kim and Mauborgne, *Blue Ocean Strategy.*
12. Sharon M. Flanagan and Carl-Martin E. Lindahl, "Driving Growth in Consumer Goods," *McKinsey Quarterly*, October 2006, www.mckinseyquarterly.com/links/24009; accessed on November 4, 2009.
13. Chris Zook, *Beyond the Core: Expand Your Market without Abandoning Your Roots* (Boston: Harvard Business School Press, 2004).
14. Sun Tzu, *The Art of War* (London and New York: Oxford University Press, 1971, 1963).
15. "The Way We Read," *Wall Street Journal*, June 9, 2008, p. R3.
16. David Hunter, "DuPont: The 200th-Anniversary Update," *Chemical Week*, December 18, 2002; and "Fact Sheet: DuPont Clean Technologies" from DuPont's Media Center at vocuspr.vocus.com/VocusPR30/Newsroom/MultiQuery.aspx?SiteName=DuPontNew&Entity=PRAsset&SF_PRAsset_PRAssetID_EQ=109381&XSL=MediaRoom-Text&PageTitle=Fact%20Sheet&IncludeChildren=true&Cache=; accessed February 2, 2010.
17. Netflix 2008 Annual Report; and Larry Dignan, "Netflix: Streaming Adoption Accelerates; Earnings Follow Suit," Ziff Davis Media, ZDNet.com, January 27, 2010; accessed on February 15, 2010.
18. This identification of possible growth pathways has benefited greatly from Mohanbir Sawhney, Robert C. Wolcott, and Inigo Arroniz, "The 12 Different Ways for Companies to Innovate," *MIT Sloan Management Review*, Spring 2006, pp. 75–81. Other valuable sources were Christensen and Raynor, *The Innovator's Solution;* and Rita Gunther McGrath and Ian C. MacMillan, *Market Busters: 40 Strategic Moves That Drive Exceptional Business Growth* (Boston: Harvard Business School Press, 2005).
19. See Anthony et al., *Innovator's Guide,* Chapter 2, "Identifying Nonconsumers."
20. These shares reflect Google's overall market performance, not specifically in the small business market. Quentin Hardy, "When Google Runs Your Life," *Forbes*, December 28, 2009; and Google 2008 Annual Report.
21. C. K. Prahalad, *The Fortune at the Bottom of the Pyramid: Eradicating Poverty through Profits* (Upper Saddle River, N.J.: Wharton School Publishing, 2006).
22. Leslie Wayne, "P&G Sees the World as Its Client," *New York Times*, December 12, 2009, pp. B1–B2.
23. Amy Feldman, "Artery, Heal Thyself," *Fast Company*, February 2008, pp. 40–41.

24. "Abbott Advances Its Revolutionary Fully Bioabsorbable Drug Eluting Stent with Initiation of Next Phase of Clinical Trial," *Medical News Today*, March 25, 2009.
25. "Abbott Reports Double-Digit Sales and Earnings Growth in Fourth Quarter," *PR Newswire (US)*, January 27, 2010.
26. Kim and Mauborgne, *Blue Ocean Strategy*.
27. Sources include www.curves.com and www. blueoceanstrategy.com/abo/curves.html; accessed on February 1, 2010.
28. Stephanie Rosenbloom, "Solution, or Mess? A Milk Jug for a Green Earth," *New York Times*, June 30, 2008, p. A1.
29. John Glavin is credited with the idea of leasing Xerox 914 copiers and charging per copy, www.bulletinboards.com/v1.cfm?comcode= x2a.org&expand=y; accessed on February 5, 2010; and www.articlesbase.com/business-articles/brief-history-of-the-xerox-company–664924.html; accessed on February 4, 2010.
30. www.google.com/corporate/history.html; accessed on February 4, 2010.

Chapter 6

1. Geoff Colvin, "Xerox's Inventor-in-Chief," *Fortune*, July 9, 2007, p. 65.
2. Thomas Stewart, "Growth as Process," interview with Jeffrey R. Immelt, *Harvard Business Review*, June 2006, pp. 60–70; and David Brady, "The Immelt Revolution: He's Turning GE's Culture Upside Down, Demanding Far More Risk and Innovation," *Business Week*, March 28, 2005, pp. 64–73.
3. Scott Sanderude, "Growth from Harvesting the Sky: The $200 Million Challenge," Presentation to the Marketing Science Institute Trustees Meeting, Boston, April 15, 2005.
4. Michael Treacey and Jim Sims, "Take Command of Your Growth," *Harvard Business Review*, April 2004, pp. 127–133.
5. See, for example, Robert G. Cooper, Scott J. Edgett, and Elko J. Kleinschmidt, "New Product Portfolio Management: Practices and Performance," *Journal of Product Innovation Management*, July 1999, pp. 333–351.
6. A template for positioning projects on the risk matrix is described in George S. Day, "Is It Real? Can We Win? Is It Worth Doing?" *Harvard Business Review*, December 2007, pp. 3–13.
7. Chris Zook, *Beyond the Core: Expand Your Market Without Abandoning Your Roots* (Boston: Harvard Business School Press, 2004).

8. Clayton M. Christensen and Michael Raynor, *The Innovator's Solution: Creating and Sustaining Successful Growth* (Boston: Harvard Business School Press, 2003).

9. See George S. Day, "Which Way Should You Grow?" *Harvard Business Review*, July-August 2004, pp. 24–26; and Geoffrey A. Moore, *Dealing with Darwin: How Great Companies Innovate at Every Phase of Their Evolution* (New York: Portfolio, 2005).

10. For further discussion of explorations beyond adjacencies when discontinuities are involved, see Erwin Danneels (ed.), "Dialogue on the Effects of Disruptive Technology on Firms and Industries," *Journal of Product Innovation Management*, January 2006, pp. 2–55.

11. W. Chan Kim and Renee Mauborgne, *Blue Ocean Strategy* (Boston: Harvard Business School Press, 2005), pp. 63–64.

12. Ken Auletta, "The Bloomberg Threat," *The New Yorker*, March 10, 1997.

13. Christopher A. Bartlett and Afroze Mohammed, "3M Optical Systems: Managing Corporate Entrepreneurship," Harvard Business School Case 395017-PDF-ENG (Boston: Harvard Business School, 1999).

14. See George S. Day, "Which Way Should You Grow?" for further details on how to implement the R-W-W screen.

15. The basic logic of "reserving the right to play" is found in Hugh Courtney, *20/20 Foresight* (Boston: Harvard Business School Press, 2001). A number of tools for implementing real options analyses (and a critique of the inappropriate use of NPV calculations) can be found in Alexander B. van Putten and Ian C. MacMillan, *Unlocking Opportunities for Growth* (Upper Saddle River, N.J.: Wharton School Publishing, 2008).

16. Interview with Govi Rao, CEO of Lighting Science Group, May 2008.

17. See Larry Huston and Nikil Sakkab, "Connect and Develop: Inside Procter & Gamble's New Model for Innovation," *Harvard Business Review*, March 2006, pp. 58–66; and Henry Chesbrough, *Open Business Models: How to Thrive in the New Innovation Landscape* (Boston: Harvard Business School Press, 2006).

18. This section draws from George Day's research project on innovation metrics (with Dave Reibstein and Venky Shankar) sponsored by the Mack Center for Technological Innovation, The Wharton School, University of Pennsylvania; and Scott D. Anthony, Mark W. Johnson, Joseph V. Sinfield, and Elizabeth J. Altman, *The Innovator's Guide*

to Growth: Putting Disruptive Innovation to Work (Boston: Harvard Business School Press, 2008).

Chapter 7

1. Case based on Fidelity Investment interviews and George S. Day, "Aligning the Organization with the Market," *Sloan Management Review*, Fall 2006, pp. 41–49.
2. Day, "Aligning the Organization with the Market."
3. Bill Doyle, "Case Study: Charles Schwab Storms Back by Focusing on Customer Loyalty," *Forrester Research*, May 21, 2008, pp. 1–7.
4. "Schwab Reports Fourth Quarter and Full Year Results," *Business Wire*, January 16, 2008, www.businesswire.com/portal/site/schwab/index.jsp?ndmViewId=news_view&ndmConfigId=1010973&newsId=20080116005274&newsLang=en; accessed on August 20, 2009.
5. Charles Schwab Corporation, 2007 Annual Report.
6. "First Direct Branchless Banking," INSEAD Case 597–028–1 (Fontainebleau, France: INSEAD, 1997).
7. Stephen S. Tax and Stephen Brown, "Recovering and Learning from Service Failure," *Sloan Management Review*, Fall 1998, pp. 75–88.
8. Fred Hassan, "Leading Change from the Top Line," *Harvard Business Review*, July-August 2006, pp. 90–97.
9. See www.theplannedlife.com/insurance/auto-usaa.htm; accessed on August 15, 2009; and Jeremy Hope and Tony Hope, *Competing in the Third Wave: The Ten Key Management Issues of the Information Age* (Boston: Harvard Business School Press, 1997).
10. "Netflix Announces Q4 2009 Results," press release, January 27, 2010, www.netflix.com; accessed on February 7, 2010.
11. Lawrence F. Feick and Linda L. Price, "The Market Maven: A Diffuser of Marketplace Information," *Journal of Marketing*, January 1987, pp. 83–97.
12. Frederick F. Reichheld, "The One Number You Need to Grow," *Harvard Business Review*, December 2003, pp. 1–9.
13. This typology of effects is described in Rajendra K. Srivastava, Tasadduq A. Shervani, and Liam Fahey, "Market-Based Assets and Shareholder Value: A Framework for Analysis," *Journal of Marketing*, January 1998, pp. 2–19.
14. Sunil Gupta and Donald R. Lehmann, "Customers as Assets," *Journal of Interactive Marketing*, Winter 2003, pp. 9–24; and Sunil Gupta and Donald R. Lehmann, *Managing Customers as Assets* (Upper Saddle River, N.J.: Wharton School Publishing, 2005).

15. John H. Sheriden, "Gordon Lankton's Global Vision," *Industry Week*, April 3, 1995, p. 40.
16. Ibid., p. 39.
17. Nypro 2008 Annual Report and Dun & Bradstreet's *Million Dollar Directory*.
18. Nypro 2008 Annual Report and Rachel Halmesmaki Lahti, "Nimble Nypro Boasts Record Year for Sales, Profits," *Worcester (Massachusetts) Telegram & Gazette*, February 2, 1990.
19. Don Peppers and Martha Rogers, "Return on Customer: A New Metric of Value Creation," *Journal of Direct, Data and Digital Marketing Practice*, April-June 2006, pp. 318–332.
20. Leonard M. Lodish and Carl F. Mela, "If Brands Are Built over Years, Why Are They Managed over Quarters?" *Harvard Business Review*, July-August 2007, pp. 104–112.
21. Natalie Mizik and Robert Jacobson, "Myopic Marketing Management: Evidence of the Phenomenon and Its Long-Term Performance Consequences in the SEO Context," *Marketing Science*, May-June 2007, pp. 361–379.

Chapter 8

1. Case drawn from Pearle interviews performed by Wharton School MBA students.
2. Gary Loveman, "Diamonds in the Data Mine," *Harvard Business Review*, May 2003, p. 5.
3. Philip E. Pfeifer and Paul W. Farris, "Customer Profitability," University of Virginia Note HBS–UV0407 (Charlottesville, Va.: University of Virginia, 2005); and Elie Ofek, "Customer Profitability and Lifetime Value," Harvard Business School Note 9–503–019 (Boston: Harvard Business School, 2002).
4. We also recommend that companies calculate customer equity, which is the sum of the lifetime values of their customers, and customer equity share, which is the value of a company's customer base divided by the total value of the customers in the market. A good discussion of both metrics can be found in Roland T. Rust, Valarie A. Zeithaml, and Katherine N. Lemon, "Customer-Centered Brand Management," *Harvard Business Review*, September 2004, pp. 110–120; and Roland T. Rust, Christine Moorman, and Gaurav Bhalla, "Rethinking Marketing," *Harvard Business Review*, January-February 2009, pp. 94–99.
5. Sunil Gupta, Donald R. Lehmann, and Jennifer Stuart, "Valuing Customers," *Journal of Marketing Research*, February 2004, pp. 7–18.

6. The formula is:

$$\text{CLV}_c = \sum_{t=1}^{N} M_c \left[\frac{r_c^{t-1}}{(1+i)^{t-1}} \right] - \text{AC}_c$$

7. The lifetime value of the average customer in a segment can be calculated using the same formula as that for the individual customer. Once the individual value is derived, it can be multiplied by the number of customers in the segment in order to derive the total value of the segment.

8. V. Kumar, *Managing Customers for Profits* (Upper Saddle River, N.J.: Pearson, 2008).

9. Sunil Gupta and Donald R. Lehmann, "Customers as Assets," *Journal of Interactive Marketing*, Winter 2003, pp. 9–24; and Sunil Gupta and Donald R. Lehmann, *Managing Customers as Assets* (Upper Saddle River, N.J.: Wharton School Publishing, 2005). Gupta and Lehmann offer the following formula to make an infinite estimation. Notice that it is not summed by year, which reflects its infinite life view:

$$\text{CLV}_c = M_c \left[\frac{r_c}{1 + i - r_c} \right] - \text{AC}_c$$

10. V. Kumar and Denish Shah, "Expanding the Role of Marketing: From Customer Equity to Market Capitalization," *Journal of Marketing*, November 2009, pp. 119–136.

11. We use the following approach:

$$\text{PLV}_c = (\text{AR}_c * \text{CLV}_c) - \text{AC}_c$$

In this approach, AR_c is the average customer's acquisition rate, which is the likelihood that a member of the segment will be acquired, AC_c is the average customer's acquisition cost, or how much the company must spend to acquire the customer, and CLV_c is the segment's CLV (you may use the infinite life assumption to simplify).

12. Cecilie Rohwedder, "Stores of Knowledge," *Wall Street Journal*, June 6, 2006, p. A1.

13. Doug Desjardins, "Retailer's Largest Store a Learning Lab," *Retailing Today*, November 6, 2006, p. 26; and Kris Hudson, "Boss Talk: Turning Shopping Trips into Treasure Hunts," *Wall Street Journal*, August 27, 2007, p. B1.

14. Adam Braff, William Passmore, Michael Simpson, and Ashley Williams, "Opportunity of a Lifetime: A More Scientific Approach to Managing the Customer Lifecycle can Create Significant Value," in *McKinsey on Marketing* (McKinsey & Company, March 2004, www.mckinsey.com/practices/marketing/ourknowledge/compdocumenttype.asp#1; accessed on March 1, 2010.

15. Kumar and Shah, "Expanding the Role of Marketing."

16. Tom Peters, "A Passion for Customers" (Des Plains, Ill.: Video Publishing House, 1987).

17. Don Peppers and Martha Rogers, *Enterprise One to One* (New York: Doubleday, 1997), p. 169.

18. Interview with Marc S. Pritchard, Global Marketing Officer, P&G, April 2009. A podcast of the interview is available at www.cmosurvey.org. For a depiction of the photo mosaic and more detail, see www.shunyagroup.com/english/news/news4.html; accessed on January 26, 2010.

19. Gurse Ilipinar, Sarah Moore, and Jifeng Mu, "Innovation and Co-Creation," MSI Conference Summary Report 08–304 (Boston: Marketing Science Institute, 2008), p. 5.

20. Verizon has used the same strategy with its "volunteer customer service." Steve Lohr, "Customer Service? Ask a Volunteer," *New York Times*, April 25, 2009, p. 4.

21. Interview with Judson Linville, CEO and President, U.S. Consumer Services, American Express, October 8, 2009.

22. Rohwedder, "Stores of Knowledge."

23. There is now an enormous amount of literature on this point. However, the key ideas are best summarized in C. K. Prahalad and Venkat Ramaswamy, *The Future of Competition: Co-creating Unique Value with Customers* (Boston: Harvard Business School Press, 2004).

24. Kapil Tuli, Sundar Bhardawaj, and Ajay Kohli, "Ties That Bind: The Impact of Multiple Types of Ties with a Customer on Sales Growth and Sales Volatility," *Journal of Marketing Research*, February 2010, pp. 36–50.

25. Given that the value of the customer is maximized through growth activities, this section has important parallels to Imperative 2.

26. Judson Linville interview.

27. Harley-Davidson 2008 Annual Report, p. 18.

28. George S. Day, "Achieving Advantage with a New Dominant Logic," in "Invited Commentaries on 'Evolving to a New Dominant Logic for Marketing,'" *Journal of Marketing*, January 2004, pp. 18–19.

29. Mike Shields, "The Knot Tightens Focus on 'Nesties' Demo," *AdWeek*, June 12, 2009.
30. See www.ireport.com; accessed on December 19, 2008.
31. Max Chafkin, "The Customer Is the Company," *Inc.*, June 2008, pp. 89–96.
32. Robert Blattberg, Gary Getz, and Jacquelyn Thomas, *Customer Equity: Building and Managing Relationships as Valuable Assets* (Boston: Harvard Business School Press, 2001). Firms use geographic, demographic, lifestyle, and behavioral variables in regression models to predict the value of acquiring new customers from the targeted region. Indexes can also be used. This involves creating ratios of the firm's customers to the total number of customers that fit a criterion.
33. H. Drouet, "HSBC Global Research," January 17, 2007; and MTN Group 2008 Annual Report.
34. Doug Desjardins, "L.A. Landing Puts Tesco on Map," *Retailing Today*, www.retailingtoday.com; accessed on December 10, 2007.

Chapter 9

1. Frank Cespedes and V. Kasturi Rangan, "Becton Dickinson & Company: VACUTAINER Systems Division (Condensed)," Harvard Business School Case 9-592-037 (Boston: Harvard Business School, 1991).
2. Niraj Dawar, "What Are Brands Good For?" *MIT Sloan Management Review*, Fall 2004, pp. 31–37.
3. The United States will adopt the International Financial Reporting Standards (IFRS) by 2011. Under FASB rules, brand value has been relegated to the ambiguous "goodwill" balance sheet category. With the adoption of the IFRS standard, brand value will be included under intangible assets. The change in accounting standards will increase scrutiny of the return on marketing dollars.
4. For an in-depth treatment of the cognitive underpinnings of strong brands, see Kevin L. Keller, *Strategic Brand Management*, 3rd ed. (Upper Saddle River, N.J.: Pearson, 2007).
5. Conjoint analysis is a tool that is commonly used to measure customers' overall preference for products with different attributes, benefits, and brand names. These overall preferences are then decomposed to determine the value of one over the other and the optimal value of each from the customer's point of view.

6. See CNN.com, www.cnn.com/2007/TRAVEL/02/15/passengers
.stranded/index.html; accessed on November 25, 2008. For an article
on how CEO Neeleman handled the crisis, see www.forbes .com/2007/
02/20/neeleman-jet-blue-lead-cx_tw_0220jetblueceo.html; accessed on
November 26, 2008.

7. Martin A. Koschat and Willem Smit, "The Battle for Consumer
Minds," *IMD Research Challenges*, 2008, www.imd.ch/research/
challenges/TC080-08.cfm?bhcp=1; accessed on February 5, 2010.

8. Michael Arndt, "Burrito Buzz—And So Few Ads," *Business Week*,
March 12, 2007, pp. 84–85.

9. One interesting statistic can be derived by comparing the 100 firms on
Fortune's "Best Global Brand" list and the 100 top firms on *Fortune*'s
"Best Companies to Work For" list. Removing non-U.S. firms to make
the lists comparable, 11 of the 50 firms (22 percent) were on both lists,
including Google, Cisco, Starbucks, Goldman Sachs, American
Express, eBay, Marriott, Nike, Microsoft, Yahoo!, and FedEx.

10. For example, Natalie Mizik and Robert Jacobson, "Valuing Branded
Businesses," *Journal of Marketing*, November 2009, pp. 137–153; and
John Gerzema and Ed Lebar, "The Trouble with Brands," *Strategy+
Business*, Summer 2009, pp. 48–57.

11. For example, Lopo L. Rego, Matthew T. Billett, and Neil A. Morgan,
"Consumer-Based Brand Equity and Firm Risk," *Journal of Marketing*, November 2009, pp. 47–60.

12. Kevin L. Keller, "The Brand Report Card," *Harvard Business Review*,
January-February 2000, pp. 147–156.

13. This material is drawn from Douglas B. Holt, *How Brands Become
Icons* (Boston: Harvard Business School Press, 2004).

14. Share includes Mountain Dew and Mountain Dew Code Red. Figures
from Mintel Report, "Carbonated Soft Drinks—US—June 2009," and
"Carbonated Drinks—US—May 2008" academic.mintel.com; accessed
on February 10, 2010.

15. Mintel Report, "Portable Technology—US—2009" academic.mintel
.com; accessed on February 1, 2010; and Philip Elmer-DeWitt, "Good-
bye iPod, Hello iPhone," CNNMoney.com, August 5, 2009; accessed
February 2, 2010.

16. Mintel Report, "Portable Technology" academic.mintel.com; accessed
on February 1, 2010. The quote was taken from a blog entry at
www.businessweek.com/technology/ByteOfTheApple/blog/archives/
2009/01/zune_sales_go_h.html; accessed on August 18, 2009.

17. David A. Aaker, "Leveraging the Corporate Brand," *California Management Review*, Spring 2004, pp. 6–18.
18. Jud Linville, CEO and President, U.S. Consumer Services, American Express, speech at Duke University, The Fuqua School of Business, October 17, 2008.
19. Gail McGovern and John A. Quelch, "Measuring Marketing Performance," Harvard Business School Simulation 507701 (Boston: Harvard Business School, 2007).
20. Thermo Electron 2003 Annual Report and Thermo Electron 2005 Annual Report.
21. Reinhard Angelmar and Christian Pinson, "Zantac (A)," INSEAD Case 592–045–1 (Fontainebleau, France: INSEAD, 1992).
22. Ove Haxthausen, "Secrets of Challenger Brands," *Marketing Management*, May-June 2004, pp. 35–38.
23. Passed in 1998, this legislation, known as the Sonny Bono Act, extended copyright terms in the United States by 20 years.
24. Betsy D. Gelb and Partha Krishnamurthy, "Protect Your Product's Look and Feel from Imitators," *Harvard Business Review*, October 2008, p. 36.
25. "The Thin Red Line: Questioning Alleged Trade Dress Infringement," *Global Cosmetic Industry Magazine*, November 2008, pp. 8–9.

Chapter 10

1. John Carey, "Under Armour: A Brawny Tee House? No Sweat," *BusinessWeek*, May 25, 2006, p. 1; and Stephanie Mehta, "Under Armour Reboots," *Fortune*, February 2, 2009, pp. 29–33.
2. Carey, "Under Armour."
3. Vanessa O'Connell, "Is Discount a Good Fit for Vera Wang?" *Wall Street Journal*, September 5, 2007, pp. B1–B2.
4. Pallavi Gogoi, "Discount Designers," *BusinessWeek Online*, September 12, 2008.
5. Louisa Lim, "Marketing to Millions: China's Changing Tastes," National Public Radio Morning Edition, August 21, 2006.
6. William J. Morrissey, "Leveraging Environmental Sustainability for Growth," Marketing Science Institute Board of Trustees Meeting on Sustainable Marketing Strategy, San Francisco, November 13, 2008.
7. Richard Ettenson and Jonathan Knowles, "Merging the Brands and Branding the Merger," *MIT Sloan Management Review*, Summer 2006, pp. 39–49.
8. Ibid.

9. Theodore Levitt, "The Globalization of Markets," *Harvard Business Review*, May-June 1983, pp. 92–93.
10. M. De Mooij, *Global Marketing and Advertising: Understanding Cultural Paradoxes* (Thousand Oaks, Calif.: Sage, 1998).
11. Marc Langefeld, "Tesco: Consistent Earnings Growth at Attractive Price," *Seeking Alpha*, September 4, 2009, accessed on February 2, 2010.
12. Darrell K. Rigby and Vijay Vishwanath, "Localization: The Revolution in Consumer Markets," *Harvard Business Review*, April 2006, pp. 2–12.
13. Ibid, p. 4.
14. The ideas in this section are drawn from David Aaker and Erich Joachimsthaler, "The Lure of Global Branding," *Harvard Business Review*, November-December 1999, pp. 137–144.
15. Reinhard Angelmar and Christian Pinson, "Zantac (A)," INSEAD Case 592–045–1 (Fontainebleau, France: INSEAD, 1992).
16. The CMO Survey (www.cmosurvey.org) reports that the following percentage of firms use each of the social media: social networking (e.g., LinkedIn), 65.4 percent; video and photosharing (e.g., YouTube), 52.3 percent; blogging, 50.9 percent; microblogging (e.g., Twitter), 44.4 percent; podcasts, 24.8 percent; communities and forums (e.g., Google groups), 23.4 percent; product reviews (e.g., Amazon), 17.3 percent; social bookmarking (e.g., Digg), 15.9 percent; product design or co-creation (e.g., NikeID), 6.5 percent; and virtual reality (e.g., Second Life), 3.7 percent. Results from the August 2009 CMO Survey, www.cmosurvey.org/survey_results/; accessed on January 5, 2009.
17. Shar Van Boskirk, "US Interactive Marketing Forecast 2009 to 2014," *Forrester Research*, July 30, 2009.
18. Bruce Horovitz, "Domino's Nightmare Holds Lessons for Marketers," *USA Today*, April 16, 2009, p. 3B; and Ben Levisohn and Ellen Gibson, "An Unwelcome Delivery," *BusinessWeek*, May 4, 2009, p. 15.

Chapter 11

1. Don Peppers and Martha Rogers, *Return on Customer* (New York: Doubleday, 2005).
2. Theodore Levitt, "Marketing Myopia," *Harvard Business Review*, July-August 1960, pp. 45–56.

3. Case based on a presentation made by Bob Woodard at the Marketing Science Institute Board of Trustees Meeting and Conference on Sustainable Marketing Strategy, San Francisco: Marketing Science Institute, November 14–15, 2008.

4. The ad tagline is *"Po doushe I na polzu"*—"It's good, and good for you." *Dousha* is used in the "it's good" part, which literally means something like "agreeable to your soul."

5. See www.reuters.com/article/pressRelease/idUS217725+01-Jul-2008+BW20080701 and www.moscowtimes.ru/article/850/49/195569.htm; accessed on January 20, 2009.

6. See www.reuters.com/article/rbssConsumerGoodsAndRetailNews/idUSN1652082220090316; accessed on February 15, 2009.

7. See www.reuters.com/article/pressRelease/idUS217725+01-Jul-2008+BW20080701 and www.moscowtimes.ru/article/850/49/195569.htm; both accessed on January 20, 2009.

8. John Sculley, *Odyssey: From Pepsi to Apple* (New York: Harper & Row, 1987).

9. Bronwyn Fryer and Thomas A. Stewart, "Cisco Sees the Future," *Harvard Business Review*, November 2008, p. 74.

10. For a good summary of Red Team exercises used in the military and in business, see en.wikipedia.org/wiki/Red_Team; accessed on January 23, 2009.

11. Hugh Courtney, John T. Horn, and Jayanti Kar, "Getting into Your Competitor's Head," *McKinsey Quarterly*, February 12, 2009, pp. 128–137.

12. Burger King's 2006 Manthem ads point to this craving for giant portions: www.youtube.com/watch?v=v9e4QD1zmoQ; accessed on February 7, 2010. Looking back, we see the same sparring around McDonald's 1991 introduction of a lean burger, the McLean. Burger King did not follow and felt quite smug when McLean flopped, reaching only an estimated 2 percent of sales. Scott Hume, "When It Comes to Burgers, We Crave Beef, Not McLean," *Advertising Age*, March 1, 1993, pp. 3–4.

13. George S. Day, *The Market Driven Organization* (New York: Free Press, 1999).

14. Associated Press, "Procter & Gamble Cranks Up Its Own Online eStore," *USA Today*, January 15, 2010, p. 5B.

15. Dev Patnaik, *Wired to Care* (San Mateo, Calif.: Jump Associates LLC, 2009); and Ellen Byron, "Seeing Store Shelves through Senior Eyes," *Wall Street Journal*, September 14, 2009, p. B1.

16. Edward J. Zajac and Max H. Bazerman, "Blind Spots in Industry and Competitor Analysis: Implications of Interfirm (Mis)Perceptions for Strategic Decisions," *Academy of Management Review*, January 1991, pp. 37–56; and George S. Day and Paul J. H. Shoemaker, *Peripheral Vision: Detecting the Weak Signals That Will Make or Break Your Company* (Boston: Harvard Business School Press, 2006).

17. A good summary of IDEO's methods can be found in *The IDEO Method Cards: 51 Ways to Inspire Design* (Richmond, Calif.: William Stout, 2003). See also Edward F. McQuarrie and Shelby H. McIntyre, *Implementing the Marketing Concept through a Program of Customer Visits*, Marketing Science Institute Report 90–107 (Boston: Marketing Science Institute, 1990).

18. Within three years, reports noted, "Huggies Pull-Ups, Kimberly-Clark's disposable training pants, for example, are approaching $500 million in sales after less than two years on the market and virtually no competition" from Don Nichols, "Darwin Smith: The Man who Bet on Huggies," *Management Review*, June 1992, pp. 53–55.

19. Leonard Lodish and Dwight W. Riskey, "Expanding the Role of the Chief Learning Officer: Balancing the Costs and Value of Generating and Using New Marketing Knowledge" (Unpublished working paper, The Wharton School, University of Pennsylvania, July 1997).

20. Thomas H. Davenport and Jeanne G. Harris, *Competing on Analytics: The New Science of Winning* (Boston: Harvard Business School Press, 2007).

21. David A. Aaker, *Spanning Silos: The New CMO Imperative* (Boston: Harvard Business School Press, 2008).

22. Christine Moorman, Gerald Zaltman, and Rohit Deshpandé, "Relationships between Providers and Users of Market Research: The Dynamics of Trust within and between Organizations," *Journal of Marketing Research*, August 1992, pp. 314–328.

23. Vince P. Barraba and Gerald Zaltman, *Hearing the Voice of the Market* (Boston: Harvard Business School Press, 1991).

Chapter 12

1. There are more than 3,500 academic journal articles and many books on this topic. Organizations that are designed and operate this way are referred to as market-driven, market-oriented, and customer-focused. The central theme of these works mirrors our focus: to identify the types of core organizational approaches that make an

outside-in approach to managing strategy and tactics a reality. For a broader reading of this important literature, we recommend George S. Day, *The Market-Driven Organization* (New York: Free Press, 1999); Ajay K. Kohli and Bernard J. Jaworski, "Market Orientation: The Construct, Research Propositions, and Managerial Implications," *Journal of Marketing*, April 1990, pp. 1–18; John Narver and Stanley F. Slater, "The Effect of a Market Orientation on Business Profitability," *Journal of Marketing*, October 1990, pp. 20–35; and George S. Day, "The Capabilities of Market-Driven Organizations," *Journal of Marketing*, October 1994, pp. 37–52. A good summary of the literature and results over a 15-year period can be found in Ahmet H. Kirca, Satish Jayachandran, and William O. Bearden, "Market Orientation: A Meta-Analytic Review and Assessment of Its Antecedents and Impact on Performance," *Journal of Marketing*, April 2005, pp. 24–41.

2. Peter F. Drucker, *The Practice of Management* (New York: Harper & Brothers, 1954).

3. Day, *The Market-Driven Organization*.

4. A. G. Lafley and Ram Charan, "The Customer Is Boss," Chapter 3 in *The Game-Changer* (New York: Crown Business, 2008).

5. Theodore Levitt, "Marketing Myopia," *Harvard Business Review*, July-August 1960, p. 56.

6. Ron Winslow, "How a Breakthrough Quickly Broke Down for Johnson & Johnson," *Wall Street Journal*, September 18, 1998, p. A1.

7. Paul Kaihla, "Best Kept Secrets of the World's Best Companies," *Business 2.0*, March 2006, p. 94.

8. Steven P. Brown and Son K. Lam, "A Meta-Analysis of Relationships Linking Employee Satisfaction and Customer Responses," *Journal of Retailing*, September 2008, pp. 243–255.

9. Marc Gunther, "Marriot Gets a Wake-Up Call," *Fortune*, July 2009, p. 62.

10. Marc Gunther, "Marriot Family Values," *CNNMoney Fortune 500*, May 25, 2007, money.cnn.com/2007/05/24/news/companies/pluggedin _gunther_marriott.fortune/index.htm; accessed on August 20, 2009.

11. George S. Day, "Aligning the Organization with the Market," *Sloan Management Review*, Fall 2006, pp. 41–49.

12. Ibid.

13. Roland T. Rust, Christine Moorman, and Gaurav Bhalla, "Rethinking Marketing," *Harvard Business Review*, January-February 2009, pp. 94–99.

14. "Minding the Store, Analyzing Customers, Best Buy Decides Not All Are Welcome," *Wall Street Journal*, November 8, 2004, p. A1; and as cited in Peter Kim, "Reinventing the Marketing Organization," *Forrester Research*, 2006; and Best Buy Fourth Quarter 2006 Earnings Conference Calls.

15. Philip Kotler, Neil Rackham, and Suj Krishnaswamy, "Ending the War between Sales and Marketing," *Harvard Business Review*, July-August 2006, pp. 1–13.

16. Day, "Aligning the Organization with the Market."

17. John Davis, *Measuring Marketing: 103 Key Metrics Every Marketer Needs* (Chichester, England: John Wiley & Sons, 2007).

18. A useful source is Paul W. Farris, Neil T. Bendle, Phillip E. Pfeifer, and David J. Reibstein, *Marketing Metrics: The Definitive Guide to Measuring Marketing Performance*, 2nd ed. (Upper Saddle River, N.J.: Wharton School Publishing, 2010).

19. Roland T. Rust, Christine Moorman, and Peter R. Dickson, "Return on Quality: Revenue Expansion, Cost Reduction, or Both?" *Journal of Marketing*, October 2002, pp. 7–24.

Chapter 13

1. Nirmalya Kumar, *Marketing as Strategy: Understanding the CEO's Agenda for Driving Growth and Innovation* (Boston: Harvard Business School Press, 2004).

2. This section draws heavily from Gail McGovern and John A. Quelch, "The Fall and Rise of the CMO," *Strategy+Business*, Winter 2004, pp. 45–51, and is consistent with Edward Landry, Andre Tipping, and Jay Kumar, "Growth Champions," *Strategy+Business*, Summer 2006, pp. 60–69 and David A. Aaker, *Spanning Silos: The New CMO Imperative* (Boston: Harvard Business School Press, 2008).

3. See Christian Homburg, Ove Jensen, and Harley Krohmer, "Configurations of Marketing and Sales: A Taxonomy," *Journal of Marketing*, March 2008, pp. 133–154; and George S. Day, "Aligning Organization Structures to the Market," *Business Strategy Review*, Autumn 1999, pp. 33–46. Using a clustering procedure, the Homburg et al. study found five archetypes that generally support our typology. We have combined their "sales rules" and "sales-driven symbiosis types."

4. Philip Kotler, Neil Rackham, and Suj Krishnaswamy, "Ending the War between Sales and Marketing," *Harvard Business Review*, July-August 2006, pp. 68–78.

5. This section is adapted with appreciation from Sean Meehan, "The Philips Marketing Journey (A, IMD–5–0729), (B, IMD–5–0730), and (C, IMD–5–0731)" (Lausanne, Switzerland: IMD, 2007).

6. Ibid., Part A, pp. 3 and 5.

7. Ibid., Part B, p. 7.

8. Company records; and ibid., Part B, p. 8.

9. Interview with Geert van Kuyck, February 11, 2009. All quotes attributed to Mr. van Kuyck were collected during this interview.

10. Gary McWilliams, "Wal-Mart Sets Fleming to Oversee Merchandising," *Wall Street Journal*, January 25, 2007, p. B7.

11. Interview with Stephen Quinn at The Fuqua School of Business, Duke University, December 1, 2009.

12. Jack Neff and Emily Bryson York, "ANA Urges Marketers: We Must Be the Ones to Lead the Country out of Recession," *Advertising Age*, November 9, 2009, pp. 3–4.

13. Ibid.

14. Tim Craig, "Smart Network Will Need Brilliant Proof of ROI," *Retailing Today*, September 22, 2008, p. 3.

15. From a speech made by Stephen Quinn to The Fuqua School of Business, Duke University, December 1, 2009, as part of the Distinguished Speaker Series.

16. Mya Frazier and Nat Ives, "Reinventing Their Brands," *Advertising Age*, October 9, 2006, p. 10.

17. Jack Neff, "Why Walmart Is Getting Serious about Marketing," *Advertising Age*, June 8, 2009, pp. 1–2.

18. Alan Cane, "Philips Tackles Its 'Old, Dull, and Dutch' Image," *Financial Times*, June 17, 2004, p. 10.

19. Neff, "Why Walmart Is Getting Serious."

20. Alice Z. Cuneo, "Ragnetti Looks to Showcase Philips' High-End Technology," *Advertising Age*, February 9, 2004, p. 46.

21. "Interview: Marketing Executive," *Marketing Insights*, London Business School, September 2004, p. 5.

22. Pat Dillon, "Values Don't Change," *Fast Company*, September 30, 1998; and "Interview: Scott Cook," November 18, 2003, www .pcmag.com/article2/0,2817,1386870,00.asp; accessed on February 3, 2010.

23. Lesley Neadel, "Stephen Quinn, CMO of Walmart, Shares Their Customer-Centric POV," November 6, 2009, ana.blogs.com/ maestros/2009/11/stephen-quinn-cmo-of-walmart-shares-their-customer-centric-pov.html; accessed on February 6, 2010.

24. Kerry Capell, "Thinking Simple at Philips," *Business Week*, December 11, 2006, p. 50.
25. Neff, "Why Walmart Is Getting Serious."

Conclusion

1. This case is based on Nicolaj Siggelkow, "Change in the Presence of Fit: The Rise, the Fall, and the Renaissance of Liz Claiborne," *Academy of Management Journal*, August 2001, pp. 838–857.
2. Anthony J. Mayo and Mark Benson, "Liz Claiborne and the New Working Woman," Harvard Business School Case 407060-PDF-ENG (Boston: Harvard Business School, 2008), p. 1.
3. "Liz Claiborne Earnings," Dow Jones News Service, February 23, 1998.

Acknowledgments

Conceiving and writing a book is like making an ancient caravan journey. It takes a vision of the destination, no small amount of bravado to get started, considerable resources to maintain the effort, and the support of countless friends, colleagues, and family members to reach the end. We came together on this journey because of mutual respect. We created the book from a shared belief that managing from the outside in is the only way to sustain a profitable organization over the long run and the worry that many firms were going astray.

We stayed on our compass heading with the help of many thought leaders, scholars, and business leaders. While on our course, we connected with many who share our belief that marketing is a critical general management responsibility through the American Marketing Association and the Marketing Science Institute.

To all our colleagues at Wharton and Duke, you were invaluable at many stages in the journey. We wish we could single out each of you, but you will recognize your intellectual fingerprints in our work and should know that we felt your support throughout the process. Chris also wants to acknowledge the impact of all her advisors at the University of Pittsburgh, especially Jerry Zaltman, for helping her see that good theory can make for good practice for the benefit of customers. We both must acknowledge the inimitable Peter Drucker, a giant on whose shoulders we stand.

During our journey we benefited from clients, such as General Electric, Medtronic, W. L. Gore and Associates, Tyco Electronics, and others, which allowed us to apply our ideas to their problems and gave us invaluable feedback. Some of the best guidance came from our students in MBA, EMBA, and executive education courses, where the practicality of the ideas were first tested. We listened carefully to your questions and ideas and used them to guide our efforts. Julia Tarasova and Maureen Atkins, both Duke MBAs, provided outstanding research assistance in fact-checking our work.

Many books are started, but few reach their destinations. Tim Ogden and Laura Starita of Sona Partners provided invaluable editorial help in the final stages. They were like the ship's harbor pilot, taking the reader's point of view to rewrite and integrate the ideas into a persuasive narrative. We also could not have finished without the assistance of Ed Holub, who offered advice on our chapters across many versions, and Cristin Harris, who kept the manuscript moving forward with competence and unfailing good cheer.

Above all, we acknowledge the understanding and the unconditional support and love of our dear families, who inspired and sustained us as we created the book together. This book is dedicated to them.

George Day
Bryn Mawr, Pennsylvania

Christine Moorman
Durham, North Carolina
June 2010

Index

About the Authors

George S. Day is the Geoffrey T. Boisi Professor and codirector of the Mack Center for Technological Innovation at the Wharton School at the University of Pennsylvania.

He has been a consultant to numerous corporations such as General Electric, IBM, Metropolitan Life, Marriott, Unilever, E. I. DuPont de Nemours, W. L. Gore and Associates, Coca-Cola, Boeing, LG Corp., Best Buy, and Medtronic. He is chairman of the board of directors of the American Marketing Association and a trustee of the Marketing Science Institute. His primary areas of activity are marketing, the management of emerging technologies, organic growth and innovation, and competitive strategies in global markets.

Professor Day has authored 15 books in the areas of marketing and strategic management. His most recent books are *Peripheral Vision: Detecting the Weak Signals That Can Make or Break Your Company* (with Paul Schoemaker) published in 2006, *Wharton on Managing Emerging Technologies* (with Paul Schoemaker) published in 2000, and *The Market Driven Organization*, published in 1999.

He has won 10 best-article awards with 2 of these articles among the top 25 most influential articles in marketing science in the past 25 years. He was honored with the Charles Coolidge Parlin Award in 1994, the Paul D. Converse Award in 1996, the Sheth Foundation Award in 2003, and the Mahajan Award for Career Contributions to Marketing Strategy in 2001. In 2003 he received the AMA/Irwin/McGraw-Hill Distinguished Marketing Educator Award.

Christine Moorman is the T. Austin Finch, Sr. Professor and founder of The CMO Survey (www.cmosurvey.org) at The Fuqua School of Business, Duke University. Professor Moorman is the author of over 60 journal articles, reports, and conference proceedings. She has coedited the book *Assessing Marketing Strategy Performance* (with Don Lehmann) and has made over 100 presentations of her work at universities and companies all over the world. Her primary areas of activity are marketing strategy and firm learning about customer-focused innovation.

Professor Moorman has served on the board of directors and chair of the Marketing Strategy Special Interest Group for the American Marketing Association, as director of public policy for the Association for Consumer Research, and as a trustee for the Marketing Science Institute. She won the 2008 Mahajan Award for Career Contributions to Marketing Strategy from the American Marketing Association and the 2008 Distinguished Marketing Educator from the Academy of Marketing Science.

Professor Moorman's research has won two best-paper awards and has been published in *Journal of Marketing Research*, *Journal of Consumer Research*, *Marketing Science*, *Journal of Marketing*, *Journal of Public Policy & Marketing*, *International Journal of Research in Marketing*, *Academy of Management Review*, and *Administrative Science Quarterly*. Her research has been supported by grants from the Marketing Science Institute, the Institute for the Study of Business Markets, and the National Science Foundation.